CAN CAPITALISM
COMPETE?

A CAMPAIGN FOR
AMERICAN FREE ENTERPRISE

BY

Raymond W. Miller

THE RONALD PRESS COMPANY

New York

FOREWORD

Increasingly in recent years we have been coming to recognize that the great increase in industrial productivity and the consequent startling rise in our material standard of living is by no means the whole of the message which we have for the rest of the world. Indeed, although we frequently continue to behave as if it were, we really know that it is the ideals of human dignity and the enhancement of the opportunity of each person to function to the fullest of his capacity that is of major consequence.

It is sadly too true that we have been slow to take the first steps in such understanding, principally, I believe, because we have been slow to put ourselves in the shoes of other peoples. We have not really tried to look at the world from the point of view of, and with the values of, our neighbors in other lands, particularly those which have been less well developed industrially.

In recent months our need to take these steps has been emphasized in many ways. From a wealth of personal experience in many parts of the world Raymond Miller has pulled together and accented this message in a way which I hope will have a widespread impact. If such efforts as this can be understood widely, we can, I think, make real progress in what in the long run may determine the future of the United States.

Stanley F. Teele
DEAN, GRADUATE SCHOOL OF
BUSINESS ADMINISTRATION
HARVARD UNIVERSITY

PREFACE

The struggle for loyalties of men between totalitarian imperialism and democratic freedom has been one of my prime concerns for many years. In particular, for more than a decade I have tried to play my part in the world-wide conflict between the Communist economic ideology and the modern capitalist system as it has evolved in North America.

In their passionate search for economic progress, the peoples of the world are faced with a choice. On one side, the Communist propagandists are extolling their own advances and painting the capitalist system as black as they can. This they do by carefully selecting materials describing the exploitive type of capitalism that a generation ago was regarded by most of the world as the accepted method of doing business. On our side, we have not been doing enough to show that this exploitive capitalism is largely a thing of the past, at least in the United States and Canada. There has emerged on this continent a new concept of the use of money, corporate organization, and economic power. This new kind of capitalism—which I call throughout this book "American service capitalism"—is based on the idea of a fair profit for free business enterprise combined with enlightened service to the community as a whole.

Over the past decades American service capitalism has been responsible for some of the most rapid advances in both material and spiritual welfare in the history of man. Yet its power for good is at present largely unknown, or completely misunderstood, throughout most of the world. Even in the United States and Canada, too few of us have any idea that we are living in the second generation of one of the greatest revolutions that has ever happened. It is the main purpose of this book to underline the fact of this revolution and to suggest ways in which its benefits can be made better known abroad as well as at home.

My interest and experience in this field have been steadily expanding as the years go by. From 1949 to 1956 it was my privilege to act as public relations adviser to the Director General of the Food and Agriculture Organization of the United Nations. In this capacity and others, I traveled some four hundred thousand miles meeting the people of the world's rural areas—where the battle for the minds of men is really being waged. I had the opportunity to visit many heads of state and leading citizens in Asia and Latin-America and to become acquainted with a cross-section of businessmen in over fifty countries. During these years I have also had numerous occasions to address classes and larger audiences at colleges and universities overseas. Whatever the original topic of my talk, I was always struck by the eager questions on one special theme: "Can capitalism be of any benefit to us?" It is my thesis that all North Americans must cooperate to answer this question in the affirmative.

Meanwhile, I had been developing a series of seminars on modern American capitalism at the Graduate School of Business Administration of Harvard University. In the fall of 1955, Donald K. David, then Dean of the School, and Stanley F. Teele, the present Dean, told me they thought the Ford Foundation might be interested in exploring this whole problem of finding a way of communicating overseas the fundamental principles of American capitalism. They asked whether I would be interested in searching for an answer or a partial answer. I immediately accepted the task, and since March, 1956, I have devoted my entire available time to this study.

The observations and conclusions in this book constitute an attempt to mirror a mosaic of the ideas and opinions of hundreds of men and women from most of the countries of the world, as gathered from personal interviews; from reading thousands of pages of current literature from other lands; and from conversations with hundreds of our own citizens both at home and abroad. My report, of course, is not intended to offer a complete answer to the complex problems involved. It is hoped, however, that it may serve as a sort of signpost along the rough and rocky road to a better understanding, and that it will to some extent reflect the vocal thoughts of the free world and, perhaps, the silent thoughts of the slave world.

I am grateful to many people, in many parts of the world, for making this book possible. Special thanks go to Dr. William S. Barnes of the Harvard Law School, whose survey of methods of communicating with Latin-American peoples has formed an integral part of this work; and to my son, Robert W. Miller, who as Executive Vice President of Public Relations Research Associates has made a special study of the situations in Puerto Rico and Europe. Both have contributed their time and advice unstintingly toward the preparation of this book as a whole; and their conclusions on their special topics of study appear in their own words in this volume. I am also deeply grateful to Monsignor L. G. Ligutti, the Reverend James L. Vizzard, S.J., Dr. Cameron P. Hall, and Dr. Louis Finkelstein for contributing their points of view as religious leaders.

Among the many others that have helped, I can single out only a few for special mention: Dr. Herbert R. Grossman, who devoted an enormous amount of time to reading and research for the benefit of this study; Dr. A. Ladru Jensen, who offered many suggestions and illustrative citations; Professor N. G. D. Joarder, formerly of India and now an American citizen, who has truly been a "one-man reference library"; George Baker, John Chapman, Saville Davis, Bertrand Fox, Horace G. Holmes, Vincent W. Lanfear, Peter Miller, Charles H. Seavers, Donald Stone, Robert West, and Ray Zimmerman, who all read the manuscript and made valuable comments; Nicholas DeWitt, who gave advice on the sections on communism; Robert Updegraff, who suggested the title; Reuben E. Slesinger, who helped greatly with the final draft; William Robinson, whose sure editorial touch can be seen throughout; Mrs. Toba Wilensky and Mrs. Miriam Kary for faithful secretarial aid; and Mrs. Ruth C. Hetherston, Associate in Research, Harvard Graduate School of Business Administration, without whose research and constructive editorial criticism the manuscript could never have reached its final form. To all these friends, and many others, go my sincere thanks.

Washington, D.C.   Raymond W. Miller
January, 1959

CONTENTS

CAN CAPITALISM
COMPETE?

I

INTRODUCTION

In March, 1949, the Rotary Club of New Delhi held a dinner at which I was a guest in company with executives of the Boy Scouts of India. The speaker that evening was a representative of the Embassy of the Union of Soviet Socialist Republics, who spoke on the accomplishments of the Communists in Russia and compared them with the lack of accomplishments of the "capitalistic czars." He told of the Soviet achievement of increasing literacy, the rising standard of living, the accentuated interest in the teaching of science, the studies that were being made in human behavior. He concluded his talk with a statement to this effect: "Capitalism, which means benefits for the few, could never educate or help the people of Asia to a higher standard of living because capitalism is based upon human selfishness, while Soviet communism is of the people, by the people, and for the people. This is the first time in human history that there has been a people's government."

After his speech, there was time for questions. An Indian gentleman in the audience gave a polite recital of some of the benefits that Asia had received from the British. Among others he listed trade and commerce, the stability of law and order, and the general improvement of the people. He said that India had now gained liberty from its conquerers but that India had no deep-seated resentment against the British as individuals nor the system of private enterprise and law which they had brought to

India. India, he believed, would try the experiment of liberty and of a "progressive capitalism" which it had learned from its deposed rulers. He said that he doubted whether a part of the Communist area would "withdraw" from its "masters" and have enough respect for its system to stay with them. He prophesied that India would stay in the Commonwealth because of its respect for the law which the British had brought and for the opportunity to progress within a capitalistic economy. He said that although the Labour government then in power in Britain was committed to "socialism," not to "communism," he would rather look forward to a future under the system of restricted capitalism than the dictatorship of the Soviets. He ended by asking the Russian this question: "Is it not true that you teach the fundamental atheistic doctrines of Soviet communism in all of your schools, and make it impossible for your students even to judge the truth or falsity of other beliefs—economic, spiritual, and political?"

The Soviet representative, who sat about four seats from me at the head table, turned to the speaker and courteously said: "May I ask the visitor from America, whom I have never met before, a question?" The speaker asked me if this was permissible, and I replied, "Certainly."

The Soviet representative then queried: "I have never been in your country, but I have studied much of it. My studies lead me to believe that perhaps the best way for me to answer this gentleman's question is to ask you a question. Is it not true that in your schools you teach the fundamentals of democracy and capitalism as you see them?"

I answered, "Yes, sir, you are right. We believe that the fundamentals we teach ultimately mean the greater dignity of the individual, the freedom of man."

The speaker then faced the audience and said: "Gentlemen, you have your answer from our American friend. We believe in what we teach, and we know that communism will ultimately triumph and that capitalism, which is at the root of most of the world's problems, will disappear from the earth."

This verbal exchange underlies the basic reason why this book was written. After I had answered the Russian, I then began asking myself, "What do we really teach? Do our people understand the fundamentals of democracy? Is capitalism, as a responsible service agency, really understood, or do our economic textbooks and teachers merely belabor the dead devil of nine-teenth-century capitalism?" As my contacts widened throughout many parts of Asia, Africa, and Latin-America, I sought the answers to the same questions as applied to other countries and, more importantly, listened to the ideas and questions of people in other lands. The challenges these raised led me to welcome the opportunity to make this study, probing methods of com-municating abroad the nature of American capitalism.[1] The research was undertaken because of a belief that a unique form of business enterprise, that may be termed "dynamic" or "service" capitalism, has developed in North America. There are, how-ever, other places in the world where the same recognition exists that the dual purpose of business should be to earn a profit for its owner and serve the community needs.

Of what value may such a study be to freedom-loving people in our times? This important question and many more have been posed to me by scores of people with whom I have discussed this whole subject.

Out of the total population of the world today, roughly one-third are dominated by the militaristic exploiters of the theories Karl Marx expounded in 1848, one-third have and believe in some form of democratic existence (ranging from those who believe in the advancement of the welfare state to those who are in favor of the status quo or even of turning history back a hundred years), and one-third are variously wavering and trying to find the way they want to travel. We are in the midst of a battle of ideas in a world-wide arena.

Under the form of dynamic capitalism that has developed in North America, there have emerged together the highest stand-ard of living ever known to man and a political democracy that preserves the dignity of man as an individual. This recent development has proved so worthwhile in men's lives, in both

---

[1] "American capitalism" as used in this book includes the capitalism of Canada and the United States, which have developed very similar social and economic systems.

its material and spiritual phases, that if it can be expanded and interpreted, it should be of inestimable value to people throughout the world who are groping for ideas as to how they may individually participate in better twentieth-century living.

But dynamic capitalism must be properly interpreted. The whole matter of interpretation is complicated by many facts and fancies, as I discovered in talking with people of all walks of life in many countries and in working on projects both here and abroad. These experiences in their entirety are too voluminous to be reported in detail, although some will be described. But out of them have appeared certain truths which are so basic that I have adopted them almost as premises in what follows.

Our overseas problem is basically one of public relations. The objective of public relations research is truth; the objective of this book is to record the results of research in the broad field of communicating overseas the fundamentals of American capitalism. Basically, communication is an area of public relations, with its many definitions. One particularly fitting in this instance is: Public relations is doing the right thing at the right time in the right way in the right place, and always respecting the opinions of others, while seeking reciprocal channels of information.

Public relations techniques recognize that emotions are far more important than facts in the making of human conclusions. Some of the various opinions reported in this book will immediately strike a spark of honest dissent or even indignation on the part of certain readers. Yet the report aims to portray sincerely the attitudes of men and women around the world today—especially what they think about the fundamentals of North American capitalism.

The fine art of public relations demands, first, that a research job be done to evaluate the situation; and second, that results of the research be implemented by action. Shakespeare recognized this truism centuries ago when he wrote: "Thought, to be worth while, must complete itself in action." When research reveals that public opinion is contrary to fact, then one of the public relations objectives is to develop and pursue ways of changing the expressed attitude to one that will accept the real facts.

Public relations attempts to change problems into projects. This research report in the field of international communications presents many problems. There is not one of them, in my opinion, that cannot be changed into an attainable project, if serious consideration will be given to it by American business-men and other leaders of thought.

The world as a whole—with, of course, some exceptions in parts of Europe, spots in Asia, and dots in Latin-America—seems to be emotionally set against our form of dynamic capitalism. In many industrial countries businessmen put their trust in restrictive cartels, and the people look to the state for their welfare.

It is hard for people in the underdeveloped parts of the world to realize that capitalism could ever be so interpreted or so practiced as to appeal to their emotions or serve their aspirations; their limited contacts and their would-be leaders have fixed in their minds a distorted picture. The followers of Karl Marx have led many of them to see communism as a new way of life almost automatically operative and as a short cut to the common welfare —not to the degradation of the individual to a mere cog in a vast economic and political machine. However much we may dis-agree with these concepts, they are the "real facts of life" for millions of people and the most powerful motivating forces in their daily attitudes and conduct.

The crucial battle upon which our future and that of our children depends is apt to be decided in our favor only when men around the world have become emotionally and affirmatively concerned about the benefits of political and economic freedom, which make possible the growth of a dynamic service capitalism. If we, as a people, believe that our freedom, as expressed in American capitalism, is worth preserving, we must assume the responsibility of interpreting it to others. We should not leave the job to the government when the very thing that we are op-posing in the battle of world ideologies is the encroachment of government upon individual lives in the economic as well as the political sphere. Only indirectly in this book is any attention drawn to the problems that are basically the responsibility of the State Department and the military. As a result of my long study of international public relations, I am convinced that our Defense and State Department organizations are doing as good a job as can be done with the means available in the face of world frictions inherent in the vast developments of the twentieth century. I personally believe that the military must be strong enough to hold the line until the competition of ideas for the benefit of mankind is won. But we cannot expect the military to do it indefinitely. As President Eisenhower put it at a press conference: "Troops are never going to win the peace. We have got to do something positive, and this must be in the field of moral and spiritual and economic and political strengthening of all these areas."[2]

Those who believe in mid-twentieth-century capitalism with its flexibility and sensitivity as having value in North America, must become so emotionally inspired with it as to explain wherever they go its value in contrast with that of communism.[3] We do not seek to transplant our system. Let others adopt the underlying principle of freedom of opportunity for all and work it out as their various circumstances permit. That is what we have had to do and will continue to do. Capitalism in America today is not the capitalism of our forefathers; and its flexibility and sensitivity will continue to readjust it to new needs, while preserving the basic freedom of opportunity. We are in an

---

[2] *The New York Times* (August 7, 1958).

[3] Harold B. Wess, in an article "We Can't Have Freedom Without Capitalism" in *Human Events* (November 19, 1958), states:

"Socialism and communism—like all forms of dictatorship—are frozen societies. The Nazis believed that they had achieved a society which would last a thousand years. The Communists believe the same. They believe that they have a system which is the ultimate in perfection and which will last forever. None of these systems tolerates any authenic change. Since change is the only constant in life, these systems must ultimately collapse or wither.

"Capitalism, on the other hand, is a way of life which has in it the inherent ingredients of growth and change. Capitalism adjusts to changing times and changing conditions. Because of its fundamental principles, capitalism makes possible peaceful revolutions like the change in the pattern of income distribution."

emotional battle for the minds of men, as *The Christian Century* has so pointedly stated:

The fact is that man throughout history has been moved less by intelligent insight and logical processes than by his emotions and imagination, by stabbing prejudices and hatreds, by volcanic passions and overweening ambitions. The reckless adventurous zeal of an Alexander; the passionate resentments of a Hannibal; the cool, calculating political ambitions of a Julius Caesar . . . the rapaciousness of an Atilla and the ferocity of a Tamerlane; the vainglory of a Louis XIV, a Charles XII of Sweden, and a Napoleon; the furies of class and race and economic interest and social tradition exemplified in the American Civil War; the raging giants of national aspirations and the monomanias of individual usurpers such as Hitler and Stalin—these are the elements of which wars have been made through the centuries and even in our own day; and these are the forces that will continue to threaten us with war.[4]

To date, the Marxist is the one who has been the most emotionally enraptured about promoting his program. I have yet to know a Marxist, or encounter one on the highways and byways and trails of Asia or South America, who was not a zealous missionary for the faith in which he believes. His text is always the same: the age of capitalism is dead, and he is preaching the new gospel that the world will be redesigned according to Marxist specifications. When he, perhaps a sincere individual, has thus cultivated the soil of human emotions and passions, he is ready to sow the seeds of blind faith in Soviet imperialism.

There is no other answer to this world problem save that given by dedicated men and women who believe in "the rules of the game"—that is, the principles and practices by which freedom of opportunity for men, women, and children may best be assured. We have found knowledge of such rules valuable in helping others understand that they themselves may play the game in their own way on their own fields with their own umpires.

Baseball became a national game in Japan because Japanese students came into personal contact with American youths who were sentimentally attached to baseball. The rules of cricket remain an essential part of the Asians' image of the British. As

4 *The Christian Century* (November 28, 1956).

an Indian told me in 1949 when I commented on the absence of hatred toward the departing British: "You know, they went out just as if they had lost the game—and you can't hate them! As an Englishman would say, that isn't cricket."

There are several simple principles which will guide us in our efforts to help the rest of the world understand this economic system that we call American private enterprise. The most important is an appreciation of the power of semantics. This was well understood by the Soviet representative in New Delhi who used Lincoln's words to lend appeal to his ideology. The fact that to other people a word can carry an overtone that was not in the mind of the user was borne out in my own experience.

In 1951 I wrote an article entitled "Our Economic Policy in Asia,"[5] covering my reactions to developments there. Shortly after its publication, three of my Asian friends drew my attention to the word "Asiatic," which I had used in defining the part of the world I was describing. They said: "Mr. Miller, 'Asiatic' is not our word even if it does appear in your dictionary. We do not like it; it has a strange twist of ridicule in it and we feel as you would if we called you 'Americanatics' or the Europeans 'Europeanatics.'" They felt this word had originated with the contempt of the colonial overlords for the natives. Naturally, I have never since used the word.

If we are going to live in harmony with the peoples of the rest of the world, we must come to understand that they have feelings about words and their associations, just as we have. When Asia, Africa, Oceania, South America, Australia, and other areas were just distant places on our maps, perhaps there was an excuse for not knowing something of them and their people. Today, we must realize that they are an integral part of the world and entitled to the same consideration we expect for ourselves. Inattention to semantics is the cause of as much international misunderstanding as perhaps any other one thing. In the field of business, this failure to recognize the importance of semantics is on a par with our lack of comprehension of the metric system, which even the British are beginning to use in

[5] *Harvard Business Review* (July, 1951).

preference to the old English system of pounds, yards, feet, and inches. These terms are still used in commerce today even though the kings whose body measurements they represented are long a part of the dust of the ages.

Other principles which should guide our communicative efforts are basically as follows: We must adjust continually to an everchanging world; the only way to get things done is through people, and to do this we must understand human emotion and recognize that most decisions are reached by emotion rather than by reason; we must know the interrelated facts of the situation that we are trying to explain; we must recognize that probably the greatest motivation of mankind has been its religion and faith, and it was conviction rooted in firm beliefs that enabled the sober man of religious faith to "endure all things."

Another thing that we must realize is that we are qualified to help other nations because we have learned to help ourselves. We, too, went through periods of colonialism, of poverty, and of illiteracy. Though our problems were not quite the same as those of today's underdeveloped countries, we do have a fund of experience on which they can draw. In the following pages will be found my reasoned conclusions as to how we can best "help others to help themselves."

II

CAPITALISM, SOCIALISM, AND COMMUNISM

§1. Too Few of Us Are Socio-economically Literate

In the Korean conflict, many Americans were taken prisoner. A few of them became imbued with the philosophies of communism, and a startlingly large percentage of those returning as exchange prisoners were found to be inoculated with the Marxist virus. Exhaustive psychological research was immediately put into operation by the military who, rather than merely criticize these men, sought to find out why this had occurred.[1] The results of these studies proved that many of our men were sent to war without understanding the fundamental principles that have made America a place of value to the ordinary man. Too few truly grasped the meaning of democracy and the nature of our capitalism.

There is an old adage, "Know thine enemy." Unfortunately, in the United States we have been so satisfied with thinking we had all the answers that we have made very little attempt to know our enemies or our friends—or understand our own political-economic system. In traveling in many countries of the world during the past few years, I have had occasion to meet

[1] Described in "The Study of Something New in History," *The New Yorker* (October 26, 1957), pp. 102 ff.

and talk with a great many Americans. I am proud to know them, proud to have them as fellow-citizens. On the whole, they represent a brilliant cross-section of the culture into which we have been so fortunately born. But let us take a look at some of their training for important overseas assignments.

Aside from a few government people, I have met very few Americans abroad who reflected previous training in the fundamental principles of our government. Nor did they understand the differences between communism, socialism, fascism, and the various concepts of democracy.

I have sat in the homes and clubs of representatives of American business, ridden with them in jeeps, and walked with them in the hills. Their conversation almost always centered around things back home. They deplored the lack of understanding and appreciation of the American philosophy of life and business by the people in the country to which they had been sent. Down underneath there was a sincere friendship and love for the people with whom they were living. But I can recall only a few occasions when these friends and hosts of mine showed any evidence that their companies had given them any briefing or taken any interest in having them understand the economics and politics of the country in which they were living. Most of them were trying to obey the laws of these countries, trying to set an example of being good American citizens, doing their jobs and keeping out of trouble.

But the great stream of thought in the nations in which they were living and working passed them by unnoticed. They knew very little of its ferment or its content. It was not their fault. How many people reading this volume have ever read a perfunctory review of the philosophy of Marx or Engels, or the translated writings of either? How many have studied the speeches of Norman Thomas, the socialist leader of America?

While I was in Europe a few years ago, a prominent member of the U.S. Congress made a public statement to the effect that the people of the United States wanted no socialist allies. The following day I attended a gathering of academic and political leaders. Never before had I met a group so polite to me or so sympathetic regarding the lack of education displayed in this speech by our representative. Every European ally of the United States, to my knowledge, is considerably socialistic. And yet, here we were telling Europe, through this member of Congress, that we wanted none of them as allies—because we had never taken the trouble to understand definitions or semantics to clarify our understanding of their evolving socio-economic systems.

We have allowed the Communists to run away with the word "socialism." Even today, many speakers on American platforms, denouncing communism and socialism, fail to recognize that the evil against which their invectives are meant to be hurled is neither of these but in reality is Soviet oligarchy and imperialism, behind the façades of socialism and Marxist communism.[2] The democratic socialists of Europe know this distinction, but we Americans have failed to cultivate our best allies by not understanding it. We have, in many cases, through ignorance of the facts of various economic societies and the meaning of words which describe their attributes, forced the democratic socialist to find his friends among those who are preaching the gospel of absolutism.

This confusion, on our part, with respect to the nature of capitalism as it exists in North America and the ways in which it differs from other socio-economic systems, is the first hurdle to be surmounted. We realize our present-day capitalism has brought us inestimable benefits. We would offer to the rest of the world the results of our experience in developing a system which serves all of society. But to effectively communicate abroad that which we would offer—and even to prepare our own people for the arguments of those convinced of the merits of other systems—we must first broaden our own knowledge.

Leaders of the millions of people in the free and neutral world are concerned with the best matrix and framework for the future of their own countries. Increasing numbers of them, whether government officials, educators, farmers, scientists, or technicians, are visiting this country wondering about the real value of capitalism to them and whether it should be placed on

---

[2] The word "communism" as used in this study, unless otherwise indicated by the context, means "Soviet imperialism," of both the Asian and European brands.

the credit or debit side of their lives. Many of their countries officially embrace socialism. All of them are subjected to Communist propaganda. The Communists are adept and battle hardened in waging their war for the minds of men. To turn the tide, we shall need to use all of the resources we possess.

The need for clear concepts of the philosophic bases and of the practical functionings of different socio-economic systems has been insufficiently recognized in America. Too few groups are embarked upon projects to better our understanding.

As a result of the Korean experience, Secretary of Defense Charles E. Wilson and the Joint Chiefs of Staff authorized a study of ways and means to help the military personnel understand America, communism, and what the battle of ideologies is all about. This study became a project known as "Militant Liberty"—the brainchild of John C. Broger, Consultant in the Office of the Joint Chiefs of Staff. The manual developed under his direction is now in use as a medium for discussion by military personnel around the world.[3] In my work on the present book, I have had the utmost cooperation on the part of Mr. Broger and his associates, and many discussions have been held as his project has developed.

To familiarize the military with the how and why of our democracy and capitalism is a proper project for government. Likewise, business, itself the objective of world-wide Communist attack, should see to it that its own personnel both at home and abroad can meet socio-economic questioning knowledgeably.

A private group which is attacking this problem is the Foundation for Religious Action in the Social and Civil Order, commonly known as "FRASCO." This action-foundation has on its National Advisory Council and Standing Policy Committee ranking representatives of the Protestant, Catholic, Jewish, and Greek Orthodox faiths. Labor unions and industry, educational

[3] *Militant Liberty, A Program of Education and Assessment of Freedom* (Washington, D.C.: Government Printing Office, 1956). Many schools, churches, and service organizations have utilized this material in their own programs seeking to foster greater responsibility to the disciplined free society. Indigenous counterparts of the study have also appeared in other countries. A follow-up study, undertaken by the U.S. Air University, evaluates the gains and losses in individual liberty during the past fifty years.

and civic groups are also represented. FRASCO's Chairman,
Dr. Charles W. Lowry, has defined its purpose, in a remarkable
"Consultation" entitled *The Ideology of Freedom vs. the Ideology of Communism* and published by the House of Representatives Committee on Un-American Activities, as follows:

> This is an all-faith organization dedicated to opposing by spiritual
> means communism and all forms of totalitarianism and, positively, to
> helping renew the religious and moral foundations of democracy in our
> own country and the whole world.[4]

Further on, Dr. Lowry adds:

> I believe that if we could forge a really vital front, not just have one
> more rump organization, if we could have Protestants, Catholics, Jewish,
> Greek Orthodox, all believers in God, all welded together as a single
> force, then I think we would have taken the first great step. The second
> step would consist of embassies of friendship and understanding to other
> great world religions.[5]

It is highly important that we implant in the minds of the
youth of North America an awareness and abiding love for the
ideals and values of democracy, and a clear understanding of the
nature of the dire threat to our free institutions which lies in
international communism.

The Council for the Advancement of Secondary Education
made an exhaustive study of what the leaders of the various
groups that constitute the United States believe are the fundamentals most needed to be taught in high school in preparing
students for entrance into the professions, business and trade,
and home and community life. Out of some 88 suggested projects for studies, these 2,000 representative Americans almost
unanimously recommended that the study of capitalism itself
was most essential in the American school curriculum.

The Council has developed a textbook which it first tried
out experimentally in over 100 high schools in nearly every state
of the Union.[6] I firmly believe not only that this project marks

---

[4] Government Printing Office (Washington, D.C.: 1958).
[5] *Ibid.*
[6] Council for Advancement of Secondary Education, *American Capitalism,
An Introduction for Young Citizens* (Washington, D.C.: The Council, 1958).

a milestone in American education, which will be of invaluable use overseas, but that the text itself contains a useful blueprint of twentieth-century capitalism and what it means.

This is by no means an exhaustive list. Nor does each project acquaint its group with all of the major forms of economic society in the world today. They are, however, among the more noteworthy movements in the needed direction of an informed American public.

§2. Exploitive Capitalism
Bears Seeds of Its Own Destruction

A detailed review of the historical development of economic and political systems would be outside the scope of this book. A brief glance, however, may be useful in portraying the background which to a large extent conditions attitudes in the world today.

Let us look first at exploitive capitalism, for this was the form within which agricultural and handicraft economies developed into industrial societies and small states became empires. It still exists in many parts of the world. In this system economic development is left entirely in the hands of private enterprisers whose sole concern is the maximization of personal or corporate profit. There was, of course, nothing new in the fact of profit and private property. Most of the laws under the codes of Justinian and other ancient lawgivers had to do with regulating the use or disposal of private property.

The term "exploitive capitalism" was suggested to me by the context of Marx's writings. As it is used in this book, it means the private use of capital characterized by disregard for proper conservation of natural resources, withholding from labor its fair share as a factor of production, engaging in unfair competition, paying too large a share of economic gains for managerial services, absence of interest in community welfare, a lack of due regard for the dignity of man as an individual, and particularly the exaction from the ultimate consumer of an excessive and unreasonable return. While private enterprise might have one or some of these characteristics to a minor degree without being considered exploitive, it would clearly belong in that category if it carried any one of these factors to excess. Another aspect frequently associated with exploitive capitalism, though technically a function of the state, was colonialism.

It is an impossibility, without some mention of colonialism, to discuss the methods by which we might be able to get the rest of the world to understand and use the principles of service capitalism which we have developed in America. This is because, in most of the developing parts of the earth, colonialism and capitalism are looked upon as synonymous. It is immaterial whether we like it or not, whether we played any part in the development of this thinking or not; the fact remains that people in other parts of the world are debating whether they will come with us, go Marxist, or try to develop a "middle road" of their own. In their minds colonialism and capitalism are inseparable.

This association is understandable, for in colonialism exploitive capitalists and the state were closely linked. Each served the other. In simplest terms the typical cycle ran thus: early explorers claimed distant lands for their home countries; the home government granted exclusive rights to certain businessmen or organizations to exploit the resources of the new territory; this exploitation—whether the distant society was composed of indigenous peoples or settlers—increased the power of the governing state, directly through tax or other revenues and indirectly through trade advantages.

Rather than take an example from the Far East or the Southern Hemisphere, let us take one closer to home which is probably typical of the sort of thing which has left this aftermath of resentment against the words "capitalism" and "colonialism."

The island of Newfoundland was discovered, and its development in the field of fisheries began, at approximately the same time as the establishment of the Colonies in the United States. Newfoundland waters had great quantities of fish which were valuable in the British market. The then all-powerful royal government gave vested interests in fishing to certain merchants on the coast of England. These men were allowed to outfit fishing boats, gather crews, and send them during the fishing season into the Newfoundland area. In order that these vested rights might not be disturbed, it was proclaimed by royal decree that the island of Newfoundland was not to be settled or colonized by permanent residents. The person who built a home or established a wharf broke the laws of the realm. This vast area was looked upon purely and simply as a private domain, which the few English merchants who controlled the fishing boats could exploit for the primary benefit of themselves and perhaps the royal family. On various occasions, the king's troops were dispatched to destroy the habitations which were erected there and to take into custody those who dared to defy the royal edict.

The reason that Newfoundland was chosen as an example is the fact that all the people involved were members of the same race and country; this was not the exploitation of an undeveloped people of another color or race or nationality. It was political power used for economic gain among people of the same race. After a century or more settlers were eventually admitted.[7] But it is only in recent times that Newfoundland has become an integral part of the modern world. Because the Newfoundlanders were largely British, they remained loyal to the Crown. Their economic distress for at least two centuries was a direct result of this colonial attitude. Even today Newfoundland is handicapped by the results of the long exploitation.

We are all familiar with the story of the hard-won liberty of the United States. We have often stressed political and religious liberty, which were of tremendous importance; but equal in importance is economic liberty. Without economic liberty other liberties are, in effect, restricted. Contributing reasons for the American Revolution may be illustrated by the fact that the fishermen from Gloucester and Boston were forbidden to fish the waters of the Newfoundland Banks because they were no part of the vested-interest group. The well-known Boston Tea Party —in fact, there were several of them—was engendered not by taxation but by the exclusion of New England merchants from the profitable tea trade operated by a monopoly granted the East India Company and its agents. The American Revolution was born largely of economic inequities.

[7] See J. A. Cochrane, *The Story of Newfoundland* (Boston: Ginn & Co., 1938).

Examples of colonialism in North America are given not to reopen old wounds, but to put into historical perspective some of the problems confronting those who would make available to the rest of the world the concept of economic democracy or responsible service capitalism that has recently emerged in North America. Our own experience has shown that attitudes can change when people have the opportunity to work out their own political and economic destiny and to discover the ideals which they have in common with their former oppressors. We in North America have overcome our resentment against those who were the perpetrators of our colonial troubles; they are the closest of our international friends. Moreover, we find ourselves in alliance, both political and economic, with some peoples with whom we were at war a relatively few years ago, and in irreconcilable conflict as to the future socio-economic patterns of nations with Russia, our former military ally.

It was, however, not until Western civilization had reached the machine age and experienced the industrial revolution that we get capitalism in the developed, characteristic modern meaning of the term. Capitalism as a term was first used in 1854. It properly denotes a system in which money is translated into machines with the power to multiply many fold the utility of labor and to produce goods in abundance. The end result of the purchase of these goods is profit added to capital to a degree and at a rate unknown in the pre-industrial ages.

I owe the above suggestive remarks to a personal letter from Dr. Charles Wesley Lowry, who is also the author of the internationally famous book, *Communism and Christ*.[8] It was again Dr. Lowry who called my attention to the following eloquent tribute to capitalism:

During its rule of scarce one hundred years, [it] has created more massive and more colossal productive force than have all preceding generations together.... It has accomplished wonders far surpassing Egyptian pyramids, Roman aqueducts, and Gothic cathedrals; it has conducted expeditions that put in the shade all Exoduses of nations and crusades.[9]

[8] Charles W. Lowry, *Communism and Christ* (New York: Morehouse-Gorham Co., Inc., 1952).
[9] Max Eastman (ed.), *Capital, The Communist Manifesto, and Other Writings by Karl Marx* (New York: Random House, Inc., 1932), p. 324.

These words were not uttered in a recent speech by an American corporation executive. They are not a modern public relations product. They are not an expression of faith in the capitalistic system at all. They were written more than a hundred years ago by Karl Marx in a tract called *A Communist Manifesto*. As a matter of fact, the word to which "it" refers in the quote above is not "capitalism" but "bourgeoisie," the word Marx used in this tract to denote the owning and exploiting class. The words "capital" and "capitalist" are not used until his later publications.

Yet throughout this superb technological revolution capitalism remained exploitive in nature. In addition to the selfish use of foreign areas as sources of raw materials and as markets, there was also an internal exploitation. Since industrial developments were located almost entirely within the independent powers, the particular evils of the factories fell on the populations of the Western nations. In these countries unscrupulous management —the twelve- to sixteen-hour work day, child labor, and working and living conditions which were crowded, poorly lighted, insanitary, and hazardous—was added to the long-borne curses of poverty, disease, illiteracy, and lack of opportunity.

The vast outpouring of goods, with its intensified and sometimes profitless competition, gave impetus to the further development of an old phase of exploitive capitalism—the cartel. Business organizations thus attempted to wring the maximum profit from existing markets through mutual agreements among competitors on such protective measures as allocation of raw materials and markets, restriction of production, and maintenance of stipulated prices. Whole populations thus became economic pawns with escape doors firmly battened.

Unfortunately, world leaders of nineteenth-century capitalism failed to observe, or admit, as the case may be, that their system was patently infected with certain inherent human social and economic errors, evils, and deficiencies, most of which were preventable or remediable. They lacked the vision or the will to exercise their corrective powers, not suspecting that the weaknesses in their structures would some day, not long postponed, destroy their edifice and themselves.

§3. WHAT IS SOCIALISM?

There is nothing in the world so powerful as an idea whose time has come.   —Victor Hugo

Never has this been proved so true as in the case of some of the ideas promulgated in the *Communist Manifesto* in 1848 by Karl Marx and since then by his disciples. With their pens and voices they attacked the exploitive types of private property which they defined in the all-embracing term of "capitalism." The time had come when the people generally believed that large accumulations of private property used for production should be managed in the public interest. The disciples of Christ and the followers of Mohammed, even in their hope of world acceptance of their ideas, never contemplated anything that moved and is still moving as rapidly as many of the ideas of Marx.

Even before Marx the human misery accompanying exploitive capitalism had not been overlooked. Here and there a sovereign had decreed a palliative measure such as setting a minimum wage for apprentices. But the whole system was so riddled with injustices that thoughtful people searched for some totally different formula which would distribute the benefits of the industrial revolution to the many rather than to the few. Socialism was the foremost panacea put forward early in the nineteenth century in England and France.

There have probably been as many varieties of socialism as there are sects within the Christian or Buddhist religions.[10] Socialists have differed among themselves with regard to such matters as the part to be played by cooperatives, abolition of all private property, voluntary versus obligatory labor, the place of religion, equal rewards to all versus distinctions on the basis of individual contribution, and support of one's government in time of war.

But one thing they have in common—the conviction that capitalism does not promote the common good and that eco-

---

[10] In response to a question by the author at a seminar at the University of Utah in June, 1958, Dr. Henrik Virkkunen, a professor from Finland said, "A socialist is a constitutional proponent of the welfare state."

nomic and social justice can be accomplished only by collective or governmental ownership of the basic elements of production and distribution.

Along with this most socialists advocated universal suffrage, abolition of child labor, free education for all, and governmental responsibility for decent housing and for adequate care of the sick and the aged. The goal was, and is, a classless society. Few early socialists were concerned with colonialism as such. But virtually all believed that wars are the result of the competition of capitalists for world resources and markets and can be averted only as socialist states cooperate in their common interest. Those who considered the practical problems of achieving a socialist state relied on recognition of human and moral values and on a widely based voting power to gradually bring about the reforms.

The doctrines of Marx presented a completely new analysis and direction which to this day marks the significant line of cleavage among socialists. His study of history convinced him that capitalism was temporary and was doomed by its inherent conflict between the greed of capitalists (bourgeoisie) for large profits and the equal desire of the workers (proletariat) for a larger share in the results of their labor. He taught that a state is always subjugated to the dominant economic class and that capitalist exploitation would increase to the point where the class struggle would inevitably proceed from the economic to the intellectual and political fronts. Revolutions of the workers, led by Communists,[11] would take over states, destroy private capital, and preserve the fruits of its efforts for new socialist states. These initially would have to be proletarian dictatorships which would eradicate all class distinctions and ultimately give way to world-wide equalitarian communal societies.

Seldom has the world encountered a more terrific shock from an idea. Today, approximately one-third of the human race is under the domination of a country or countries whose expressed objective is the subjugation of the people of the earth to the Marxist program. No person in the world is unaffected in one

[11] The Communist League of the period was composed of exiled German radicals who chose the term "Communist" to distinguish themselves from reformist or utopian socialists.

way or another by the teachings of this man. Much of his
original doctrine has been changed by addition or subtraction to
meet the whims and suit the purposes of the potential and real
dictators who have used his ideas as weapons to subjugate millions of men to their power.

Giving Marx the benefit of the doubt for being an honest
researcher, he saw the evils of the capitalism he knew—exploitive
capitalism. He rightly perceived that something dynamic and
revolutionary had come into history, namely, machines and fabu-
lous technology and emerging capitalistic corporations. However,
his prediction of ultimate communism failed to recognize the
desire of all men to acquire and possess real and personal property.

Right-wing European socialists rejected the dogma that the
state is but the servant of the dominant economic group. This
was particularly true in England where the political franchise
had already been broadened to include wage-earners, trade unions
were slowly improving working conditions, and consumer cooperatives had begun to raise living standards. These circumstances
underlay the formation of the Fabian Society whose policy was
one of reform through conventional political activities. This is
the working hypothesis today of the non-Marxist Labour Party,
French Socialist Party, German Social Democratic Party, Italian
Social Democratic Party, Austrian Socialist Party, Norwegian
Socialist Democratic Party, Danish Socialist Democratic Party,
Swedish Socialist Democratic Party, and India's Congress Party.

I hold no brief for either socialism or communism. I like our
own form of American democratic capitalism which has such
socialistic features as our people have found expedient. But, for
my Swedish friends who want much socialism, intermingled with
some private profit corporations and many democratic cooperatives, and for those of my Israeli friends who want the kibbutz,
which is pure communal living, I have no criticism because
neither of these is undemocratic or imperialistic. But when the
men in Moscow or Peking destroy the dignity of man, the freedom of the soul, under a form of tyranny and despotism more
rigid than that described by Plato in the *Republic,* then I am
against such a system.

§4. COMMUNISM THROWS DOWN THE GAUNTLET

What is communism? In answering this question we should perhaps look at the U.S.S.R., the dominant and the first country pledged to communism. Under this banner a handful of men instituted, and their successors perpetuate, a calculated dictatorship which under the guise of socialism and democracy governs every phase of the economy and of society in the Sino-Soviet bloc.[12] Communists everywhere proclaim the "scientific principles" of evolution as enunciated by Marx and Engels in the *Communist Manifesto* as the basis of their ideology and the mainspring of their actions. Lenin constantly referred to the teachings of Marx. Stalin exalted Marxist-Leninist principles (the difference is important). Although Stalin has been downgraded officially as a practitioner of communism, the party continues his recognition that its doctrines and the workings of the Soviet government reflect the adaptations of Marxism while Lenin devised and implemented.

Two basic distinctions between the original Marxism and modern Soviet communism lie in the degree to which power is to be shared by the working class as a whole, and the stress laid upon the "withering away" of the "dictatorship of the proletariat" and its replacement by a voluntarily classless society. Marx envisaged broadly based revolutions led by adherents to his beliefs, but his theoretical approach did not fill in the practical details of how the new socialist states should be governed and their future courses plotted.

Marx's disciples split irrevocably on the question of the sharing of power. Lenin believed in principle, and as a result of the unsuccessful amorphous Russian revolution of 1905, that party membership, leadership, and power should be held by a limited group of thoroughly dedicated, trained, and disciplined adherents who would guide the rest of the proletariat in their development. The methods could include violence and terrorism. Lenin's doc-

---

[12] For an authoritative firsthand report on China's scientific development, see J. Tuzo Wilson, "Red China's Hidden Resources," *Saturday Review* (November 8, 1958).

trines and leadership were adopted by the Bolsheviks who, within a few months after the 1917 revolution, wrested control away from the provisional government of Kerensky, which was attempting to establish a democratic socialist state.

The concentration of leadership is partially reflected in the fact that, in 1956, out of a population of 200 million people in the U.S.S.R., party membership was roughly 5.8 million men and 1.4 million women. These party members constitute the dedicated, disciplined corps who are assigned to penetrate every profession, farm, and factory in order to further Communist doctrines and carry out its programs. The same general pattern is followed in Communist China.

Actual power, however, is restricted to a very small party group whether this group is the summit 13-member party Presidium (formerly called the Politburo), as under Stalin's domination, or the next ranking 120-member Central Committee, as at present under Khrushchev. Under the constitution of the U.S.S.R. neither one is a formal part of any branch of the government. But as a matter of practice it is these groups which have decided who shall be nominated to government posts and have dictated state policies and programs. To quote Stalin:

> Here in the Soviet Union, in the land of the dictatorship of the proletariat, the fact that not a single important political or organizational question is decided by our Soviet and other mass organizations without direction from the Party must be regarded as the highest expression of the leading role of the Party. *In this sense,* it could be said that the "dictatorship" of its vanguard, the "dictatorship" of its Party, is the main guiding force of the proletariat.[13]

It is not by accident that Khrushchev, like Stalin, became both First Secretary of the party and Premier of the U.S.S.R., and that many high party officials also hold leading government positions.

The dissolution of proletarian dictatorships into equalitarian communal states as prophesied by Marx receives little attention from Communists today. Marx was vague as to its timing. Many

---

[13] From Stalin, *Problems of Leninism,* quoted in *Brief on Communism: Marxism-Leninism,* p. 16, prepared and privately printed by the American Bar Association, 1951.

Communists had judged it would take a generation of training before the people were ready voluntarily to live in this way. Certainly Lenin, who died in 1924, was more than occupied with the dual problems of building the new economy and society and of organizing subversive groups to promote workers' revolutions in other countries. But forty years have elapsed in which the party has had full sway. Stalin throughout the 1930's justified strengthening dictatorial power as necessitated by the enmity of capitalist nations. Current Soviet pronouncements refer to the encirclement by our military bases as evidence of our hostile intentions; and the dictatorship continues. The Communist Party is no exception to the rule that absolute power is seldom voluntarily surrendered.

What does this mean in terms of the economy and of the daily life of a people whose justifiable discontent under the exploitive capitalism of the Czars enabled the Communists to seize control? All of the developments, both social and economic, are planned and carried out by the state. Land and facilities of production and distribution are owned by the state. The state decides just what facilities shall be created and where, what products shall be made—where and how many—where they shall be marketed and at what price. Despite the Communist line that profits are iniquitous, prices in the U.S.S.R. are not limited to the cost of production. There is a planned gap between predetermined factory costs and set factory prices. This "profit" goes to the state. If factory costs are in actuality reduced—for instance, if unit costs are lowered by production over the quota (and this is *expected* of a factory)—factory prices are not reduced. Of the resulting extra profit a small part goes to the state. The bulk of this extra profit remains at the plant as a Director's Fund to be used at his discretion for vacations, rest houses, recreational facilities, housing, and the like, and to serve as an incentive for increased production. The same principles are applied to other forms of Soviet enterprise except that in agriculture profits from overfulfillment of the quota go to the individuals in the collective rather than to a Director's Fund. There is no "middleman's profit" as such, since there is no private ownership of goods except those for individual use, but the markup from factory price to sales price, the so-called "turn-over tax," is the major source of capital formation in the Soviet Union.

Let us make no mistake about it, the successive five-year plans have brought about some great advances. In the field of social services primary and secondary education is free and compulsory, and evening schools are available for adults, with an attendant rise in the literacy rate from under 50 to a claimed 95 per cent. University and graduate education plus a stipend is available to those of proved ability. Health services are the right of every citizen. Child care units are adjuncts of factories and collective farms. Cultural and recreational centers serve the people in varying degrees of elaboration in cities and hamlets. As a worker no one need fear unemployment. The doors of opportunity have been opened in the professions, science, management of industrial or agricultural developments, and, after assiduous indoctrination and screening, in the party and in the government. In the arts, sciences, and professions, such international contacts as have been allowed show that the Soviet Union is among the most advanced nations. Production basic to both military might and the civilian economy has moved forward rapidly.

Such are the facts with which Communists solicit new converts and which we must acknowledge and put into perspective if we are to reach the minds of those peoples seeking the best road for their own development. Are the industrial advances to be taken at face value? And what is the price exacted for the social benefits?

In appraising the industrial figures, economists have pointed out that these long-term advances occurred in spite of two wars and the upheaval of revolution, and that the concentrated effort of Soviet five-year planning did not begin until 1928. However, we should not forget the part played by the U.S. Lend-Lease assistance of $9 billion and subsequent UNRRA aid. Another factor in increasing production rates was the territorial expansion of the U.S.S.R. after World War II. Still another *caveat* in accepting Soviet figures lies in the area of quality. The Polish Communist economist Oskar Lage states:

> It is necessary to stop the race for purely quantitative indices which are attained thanks to low quality and to high own costs. This brings

about purely fictitious results, the usage of raw materials and of human labour for production of goods which do not produce the intended economic, and often even the intended technical effects (e.g., agricultural machinery improper to any use after a few weeks).[14]

Also, as Nutter points out, most industries tend to grow more slowly percentage-wise as they grow older. The growth of the relatively youthful Soviet industries during the 1913–1955 period was at roughly the same rate as took place in the United States from 1880 to 1920. According to Gabriel Hauge, then assistant to President Eisenhower:

Over the same 40 years which encompass the Soviet experience, Canada grew at least as rapidly as the Russian economy and this growth was far better, balanced between agriculture and industry, than Russia's.[15]

More significant for today and tomorrow are measures with more recent benchmarks. Annual growth rates of *total* production in the 1950–1955 period ranged from 7.7 to 11.7 per cent.[16] Another estimate shows that total industrial output, using 1950 as 100, grew to 178.2 by 1956.[17] John Gunther makes meaningful observations: from a share of only 1 per cent of total world industrial production in 1917, the U.S.S.R. now stands, second only to the United States, at over 19 per cent; recent annual growth rates were 10 to 11 per cent; and the current seven-year plan and the one to follow would "put the U.S.S.R. neck and neck with the United States on most categories of basic industrial goods by 1972."[18]

[14] Quoted by G. Warren Nutter in "Some Observations on Soviet Industrial Growth," *American Economic Review* (May, 1957). Oskar Lage, *For a New Program* was translated from the Polish by J. Vanek and reproduced for private circulation by the Center for International Studies, Massachusettes Institute of Technology, October, 1956. The article originally appeared in *Zycie Gospodercze* (Warsaw) for July 16, 1956. The quotation is taken from p. 5 of the translation.

[15] Reported in *U.S. News and World Report*, "The Truth About Russia" (April 25, 1958), p. 61.

[16] G. Warren Nutter, "Measuring Production in the USSR: Industrial Growth in the Soviet Union," *American Economic Review* (May, 1958), p. 408.

[17] Demitri B. Shimkin and Frederick A. Leedy, "Soviet Industrial Growth— Its Cost, Extent and Prospects," *Automotive Industries* (Jan. 1, 1958), p. 51.

[18] See John Gunther, *Inside Russia Today* (New York: Harper & Bros., 1957, 1958), chap. xvii, "Aspects of the Economic Picture," pp. 354–77.

These objectives may seem unrealistic in the face of the failure of the last five-year plan to reach its goals. But the decentralization of industrial production undertaken in 1957 was planned, partly for military reasons, but more importantly to eliminate the admittedly gross inefficiency caused by the bureaucratic rivalries of the former industrial ministries. Each of these, from its headquarters in Moscow, ran its own industry in minute detail. Khrushchev termed it "administrative chaos."[19] The new setup with over-all planning centralized in the State Planning Commission and residual autonomy and opportunity for initiative resting in the regional councils may, after an initial shakedown period, go a long way toward achieving the Soviet industrial goals.

The price the Soviet citizen pays for the industrial advances and social services is *freedom*. From birth he is molded and utilized by the state for the state. The seven- and ten-year schools impart heavy Communist indoctrination along with excellent education. Those who go on to vocational schools are required by law to spend three years in practical work in the specialty for which they were trained. Theoretical university training for those of superior ability is offered only in the subjects and only to the number of students for which the state plans indicate a need.

Freedom of choice in disposing of income is severely limited. The factory worker is caught in the vise of low wages and high prices from which there is no escape. Both are set by the state with the objective of conserving material and human resources for industrial, scientific, and military developments. How little a Soviet factory worker could have beyond basic necessities can be indicated by a sampling of prices in terms of his working time as compared with the working time the same type of item would cost the factory worker in the United States. Bread in the U.S.S.R. costs nearly twice as much working time as in the United States, a cake of soap about 6 times, a pound of butter about 10 times, a woman's dress about 8 times, a man's shirt almost 17 times, man's shoes over 11 times, and a man's suit

19 *Ibid.*, p. 366.

almost 14 times.[20] While housing costs are lower than in the United States, Gabriel Hauge stated:

... a recent United Nations study showed urban housing standards in the Soviet Union to be the lowest in Europe [about 13 by 13 foot living space for the average family of four]. ... At the risk of some oversimplification which does no violence to the facts one can say that 40 years of Communism has given the average Russian citizen one more shirt for his sacrifices.[21]

The industrial worker has a trade union, but it is controlled by the party, and its primary responsibility is to increase production. Secondarily, the union can seek specific wage adjustments within the narrowly set range of wage rates and confer on the use of the Director's Fund. From all reports agricultural workers are no better off in terms of real wages. The economic bind does not exist for intellectuals, scientists, government officials, and those gifted in the arts, for they are well paid. But the limited production of luxury goods gives these people, too, little choice in disposing of their income. Nor can they count on their savings when these can be virtually expropriated as they were in 1957.

Freedom is limited in nonmaterialistic areas. Religion is now tolerated, but to be a party member one must be an atheist. Freedom to travel, even within the U.S.S.R., is restricted. Unauthorized absence from school or work is a criminal offense. Freedom of inquiry is stifled since there is no freedom of the press or of any form of mass communication. There is no political freedom. Overt questioning of the official party line is tantamount to a crime against the state. The opportunity, at election time, to write in candidates in place of the official single slate in no wise jeopardizes the absolute dictatorship of the Communist party.

The subjugation of all resources, human as well as material, takes on enormous significance in evaluating the power behind the prime Communist objective—world domination. The interna-

[20] Based on *U.S. News and World Report*, "Sputnik: Russia's Living Costs Are Sky-High, Too" (November 29, 1957), p. 61.
[21] *U.S. News and World Report*, "The Truth About Russia (April 25, 1958), pp. 61–62.

tio..al role to be played by the Soviet Union was clearly set forth by Lenin and Stalin.[22]

Lenin:

We are living not merely in a state but in a system of states and the existence of the Soviet Republic side by side with imperialist states for a long time is unthinkable. One or the other must triumph in the end. And before that end supervenes, a series of frightful collisions between the Soviet Republic and the bourgeois states will be inevitable. That means that if the ruling class, the proletariat, wants to hold sway, it must prove its capacity to do so by its military organization. (*Report of Central Committee at 8th Party Congress,* 1919)

Stalin:

The tasks of the Party in foreign policy are: 1) to utilize each and every contradiction and conflict among the surrounding capitalist groups and governments for the purpose of disintegrating imperialism; 2) to spare no pains or means to render assistance to the proletarian revolutions in the West; 3) to take all necessary measures to strengthen the national liberation movement in the East; 4) to strengthen the Red Army. ("Party After Seizure of Power," *Pravda* [August 28, 1921])

The taking over of small nations after World War II and the U.S.S.R.'s actions toward its satellite nations are clear evidence that communism is nothing short of Soviet imperialism.

Essentially the thinking has not changed since Lenin's time, in spite of current Soviet propaganda for "peaceful coexistence." It is quite possible that the Kremlin leaders are now convinced that actions short of war would best suit their purposes. This is still in keeping with Lenin's dictum:

Lenin:

The strictest loyalty to the ideas of Communism must be combined with the ability to make all the necessary compromises, to "tack," to make agreements, zigzags, retreats, and so on, in order to accelerate the coming into power of the Communists.[23] (*Selected Works* [New York, 1943], Vol. X, p. 138)

Even in the propaganda, aggression is merely shifted from the force of arms to the battle for men's minds. Soviet adeptness in

[22] U.S. Department of State, *The Kremlin Speaks,* Publication No. 4264 (Washington, D.C.: Government Printing Office, 1951), p. 4.
[23] *Ibid.,* p. 17.

the latter area is well illustrated in Khrushchev's letter to Eisenhower, suggesting a meeting between representatives of capitalist and Communist states:

> What we advocate is that the superiority of any particular system be proved not on the field of battle, but in peaceful competition for progress and for improved living standards of the people.[24]

We have only to look at present living standards in the Communist world relative to those in the United States to realize that the suggested test is in the area where the increasing Soviet industrial potential could show up to the greatest advantage. Could the arena be so narrowed, Khrushchev's predictions "we will bury you" and "your grandchildren in America will live under socialism" might indeed come true. This only emphasizes the need for communicating to others the totality of the benefits which are intrinsic to American capitalism.

[24] *The Washington Post* (December 19, 1957).

III.

AMERICAN SERVICE CAPITALISM

§1. What Does Modern American Capitalism Offer?

What, then, is this "capitalism" which the Marxists and Communists are seeking to destroy, and yet which we Americans (and others) feel is the servant of all mankind?

Capitalism has been defined as follows:

> ... an economic system in which capital and capitalists play the principal part; specifically, one in which the ownership of land and natural wealth, the production, distribution, and exchange of goods, and the operation of the system itself, are effected by private enterprise and control under competitive conditions.[1]

With this I would not quarrel—insofar as it goes. But it carries little hint of the philosophies, attitudes, and the democratic framework which in the United States and Canada have produced a dynamic North American capitalism which is unique in its functioning. There is no one definition of American capitalism. It is of necessity a definition that varies with experience and viewpoint. American capitalism is evolving and therefore has to be defined in its condition at a particular time; but it is the North Star of hope for mankind if it is to find a way out of the morass caused by exploitive capitalism—the very

[1] *Webster's New Collegiate Dictionary* (Springfield, Mass.: G. & C. Merriam Co., 1956).

34

morass which prompts the Marxists to condemn all capitalism. Its essential characteristic is that *mid-twentieth-century American capitalism participates in producing economic progress through social justice by democratic means.*

In contrast to socialism or communism, under capitalism the basic economic decisions are determined by the sum of countless individual decisions of all the people, rather than by the state. Under North American capitalism the ultimate consumer, in the long run, determines the types of goods that are to be made and sold. The previously mentioned study made by the Council for Advancement of Secondary Education, of which the author is a trustee, points out: "Free enterprise assumes that individuals are in the long run the best judges of their own interests, and that an economic system that makes it possible for them to pursue those interests will achieve the greatest welfare for all."[2] The basic foundations of the system are *private property, profit motivation, competition, and economic freedom.* Further definition of the latter develops particular economic freedoms:

Freedom of enterprise is the right of the individual businessman to decide what business to enter, and what goods to produce or what services to render. Once his business is established, it is his right to conduct his enterprise responsibly in pursuit of profits. His decisions, of course, are guided by market conditions; they are not arbitrary ones.

Freedom of choice assures a person the right to live where he pleases, to work at what he can do best, and to buy the goods and services he prefers. Many believe this to be the most fundamental economic freedom—the one that especially distinguishes a free-enterprise economy from others and that is most essential to a democracy.

Freedom of contract means the right of consumers, producers, workers, and owners of property to bargain with one another, and to exchange goods and services on terms acceptable to all concerned.[2]

Noting that certain modifications of free enterprise have been developed in this country the study describes the foundations of American capitalism as follows:

(1) Its property and enterprises are *predominantly* privately owned. (2) The profit motive provides a *major* incentive for its operation. (3) Ac-

[2] These quotes are taken from Council for Advancement of Secondary Education, *American Capitalism, An Introduction for Young Citizens* (Washington, D.C.: The Council, 1958), pp. 21, 22, 23.

tive and *substantially* free competition exists. (4) The maximum *desirable* economic freedom is assured.[2]

These four foundations support our market economy in which individual decisions and initiative determine what consumer or capital goods are to be created—where, how many, and at what price—how to organize for the most effective production and distribution, and who should receive the products.

The italicized words in the definitions of the four foundations of American capitalism are indicative of the developments by which we have moved away from exploitive capitalism. Underlying the changes is the basic philosophy that business should serve as well as get. To this end it should be subject to reasonable regulation by the state when the people through their freely chosen representatives determine that the public interest so requires. In speeches in Congress, Senator Ralph E. Flanders of Vermont has recognized this situation several times. He sent me the following statement during the Suez crisis:

> This closing off of Western Europe's supply of oil has brought problems to this country. The oil companies have raised the price of oil and its products to American customers. On the basis of free enterprise of which I am an ardent supporter, it can be argued that they can and may charge all that the market will bear. This, however, is not in the long-range self-interest of the oil companies. If they continue to take advantage of a foreign situation when their stocks are high and their production capable of great expansion, they may look for legislation in the near future which will declare the oil industry to be a public utility in which prices will be determined by the government instead of competitively. The principle of free enterprise is best served when the free enterprisers regard their long-range interests instead of looking for immediate profit.

If a job is too big for private enterprise, or if private business has failed to perform a necessary service for a reasonable price, the people should and do determine by their individual votes or by the votes of their representatives whether they wish the state or the community to assume some function normally performed by private capitalism. Congressman Brooks Hays of Arkansas, until 1959 a member of the House Foreign Affairs Committee, in a statement prepared for inclusion in this study, sums up what

I believe is a cross-section of Congressional opinion in regard to capitalism, as follows:

Capitalism is private enterprise with a conscience. If the conscience is lacking, then no amount of technical proficiency or managerial genius can prevent the breakdown of the system. Where there is no self-imposed moral discipline, government will inevitably take notice of the problems created. The breakdown thus leads to some form of statism which marks the end of industrial freedom.

Under the modern Sino-Soviet system, state capitalism is blended with a political oligarchy.[3] The net result is that the beneficence of service capitalism is something that does not need to be taken into consideration by those operating the state organizations, because they are responsible only to the political arm of government for the operation of an economic function. In North America where the government, either federal or local, enters into the operation of a business, the officials are directly or indirectly responsible to the voters.

To appreciate the changes that have taken place in this century, one should read *The Age of the Moguls,*[4] which is not a muck-raking document per se but does point out the general failure to recognize social responsibility as part of the role of capitalists during the era when the United States became materially great. The revolt of the American conscience and some of the subsequent reforms in our economic society have been well presented in *The Big Change.*[5]

[3] Under the system of free enterprise capital is owned largely by individuals. The open market determines the value of goods and services. The law of supply and demand acts as a regulator of values, with the government providing the rules of "fair play."

Under the Communist system the state becomes the sole owner of working capital, and most personal possessions are taken over by the state. Capital is used both at home and internationally by the state. Prices are determined not by the rules of the ordinary buyer-and-seller transaction but by the determination of policy in line with the objectives of the state. Capital remains as an indispensable ingredient in life, but its use and values are determined by political as well as economic considerations.

[4] Stewart H. Holbrook, *The Age of the Moguls* (Garden City, N.Y.: Doubleday & Co., Inc., 1953).

[5] Frederick Lewis Allen, *The Big Change, America Transforms Itself, 1900–1950* (New York: Harper & Bros., 1952).

Due to the constant discovery by scientists and engineers of new products, and the development of means to manufacture and distribute them by fabricators and distributors, modern business manufactures many products that are obsolescent when put on the market; there is often a better one on blueprints or in the initial stages of manufacture. These dynamics of business are largely impossible where the supply and demand is regulated by the all-powerful state.

As material products become obsolescent, similarly many of the old concepts of capitalistic business have become obsolete. Some of the changes have been reflected in legislation. When exploitive monopolistic corporations were concentrating economic control in the hands of a few to the detriment of the many, Congress passed the Sherman Anti-Trust Act and Canada legislated its Combines Investigation Act. These acts, with their amendments and regulations, established the principle that every North American should have the opportunity to become a capitalist. Today's corporations largely not only accepted this principle but as a whole actively encourage individual capitalism in another sense—through widespread ownership of their stocks—by employee purchase plans and by offerings to the public. Over 8 million families are stockholders in the United States today. Many millions more are capitalists through their interests in savings, life insurance, pensions, and so forth. These funds are managed by privately operated institutions which in turn lend to or invest in private enterprise. A significant proportion of North Americans are capitalists via their ownership of farms and real estate.

For centuries, the doctrine of *caveat emptor* (Let the buyer beware) was the rule of trade. Under it, wooden nutmegs were sold to unsuspecting "natives," and dangerous medicines and adulterated foods sent many a person to an untimely grave. So extensive were these evil practices of "exploitive capitalism" that Congress saw fit to pass the Pure Food and Drug Act of 1905. Equally strict are the regulations under Canada's Food and Drug Act. However, during the last half-century North American capitalism with enlightened management has largely removed the fear of *caveat emptor* from the mind of the purchaser. The overwhelming majority of goods and services are today guaranteed to satisfy the customer. Some stores even advertise that they will refund the money for a roast if the housewife is not satisfied with its tenderness! This is a distinct step ahead from the "Let-the-public-be-damned" attitude of the later nineteenth century.

Times are changing in the direction of fair dealings in the public interest. Many an innocent investor used to be fleeced through shady practices by issuers or sellers of stocks and bonds. But the principle of *caveat venditor* (Let the seller beware) has been legislated into most of the state and provincial acts regulating securities, and particularly into the U.S. Securities Exchange Act of 1934 and amendments thereto. The latter makes subject to civil suit and criminal penalties individuals who violate its provisions, for instance, by failure to give adequate information about a company whose securities are to be issued, or taking advantage of inside knowledge, or manipulating the market. The operations of dealers and of securities exchanges can incur severe administrative penalties if they do not comply with standards set up under the act.

§2. AMERICAN CAPITALISM
IS RESPONSIBLE

North American capitalism has worked out other concepts unrelated to any compulsion of law. One of those is to help people help themselves. Just two illustrations. Within a business organization there is usually the opportunity for an individual to advance to the extent of his ability. Even more, many enterprises, recognizing latent abilities in their employees, enable them to develop their potentialties through training programs either within or outside the company. Business, as a matter of course, applies the same concept to its customers and suppliers by encouraging them to develop products which will enhance the growth of those outside enterprises.

A fundamental attribute of mid-century American capitalism is equality of respect. The patronizing attitude of the proprietor or manager in the 1890's has largely disappeared, and the man who works at the bench, or drives a truck, or sells behind the counter receives as his human due approximately the same amount of respect and consideration as does the white-collar man, or proprietor, customer, stockholder; in fact, he is often a stockholder himself. This is so far from the old concept of business that it is very hard for people in other parts of the world to understand. Largely a thing of the past is the situation where an employee would come into an office and bow as though he were appearing before a lord of the realm, or would come in "with his cap in his hand," as the old expression went. One finds in most of private business in America a fraternal relationship that is unique.

Closely related but going beyond all these is the essential ingredient of today's American capitalism—the matter of business responsibility, human or public relations, human engineering, or whatever you want to call it. The American industrialist has learned to put fellowship, truth, and honesty into business. Practically unknown until a few years ago, this philosophy is perhaps the greatest development of the genius of America in the field of economics—the discovery that business can function and still be friendly; that the businessman does not have to tell the truth to a few and some prepared story to the many; that goods can be honestly made, distributed, and sold to the consumer at a fair profit. The extent to which these ideas go beyond any legal requirements is reflected in the emphasis which today's industrialist places on the brand name he gives his products. He holds out his brand as a hallmark of integrity and of a certain quality at a suitable price, and he is careful so to design and make each item as to support the brand's reputation.

We have developed a capitalist enterprise system that has made it possible for men of all strata of society to enjoy the benefits of industry in a way that just a generation ago was the goal of the radical "soap box" orator. This is not solely due to the technique of mass production, for the needed increase in markets to support mass production depended on concepts unrecognized by exploitive capitalism. American businessmen have learned that when they set prices at a low enough level to allow more people to buy their products, the resulting increase in the market for most goods returns an increased total profit; that the new income of the additional workers needed for the increased production again increases the market potential; and that wages, which reflect a sharing of the cost savings from increasing productivity enable workers to enter the market for goods which in their grandparents' day would have been the privilege of the wealthy. The woman on Main Street can wear the same fashion in clothes as the woman on Fifth Avenue. The farmer from out where the creek forks, when he gets into the city, is hard to differentiate in appearance from the businessman. And if one were to call at their homes he would find labor-saving devices, luxuries, and evidences of culture that would make him realize that in its own way American capitalism has gone a long distance toward a classless society.

Present-day responsible American capitalism looks upon community and civic projects as something in which it should take an active part. Just a generation or so ago, it was rather uncommon for a company to understand that its employees owed any other duty during their waking hours except to the corporation. Today, this is very largely reversed, and increasing numbers of American businesses recognize that the employee who takes an interest in community development in his off-duty hours—and sometimes during working hours as well—can and does perform a service not only for himself and his company, but for democracy itself.

This same thinking prompts business leaders to accept the call of the government to fill responsible posts despite the financial sacrifice to themselves and the loss of their leadership to their companies. Private enterprise as a responsible force in our society has set up, or contributed substantially to, many foundations for research in medicine, education, and other social areas.

§3. MODERN CAPITALISM OUTSHINES "SOCIALISM OF THE CHAIR"

In the late nineteenth century there developed in Germany a concept known as "Socialism of the Chair." The term was applied, at first in ridicule, to the doctrines of a group of economists who advocated state aid for the betterment of the working class. In America our sense of responsibility has led us to take the very principles which Germany enunciated in "Socialism of the Chair" and make them a large part of the basic economic practices of our land. We have enacted laws first proposed by the socialists, among which are workmens' compensation, unemployment insurance, wage and hour laws, and veterans' insurance and health services. An increasing number of people are coming under Social Security, to which few object; we do not allow the poor to suffer at home and alone—we hospitalize them at public expense and see that they receive adequate medical service. The costs of many of these benefits are borne completely by industry; of others, business enterprises pay a significant share through their taxes. No political party in North America has made any serious attempt to undo any of the social or welfare legislation enacted under preceding administrations. This fact was illustrated by the 1957 election in Canada.[6]

In 1953, after Norman Thomas had retired as active head of the Socialist Party (having been its Presidential nominee six times), I sent him a copy of a speech I had made before the Third Annual Conference on Institutional Relations, at the University of Utah, November 28–29, 1952. It was entitled "Dynamic Capitalism." In this speech I had said:

... The study of despotic materialism is interesting. Norman Thomas, the leader of the Socialist Party, was one of the first to denounce it. He was, perhaps, the first leader of consequence in the United States to expose the men of the Kremlin as being opposed to human liberty in the Twentieth Century. He said that the world has its choice of being free or slave. Many of our politicians didn't see it that way. Many of those who thought so didn't have "nerve" to say the things that they knew were right. No one will ever successfully attack you if you say the thing you know is right. "Truth though crushed to the earth will rise again." Norman Thomas had the nerve to do it. A few months ago when he retired as leader of the Socialist Party, a big banquet was given *for*

---

[6] *Time* magazine reported: "Triumphant Tory

"Leader of Canada's Progressive Conservative (Tory) Party, which last week downed the powerful Liberals: John George Diefenbaker.

"... Politics: Accents the 'progressive' in his party's official name, Progressive Conservative. Backs flexible farm supports, social security and health measures, more federal aid to penniless Atlantic provinces. Shunning a doctrinaire stand, he goes along with Canada's pattern of government competition with private enterprise in rails, airlines, hotels, T.V . . ."—*Time* (June 24, 1957).

Norman Thomas. A thousand business, religious, political and industrial leaders came to pay their respects to him as *a man.* Mr. Thomas, following the simple rule of integrity, had said the things in which he believed and had often been called a radical. Today, many of his ideas are in the Democratic and Republican party platforms—this is a demonstration of how democracy works in the U.S.A., and this is as it should be.

In a letter to me, dated June 23, 1953, Mr. Thomas wrote:

"Thank you for your pamphlet, "Dynamic Capitalism." In these days when obviously so much rethinking is necessary, the old division lines aren't what they were. It may be that "dynamic capitalism" and democratic socialism are growing nearer and nearer together. Anyway more forthright discussion is in order. I appreciate your references to me which were, if anything, too complimentary.

In a succinct way this states the whole case of the changing status of capitalism from the laissez faire to the dynamic.

Yes, "Socialism of the Chair" and a lot more "socialistic" ideas unconsciously became a fundamental part of the American social economic and financial system; but American business has very slowly begun to realize the fact that it is living in a new and fast changing world, and that it has a chance to penetrate that new world and work cooperatively with it for mutual benefit and universal peace and prosperity. A "creeping socialism" has understandably accompanied a "creeping" (or galloping) capitalism, but it has not seriously impaired the capitalistic nature of our economy.

§4. Definitions of Capitalism Are Many and Varied

"What is capitalism?" is a question that I have asked citizens of most of the free nations of the earth, ranging from rulers in high places to students in the classroom, farmers in the field, managers in their offices, and laborers at the bench. No two definitions were the same. The great majority of answers of persons not living in America included some form of statement or prophecy to the effect that the welfare state will be an integral part of modern life—usually with an approving reference to the Scandinavian use of capital. I have asked this same question of a cross-section of North Americans, both citizens of Canada and of the United States, and find much the same answer, except with an almost universal appreciation of the fact that business now represents a great improvement over the concept of business in 1900. The belief of most people in and out of business seems to be that had not business recognized the responsibility of capitalism within a responsible society, organized business in America would have been inextricably enmeshed in the toils of state control or ownership.

The definitions of some observers of the American scene seem particularly worthy of inclusion here. Dr. Tojuro Murai, Chief Editorial Writer of the *Hokkahu Shimbun,* as well as lecturer at Toyama University and Kanazawa Women's College in Japan, had been told that our capitalism was still of the exploitive type. But because he is an astute, natural researcher, he wanted to base his opinions upon his own observations. Dr. Francis Brown of the American Council on Education arranged for him to spend a few days with us at the Harvard Business School in 1956. We made for him many other contacts, among them John Kenneth Galbraith, Professor of Economics at Harvard, with whom he developed a warm and close friendship. Dr. Murai proved to be an intense, interesting man, and his questioning about our new capitalism was among the most searching I have encountered. Dr. Murai's definition of capitalism as he found it here is included in a round-table discussion he haq with other educators upon his return to Japan. Below are some direct quotes translated from this discussion, published under the title *Capitalism Is Already Exceeding Itself*:

[Preface:] Capitalism already appears to have changed into something completely different. Capitalism is difficult to understand unless it is understood as something dynamic and different from what Marx defined. Particularly, in the changing American society, it appears that a firm, new trend is being worked out by management executives, labor union leaders, and a number of leading scholars. This trend is to discover within capitalism itself a public-ness, and to further and develop this public-ness.[7]

[7] Public-ness (kokyo-sei) is a coined word derived from kokyo, or public, as used in such terms as the public welfare, the public good (but not the general/or public opinion) and sei, or nature-ness.

[Kobayashi:] ... Today it is already a question whether we should badly say, "Choose capitalism," or "Choose communism." How has capitalism as represented by the United States today changed? Can capitalism progress further? If it can, what kind of labor-management relations will be born? As a matter of fact, already in America a new labor-management relationship may be a-borning.

If there is indeed something new in American capitalism, the big question is how to adapt it and use it in Japan. I would like all of you to give us your opinions with this background in mind. First of all, I shall call on Mr. Murai, in order to have him indicate the direction in which we should take our discussion.

[Murai:] ... I was first struck by his [Mr. Raymond W. Miller's] contention of the dynamic nature of American capitalism. The question is, of course, practically speaking, how did capitalism come to take a course different from that prescribed by Marx? Well, it seems to me that, first of all, in regard to labor, capital, management—all these important production factors in the capitalistic structure—an attitude of, what shall I say, a kind of social responsibility has been very strongly developed.

Specifically, capital, for instance, is not looked upon as one form of the right of absolute possession by an individual. It is looked upon as a wealth shared by society as a whole. Of course the starting point was the formation of an organization through which the individual would seek to gain profits. But as this concept progressed, it was looked upon simply as one factor within a common society. The main factor then came to be regarded as a whole. Management, for instance, in its relations with labor, came to look upon its ultimate aim as that of dealing with good citizens. I feel that America is proceeding and will proceed in that general direction. This is what will make capitalism dynamic, I feel.

Dr. Dale Yoder, then Professor of Economics and Director, Industrial Relations Center, University of Minnesota, now of Stanford University, participated with me and others in an Executive Development Program in Utah, in June, 1958. This program was sponsored by the Institute of Industrial Relations and the College of Business of the University of Utah. The thirty executives in attendance gave freely of their time and thought in discussing many of the ideas expressed in this book, and Dr. Yoder added greatly to a stimulating and exhaustive examination of the whole subject of twentieth-century capitalism. During these seminars he made the vital statement:

As managers of American industries have faced the growing relative scarcity of manpower and as competition for available labor supplies has become sharper, we seem to be developing a new type of economy that might be called *capitalistic socialism*. The basic Marxian precept—to each according to his needs—is increasingly implemented through our expanding program of employer-financed employee benefits and services. These "fringe benefits" provide many of the objectives advocated by Marxists, at the same time that they preserve the incentives, motivations, and freedoms that have been the distinctive contribution of the private capitalistic system. This development is a part of the emerging theory of agency management, in which managers propose to act as the agent of employee team-members. As agents, they promise to encourage the continuing personal development of their worker clients, to maximize their contributions and rewards, to coach them in their work, and thus to develop each team-member as an All-American worker.

A most significant analysis of the genius of North American freedom in developing the most highly productive economy in the world was made by Herbert Hoover before he became President of the United States. In defining the American social system he says:

We have, in fact, a special social system of our own. We have made it ourselves from materials brought in revolt from conditions in Europe. We have lived it; we constantly improve it; we have seldom tried to define it. It abhors autocracy and does not argue with it, but fights it. It is not capitalism, or socialism, or syndicalism, nor a cross breed of them. Like most Americans, I refuse to be damned by anybody's "word-classification" of it, such as "capitalism," "plutocracy," "proletariat" or "middle class," or any other, or to any kind of compartment that is based on the assumption of some group dominating somebody else.

The social force in which I am interested is far higher and far more precious a thing than all these. It springs from something infinitely more enduring; it springs from the one source of human progress—that each individual shall be given the chance and stimulation for development of the best with which he has been endowed in heart and mind; it is the sole source of progress; it is American individualism.

The rightfulness of our individualism can rest either on philosophic, political, economic, or spiritual grounds. It can rest on the ground of being the only safe avenue to further human progress.[8]

Col. Richard P. Crenshaw, Jr., a fellow-member of the Bar who has long been familiar with national and international

---

[8] From *American Individualism*, by Herbert Hoover, pp. 12–13. Copyright 1952 by Doubleday & Co., Inc. Reprinted by permission of the publishers.

affairs, has sent me the following thought-provoking paragraph regarding the value of the new capitalism:

The competitive North American free enterprise system (modern "capitalism") is absolutely indispensable to human freedom and the inevitable future world-wide system, since no other system both (1) gives the individual full incentive to work and thus throw off the bondage of want, and (2) splits up economic and thus political power, and prevents its concentration by providing many bosses and alternatives instead of (as in the Soviet) only one. A man given too much power will always abuse it and competitive free enterprise alone sees that no one man gets too much power.

Sylvia and Benjamin Selekman, authors of *Power and Morality in a Business Society,* explore how the various centers of power in our society interoperate, and come up with a research concept of our American capitalism. They say:

These critics [of capitalism] assume that, with the abolition of private property, materialistically motivated business managers will be replaced by dedicated, selfless servants of the state. Events have by now clearly demonstrated that before very long the selfless servant, in fact, turns into an absolutist commissar. Such is the logic of power. The gradual gains growing out of the exchanges of negotiation in our capitalist democracy, on the other hand, furnish convincing evidence of steady advance toward social goals without the risk of enthroning commissars. For capitalism, as it has evolved in the West, is a decentralized form of power—in contradiction to Marxian theory—with negotiation as the strategic form of administration.[9]

§5. The Structure of the North American Economy

With the growth of large business enterprises for production, transportation, and distribution of goods, there gradually emerged the general use of the capitalistic corporation—a legal device seldom needed or used until mass production made possible wide use of products. Many of these corporations, as in the automotive, electrical, steel and telephone industries, are of truly massive

[9] By permission from *Power and Morality in a Business Society,* by Sylvia Kopald Selekman and Benjamin M. Selekman, p. 172. Copyright, 1956, McGraw-Hill Book Company, Inc., New York.

size. Most large businesses, either directly or through subsidiaries or affiliates, perform in varying degree a wide variety of functions. In manufacturing, these may range from extraction of raw materials to franchising dealers in the finished products; in insurance, from selling and servicing the insured to the development and management of residential or commercial buildings in which some of their funds are invested. Perhaps size and integration are the most widely known aspects of our economic structure.

Less widely understood and deserving of emphasis is the place of small business. For despite giant corporations there is room and need for enterprises on a scale that could be duplicated in almost any part of the world. Of all retail establishments in the United States, for instance, over one-third are run by the proprietor, with no paid employees. Over another third have five or fewer employees. Together their sales volume is over one-third of all retail sales, including those of large retail chains. Even more surprising to many, perhaps, is the degree to which manufacturing offers an opportunity to the man who desires to create goods for others while making a profit for himself. There are over 100,000 manufacturing enterprises in the United States —nearly 40 per cent of all manufacturers—with fewer than five workers. Nearly 240,000, or over 80 per cent of all manufacturers, employ fewer than fifty.[10] Some of the smaller enterprises serve local needs; others have found a wider niche. Many have found a sure place for themselves simply because their very smallness allows them quick flexibility in adjusting to the changing needs or desires of those whom they would service.

The nonprofit cooperative enterprise is a fundamental part of the American business scene, recognized and respected throughout the nation. To quote the National Association of Manufacturers:

A "cooperative" is a form of business enterprise that enables a group of individuals, partnerships, or corporations, to combine together for the

[10] The figures cited are based on the latest available U.S. Census of Business, for 1954.

purpose of producing or buying or selling a commodity or service. City consumers have gotten together to buy goods and sell them. Businessmen have formed mutual fire insurance companies. Individuals join together to buy life insurance through a mutual insurance company or merchandise through a mutual wholesale purchasing association. People who save money put their funds in a mutual savings bank. Farmers join together to buy goods they use in production or to sell the things they grow. All of these are "cooperatives." They are also legitimate forms of private enterprise.[11]

One of the fields in North America in which cooperatives are most active is agriculture. The Railway Express Agency, shipping packages of a size comparable to or larger than those the Post Office accepts, is a nonprofit cooperative corporation owned by about seventy-four railroads using it as a service agency.[12] Several million American families living in small towns and rural communities secure their electric service through private cooperatively owned power companies (R.E.A.), whose original capital was borrowed from the government, and which is being repaid ahead of schedule. Every bank clearing-house, rural telephone and electric cooperative, mutual building and loan association, mutual insurance company, mutual savings bank, credit union, and cooperative apartment is a sign post pointing to the fact that people in a free society demand and have achieved freedom to organize for their own best economic interests.[13]

The area where the people choose to have enterprise owned and operated by local or federal government is not clearly defined. There is the government-owned Post Office which is universally accepted as a public business operation. Even this,

[11] National Association of Manufacturers, *NAM and Cooperatives* (privately published in New York, 1946), p. 7.

[12] "... Express companies ... have handled small packages for 118 years, even though the competition of the subsidized parcel-post service has, since 1913, been almost insurmountable.

"... The Express Agency conducts the express business for substantially all the express-carrying railroads of the country, in effect serving as the express department of each railroad. The Express Agency collects the express revenues, pays its own operating expenses and taxes, and turns the balance over to the express-carrying roads." *U.S. News and World Report* (June 21, 1957).

[13] See Joseph G. Knapp, "Are Cooperatives Good Business?" *Harvard Business Review* (January-February, 1957).

however, is sometimes challenged.[14] We have a dynamic economy, in which functions change from the public to the private sectors and vice versa as serious need may arise. As an example, there are in the United States today something over 2,000 municipally owned electric services providing power and light for communities that have decided to create or take over such functions rather than have private enterprise own and operate them. Many cities own and operate their own water supply. On the other hand, there are the facilities and services in government-owned national parks which are provided by private enterprises operating under a government franchise. There are hundreds of municipally owned airports where the state or municipality charges a fee for the use of the field or its terminals. There are wholly owned federal projects, such as the Tennessee Valley Authority, which has been one of the most controversial of all national projects, and at the same time one of the most widely heralded abroad as an American triumph.

Many of our early highways and country roads in the United States were largely privately owned toll roads at one time. Later, under the post road provision of the federal Constitution and the taxing power of the states, nearly all of them were thrown open to public use. Recently, however, there has developed a trend to special high-speed toll roads, with the state acting as operator, and borrowing the money to build them from the general public through the means of bonds, the income from which is nontaxable.

In the United States, rail and truck transportation systems are owned by profit-entity corporations highly regulated by government—city, county, state and federal. In Canada, a major part of the public transportation systems—air, rail, and water— is conducted by government-owned corporations. Canada prides itself on an excellent system of hotels owned and operated by its government-owned railways, but these are in direct competition

[14] *"Private Mail Contract Suggested by President*—Apparently annoyed at the all-out pay raise fight being made by the postal employee unions, President Eisenhower is reported to have told a group of Republican Congressmen that a lot of the Nation's postal problems could be solved by the Government turning over its postal operations to a private firm...." Joseph Young, *The Evening Star* (Washington, D.C., June 18, 1957).

in many places with hotels which are the property of the privately owned competing railway.

Banking and credit is largely in the private enterprise sector. Canada has its government-owned Bank of Canada along with the other independent banks. In both countries there are a number of federal credit agencies which lend capital to risks which private banking does not care to undertake.

Labor is organized into trade unions when the workers themselves choose to do so. Some of these organizations draw their membership from individual crafts, others represent all categories of workers in a particular industry. When a labor union is certified as representing a majority of the workers in its field within a plant or company, the employer must bargain with it regarding wages, hours, and working conditions. While organized labor's primary activity is to serve the interests of its membership through negotiation with employers, it is also active in the political sphere—primarily by endorsing or opposing either individual candidates for political office or proposed legislation which is of interest to labor. Officials of organized labor frequently serve on governmental or independent boards or agencies which are concerned with matters of public interest.

Employers, too, voluntarily organize into trade associations which without indulging in monopolistic practices serve the interests of their memberships. Some of their activities are pooling knowledge of their markets; collecting, computing, and publishing average operating figures so that individual members may judge and improve their own performance; citing individual experiences in overcoming some particular problem; and representing to the public and to the government the interests of their own group and the ways in which their industry serves society.

While not immediately a part of business, there are hundreds of organizations by which business is informally linked to the community. Among them are the Chamber of Commerce, trade associations, and service clubs. These are composed of business and professional men who as individuals bring their knowledge and their leadership to the finding of voluntary solutions to community social and economic problems. In this same category might also be included the large foundations which are set up for social purposes and whose funds originally come from corporate or individual enterprise.

I would not wish anyone to think that we in America have reached the millennium. We, too, are human. We make mistakes. Not every businessman appreciates all the values which underlay the transition from exploitive capitalism. But I do believe that in American service capitalism we have found one of the roads toward the optimum material condition of man: economic power used for profit and social justice with the government as a referee and umpire, with freedom of conscience introduced into material well-being as business tries to serve as well as to get.

IV

OBSTACLES TO THE SPREAD OF
SERVICE CAPITALISM

§1. Problem of Communicating Information About American Business

We have proved that we have the knowledge, gained from experience, to help our own people to help themselves to a standard of living previously unknown. The marvel of being able to live so that the process of living does not destroy the best purposes of life is, perhaps, the greatest contribution that mid-century America has to offer the rest of the world. We have this knowledge, but how can we pass it on to others so that they may draw from it those parts that they may find useful to their own situation? That is the problem facing us.

Coupled with this is the matter of unawareness that these benefits are available to them, or of suspicion, distrust, and disbelief on the part of many who could use them. An interesting discussion of this point is found in Dr. Marshall Knappen's *An Introduction to American Foreign Policy* in the chapter entitled "The American System and Its Appeal."

Much more serious from the standpoint of foreign policy is our inability to export our system. Americans seem to have great difficulty in finding ways to propagate beyond their own boundaries the thought-patterns and social attitudes which will enable other peoples to share in the flood of automobiles, refrigerators, television sets, and other products from the American-model horn of plenty. However many cars there may be in American garages or bathrooms in American homes, the statistics fail to arouse much enthusiasm among people of other lands. The lover's philosophy is also theirs:

> If she be not so to me,
> What care I how fair she be?

Communist agitators seem to have little difficulty in transporting to other lands their crude and often violent programs for eliminating illiteracy, instituting land reform, and beginning the process of industrialization. They are not squeamish about meddling with the internal affairs of the countries they visit or about attacking alleged evils in the existing social order, even at the expense of destroying that order. Americans, on the other hand, representing a liberal and tolerant political system, use much milder methods.... They work through existing and established governments rather than seem to question their competence or undermine their authority. Consequently their assistance often serves to strengthen and perpetuate the power of landed interests, mercantile groups, and budding industrialists whether this power is being wisely used or not. So the American missionary effort is not always as successful as the rank and file of the peoples who are supposed to benefit by it might wish.[1]

Arnold F. McKee dramatically presents the problems involved in establishing an understanding of present-day American capitalism. In an article entitled "Selling American Capitalism—A Conspicuous Failure" he says:

... Withal, the one thing the United States cannot sell (one of the most striking failures) is American capitalism itself. Curiously, a literally great volume of interest has been shown abroad in American productivity and the goods and services at the end of the chain. But while the techniques command the highest respect, the declared master-technique itself has never "gone across." Although they deeply admire and intensely study many details of the operation, foreign countries seem to display an aversion for some of its fundamental principles.

The great propaganda campaign at home and abroad to sell, not the "Bad Old Capitalism," but the "New Good Capitalism" with such modifications as "Dynamic Capitalism" and "People's Capitalism" have all failed to sell the product.

The campaign has been trying to sell the product to a customer who has a deep mistrust of capitalism for several reasons.

[1] Marshall Knappen, *An Introduction to American Foreign Policy* (New York: Harper & Bros., 1956), p. 111.

Unfortunately, the name itself has a meaning different among us from what it has abroad.[2]

Capitalism in too much of the world today embodies the same attitudes as American capitalism showed in the latter part of the nineteenth century; it is still the exploitive type of capitalism which has been slowly overcome in the first half of the twentieth century in our own continent. Capitalists in those countries often live a restricted life, spend their money in building palaces and hunting preserves, deposit their money in foreign lands, and do little to improve the community or assist it to a higher standard of living.

Dr. Nathan A. Baily, Dean of the School of Business Administration, the American University, Washington, D.C., commenting on the problems engendered by "exploitive capitalism," says the following in a letter to the author:

Our biggest problem seems to be that regardless of the terms we coin for capitalism or private enterprise, there is associated in the mind of the common man a selfish aspect to the term and to the economic system. On the other hand, the socialists and communists have been able to capitalize on a frame of reference that at least implies an interest in the general welfare, in the common good, and in the little man. Even the terms "socialism" and "communism" have these built-in implications.

There isn't much use in pointing out that individual initiative and private enterprise provide more for everybody than any other system we know of. That is an intellectual argument and not an emotional one and the problem seems to be an emotional one clearly.

General Alfred M. Gruenther put the problem most succinctly when he said, "Capitalism around the world is a bad word."[3]

§2. Land Tenure a Most Important World Problem

We cannot expect the people in the world's rural areas to understand fully the dynamics of American capitalism until they

---

[2] Arnold F. McKee, "Selling American Capitalism—A Conspicuous Failure," *Social Order* (St. Louis, Mo.: Institute of Social Order) (November, 1956), pp. 411–16.

[3] *The Commonwealth* (June 2, 1958), p. 136.

are a little farther removed from the bare necessity of producing food merely to keep alive.

Today in most of the problem areas of the world, the ruralist is in the majority. In fact, in many of the countries of the Far East, 90 to 95 per cent of the people are primary producers of agricultural or fisheries products, with many farmers producing just enough food for their own use on a restricted diet, but very little for sale to other parts of their own country or for export abroad.

If these people are to make progress, they must change the present situation and become more and more industrial. A strictly rural civilization will be poor, particularly so if it is composed of farmers whose land consists merely of tiny patches. It is not easy for an American to comprehend it, but in most of the troubled areas of the world, outside the Iron Curtain, the average cultivated farm is approximately one hectare, about 2½ acres.[4] And this, in turn, is usually split up into smaller parcels. Even in much of Germany and Holland, for instance, with all of their modern developments, one finds a farm design that is absolutely unbelievable to those of us accustomed to the situation in North America.

A few years ago I visited near Stuttgart and participated in the first Congress of German farmers since the war. Some 5,000 leaders of German agriculture were there to study the problems of the new Germany. I went out with a few of these people, visited the countryside, and called on what I believed was a typical German farmer in the Stuttgart area. He owned 7½ acres of land, divided into 27 parcels, scattered several miles apart. His means of transportation to reach these farms was a wagon pulled by two cows. We sat down under a cherry tree, which, incidentally, was the only fixture on one of his parcels, perhaps 1/16th of an acre; and it was a mile from the nearest other parcel which he owned. We calculated, with the aid of an interpreter, that if he drove his cows and his wagon and visited each of his parcels of land it would take him two 14-hour days to accomplish this. Now that type of farming is not extreme.

---

[4] This was also true in pre-1919 Russia, and the fact is considered to be a major reason for the support given the revolution by the peasants.

In Europe, flying over the lowlands of Holland and Belgium, and parts of Germany, Switzerland, Austria, and France, one can see many of these fragmented areas, ⅛th of an acre here, ¼th of an acre there. Even in Greece many farms have been split into such diminutive sizes that they have been abandoned. The two great curses of overpopulation and lack of industrialization were evident throughout Asia and much of Europe.

In India there are villages where the average farmer owns less than one acre of land, which again will be subdivided when he leaves this earth and his children take over. In India today there is a great movement toward what is commonly known as the "defragmentation" of farms. Whole communities elect some of their local leaders to temporarily own all the property, and then redivide it, in order that there may be some form of consolidation. I saw one village that had some 1,800 parcels and was finally divided so that there are now some 200 in a total of about 115 farms. However, with this improvement there still remains the same adverse relation between area and population numbers.

This whole subject of the fragmentation and defragmentation of farms is something that might well demand the attention of a study much longer than the one in which I am presently engaged. The problem is inserted here merely to bring attention to the baffling questions in many parts of the world today. The lowering of the death rate and the acceleration of the birth rate creates an everlasting population situation which produces more and more demand for more and more land; at the same time there is less and less of it to fill the need, due to the effects of land erosion and the removal of production and habitation sites taken over by roads, airports, and industrial plants. These facts create problems that will go on until organization, education, and a change of social attitudes and economic practices achieve reasonable solutions. Basically, it is situations like these that swing the balance from the right to the left. Such problems should offer challenges for the skillful handling of ideas.

What is needed in most of these spots is that some form of development of industry be started to enable farm people to drain off into manufacturing—to start creating things that will tend to raise the standard of living above the level resulting from the mere production of agricultural products for home use. Under present circumstances such countries can have nothing comparable to the modern civilization which we enjoy.

There are only two short-run ways to solve these rural problems—one is the way of the dictator that we hear about in Russia, Yugoslavia, Hungary, and Red China. The forced collectivization of farms in the areas behind the Iron Curtain is the dictatorial method of attacking this problem, which I have seen in Europe and in Asia.

This rural problem has too long been looked upon in many countries of the world as a status quo situation that can never be changed. In many countries outside the Iron Curtain the Reds come along, change the problem into a project, and capture the imagination of farmers. They do this by proposing the redistribution of the large landed estates of 1,000 to 5,000 acres. Surrounded as they are by a multitude of tiny farms, these large estates are a potent temptation to revolution.

The other method of solving rural problems is by the process of democratic education. America can help in this latter way; but, no matter how many multiplied millions of dollars it spends, it cannot do it itself. In the Marshall Plan days, in Holland, I saw the efforts of well-meaning Americans and the expenditure of literally millions of dollars fail miserably to work out a plan for the consolidation of farms in that country of tulips.

If the fragmentation problem is to be solved, the people themselves must do it, and only after having come to the reasoned conclusion that it is best for them. Denmark did it a few years ago; and now basically in Denmark a farm can no longer be subdivided below a unit of approximately 7½ acres.

Too many Americans visiting countries abroad expect everything to be as modern and mechanized as it is here—four-lane highways and all the gadgets that we enjoy. The truth is that in much of the world there is not enough land available for four-lane highways, and many of the gadgets we know are not yet even dreams. Progress for those people will move in a different direction from ours, but the same fundamental rules will work. Unless they do work, the heel of the dictator will crush their aspirations, for a change of any description is looked upon by such people with suspicion and fear. We must help them to substitute hope for fear and faith for despair.

Before the Communist doctrine won in Russia and swept out from there, much of the world was beginning to move from peonage and evil land tenure to greater personal freedom and to land reform. Following World War II, under the wise leadership of General Douglas MacArthur, Japan led the way; and most of the countries of Asia and many in South America are beginning to attack this age-old problem of human inequality and lack of opportunity.[5] The community-development projects in India, development of homesteads from the Shah's property in Iran, the land tenure laws of Burma, and the beginning of something of the sort in Pakistan—all are indications of an adjustment of agricultural and rural conditions toward a type that will fit into a beginning of capitalism as we developed it in this free land.

These developments are hopeful and should be encouraged in every way. Until the world's agricultural population feels that it has real opportunity, it will look upon the message of American capitalism with suspicion.

§3. INDUSTRY-EAGER PEOPLE FEAR CAPITALISM

Before we can explain North American capitalism effectively, we must realize that millions of people throughout the world have either a false idea of its character or no idea at all. In *An Introduction to American Foreign Policy* Marshall Knappen says:

The world has heard little about the new American system of aided and regulated free enterprise. It has instead been asked to believe that Americans have remained true to the old principles of virtually unrestricted free enterprise. To people in other lands who have already had their fill of sad experiences with unregulated nineteenth-century capitalism this has proved very confusing. Possibly in the American El Dorado there is some mysterious fountain of youth which somehow warded off the evils of a maturing, unregulated capitalistic system which gave the Marxist movement its start and with which the people of other industrialized areas were already too familiar. But from their own experience they

[5] See *Time* (October 6, 1958), p. 31.

know that in their countries pure and simple free enterprise of the nine-teenth-century variety cannot be tolerated. So they tend to lose interest in sales talks promoting the American economic system.

Actually, of course, the United States does have something new and different to offer—new because it is not pure and simple free enterprise but increasingly aided and moderately regulated free enterprise, and different because the degree of regulation and control in the American system is not of the high European order which all too often has choked and crippled the free enterprise system overseas. But the changes intro-duced in the United States have become involved in partisan politics and so are not greatly acknowledged as permanent improvements though never, in fact, substantially affected by changes in the political com-plexion of American Congresses or administrations.[6]

On February 3, 1957, Edward R. Murrow of the Columbia Broadcasting System, on his See It Now show interviewed former Prime Minister U Nu of the Union of Burma in Rangoon. It is unfortunate, but true, that the statement made by U Nu on this broadcast represents a cross-section of the thinking prevalent in Southeast Asia. The President of Burma told me much the same thing in Rangoon in 1949. Said U Nu:

> The conditions in the United States and in the countries in Asia are quite different, so if we introduce American style capitalism into the countries in Asia, I think it'll bring about undesirable economic discrep-ancies. The rich will become richer—very much richer, and the old ... the poor become—will become very much poorer, so that in that case, it will bring about much discontent and dissatisfaction, you see, throughout Asia. Then I believe it'll be a sure means of—of installing Communists in Southeast Asia, so I do not want American style capitalism to be introduced into Southeast Asia.

This statement by an illustrious, democratically minded Asian should cause every business leader of American capitalism to pause and consider, plan and study how he may do his part, individually and in concert with others, through established or-ganizations and organizations to be established, to make it pos-sible for such leaders as U Nu to understand that a responsible service capitalism is of great potential value to the Burmese people and not "a means of installing Communists" in his and adjacent countries.

[6] Marshall Knappen, *An Introduction to American Foreign Policy* (New York: Harper & Bros., 1956), p. 70.

Neutralism may be a temporary necessity of self defense, but Burma will eventually develop either toward communism or toward a dynamic service capitalism. The developing countries have awakened and change is inevitable.

A dispatch from Jakarta, Indonesia, which appeared in *The New York Times* of June 20, 1957, adds further evidence to the fact that political democracy is one thing and economic democracy is another in the minds of the people of Asia.

President Sukarno is quoted in the article as saying:

> The National Council ... is a midway form of government between the Western system and the Communist system that can adapt to the original nature of our own personality, namely gotong rojojg (mutual assistance).

> Asked why Indonesia should adopt a new style of government, the President said that political democracy alone "does not satisfy us ... we want another way which fits in with our own personality, namely social democracy, which also includes economic democracy.

Dr. A. Ladru Jensen, Professor of Corporation Law at the University of Utah, has called my attention to the first use of the phrase "economic democracy" by the United States Supreme Court. In the case of *Frost v. Corporation Commission of Oklahoma* (278 U.S. 483, 1928) Justice Brandeis dissented, with Justices Holmes and Stone, in the following forceful language, declaring for economic liberty of farmers to build their own cotton gins with their own capital:

> The act is that these two types of co-operative corporations—the stock and the non-stock—differ from one another only in a few details, which are without significance.... The farmers seek through both to secure a more efficient system of production and distribution and a more equitable allocation of benefits.... They seek through co-operation to socialize their interests—to require an equitable assumption of responsibilities while assuring an equitable distribution of benefits. Their aim is *economic democracy* on lines of liberty, equality, and fraternity.

Under our political democracy, which is a powerful force in creating dynamically responsive capitalism, our citizens have secured the liberty to organize and operate small business corporations, of both the profit-entity, and the patron-profit co-operative type, by enabling legislation in all of our forty-nine states. The principle which President Sukarno desires for his own country, and for which Justice Brandeis declared in the *Frost* case, *supra*, has been established in the United States and Canada. But we have not disseminated this information abroad to the extent that honest democratic leaders seeking to benefit their own people can utilize the legal-economic patterns which have evolved under our dynamic capitalistic economy.

To the average man in most of the developing areas of the world, whose chief economic concern is keeping body and soul together, the capitalist is the local moneylender. It would be hard to exaggerate the resistance to capitalism which is engendered by the avaricious practices of the moneylender.

This problem was dramatically brought to my attention in October, 1949, when I was legal consultant to the Technical Meeting on Cooperatives of South East Asia at Lucknow, India. Representatives of the "new countries" of that area which were just "hatching" from under the hen of colonization met there in peace and harmony with representatives of the colonial powers. Japanese were on committees with Americans as representatives of the "occupying power." A New Zealander, Dr. Horace Belshaw, was the general Secretary representing the Food and Agriculture Organization of the United Nations. I was there as his and their adviser.

Perhaps a person might pray that once in a lifetime he might reach a pinnacle experience in human relations. Well, I reached mine, and I have never come out from under its influence. Here were men whose people had just been through the greatest cataclysm in history. They were gathered together to work out a system of economic law and order under capitalism. The fear of these men was that cooperatives with individual capitalistic members might fall under the Soviet concept of "forced cooperatives," where just the name remained and whose function was the antithesis of the freedom of choice under the "true" cooperative. China, only a few hours away, was just rolling under the red carpet and these men knew that there, at least, capitalistic cooperatives would never now be tried. They were up against the hard facts of reality, and as events turned out were better prophets than many of the forecasters.

Upon one thing they agreed unanimously with a passion that one seldom sees in any meeting upon any subject: the money-lender. The local moneylender was the curse of the poor man; the moneylender was the great cause of the frustrations upon which communism feeds; unless the resentments engendered against him were alleviated by "decent" money rates, the high resolves of liberty would eventually disappear under the waves of communism. Stories of moneylenders charging 10 per cent per month were common; 25 per cent for two months was not an unusual figure.

Later I visited areas in Hong Kong where I saw small boats which were used both for fishing and for family living. Twenty feet long or less, they were home for five people and a pig and a couple of chickens. In many cases they had been mortgaged for some three generations at an interest rate of about 100 per cent of the value of the boat per year. The father passed on a debt to the son. I visited rice growers in interior Thailand who had always been in debt and probably always would be, with a millstone of 15 per cent per month interest. I visited with a farmer from what is now Indonesia who told of his community where the moneylender not only took as security the inanimate growing rice but also the wife and daughters of the farmer. From these conditions the natural resentments of man bring him sooner or later to rise up and demand a change.

The world wants to move away from the iniquitous local moneylender and "exploitive capitalism." The people in the depressed parts of the world are anxious for industry, particularly for the chance to labor in it and to gain the financial ability to purchase its products. In order to gain the advantages of industry, however, they fear that they must come under the influence of the "exploitive capitalist." Because of that fear, the tendency in most of the world is to push industry over into the public sector rather than keep it in the private domain.

But despite this fear, one of the chief desires of the people is to learn how to build for themselves, by government credit and taxation, an adequate, accessible, and relatively cheap capital for private enterprise. This has been done in the Scandinavian countries for fifty years and is one of the chief reasons why they are a bulwark against communism. This was also done effectively in America following the great depression of the 1930's by creating the Reconstruction Finance Corporation, the Farm Credit Administration, and other similar organizations whose work is still being carried on as need arises and when it is beyond the capacity of private institutions to supply the financial needs of the people at reasonable costs.

Will the people of the "developing countries" be able to get industrial products and employment under a democratic concept of economic enterprise, or will they rush to the State and get these wants largely or entirely under some form of State ownership? That is the biggest problem confronting the world today in the regions that have been and are now the providers of many of the primary materials for industrial Europe and America.

Men the world over react the same way to pain, pleasure, or the benefits of profit. It is a native human trait to desire participation. Man wants the opportunity to be a part of the current world and to enjoy owning some of it, by virtue either of his position or of his property. Man also wants to work if there is an incentive to do so. No one cares to be merely a horse on a treadmill or a slave in the galley. But man is eager to work with a will if given the incentive by which he can secure for his labor something that will give him the self-realization of respectability rather than the degradation of involuntary servitude.

It is tragic but true that too much of the business world in "developing" countries looks upon 40 per cent profit from investments and 60 per cent profit from land rent as being the reward due the capitalist. Both of such percentages breed radicals. In her book, *The Nature of the Non-Western World,* Vera Micheles Dean says:

It is not surprising that the great majority of Southeast Asian intellectuals were as profoundly influenced by Western Socialist ideas as they were by those of nationalism, and that some few among them, impressed by the victory of the Bolsheviks in the Soviet Union, embraced communism from the early 1920's onward. From their point of view, capitalism was intimately linked with the economic exploitation of their own countries by the West. In the absence of a powerful native middle class in the plural societies of the colonies, there were in fact few, if any, Southeast Asians with a vested interest in capitalism. In addition, the socioreligious tradition in Southeast Asia provided, as we saw, an unfavorable climate for economic individualism. Socialistic doctrines could fairly easily be assimilated to the traditional distrust of the capitalist, a distrust by no means alien to the new leaders, many of whom came from aristocratic—and thus inherently anti-capitalistic—families. In attacking colonialism, the new leaders were almost invariably led to attack capitalism as well, and to advocate a socialist economy and national independence at the same time. Largely however, because of the fact that the intellectual inspiration of these new leaders was predominantly derived from the West rather than from Russia, only a small minority of them turned to communism. Even then, however, nationalism and communism often seemed to go hand in hand in their attacks on the common enemy—Western dominance over Southeast Asia. This relationship is of the utmost importance for present-day developments in many parts of the area.[7]

Much of the radicalism of the world is engendered by people who are disillusioned by having to exist in eternal poverty with no opportunity for escape. The Soviets are credited with winning the minds of men. In millions of cases, however, they have never actually "won" these people—they got them entirely by default. Administrators of business, indigenous or foreign, so frustrated their laborers that they fled to the Communist side as the lesser of two evils, believing that in so doing they could not worsen their condition.

§4. Capitalism Feared as Inflationary

I have talked with a number of people who say that under our present economic system it is an impossibility to curb inflation without government intervention; that the numerous raises in steel prices since the great depression of the 1930's, accompanied by general wage and price rises, have developed a pattern in our present capitalistic society to which there is no foreseeable end. I disagree with these men because there are a few fundamental facts in man's nature that seem to guarantee that the idea of responsible capitalism can succeed and will be

[7] By permission from *The Nature of the Non-Western World*, by Vera Micheles Dean, pp. 138–39. Copyright, 1957, Vera Micheles Dean. Published by The New American Library, New York.

helpful and beneficial to mankind the world over, just as it has been in North America, provided we will study it seriously and do something about it.

Most of the world has been cursed with inflation. North America has been afflicted in a minor way when contrasted with the evils of inflation in several other countries.[8] Inflation is not confined to capitalist countries, and in America businessmen have an opportunity and obligation to combat it vigorously. In 1950 I made a speech before a group of executives of The Life Insurance Companies of Massachusetts, and I quote from that speech because it expresses my thoughts of several years ago:

> You have a direct and continuing line of communication to the family unit. In almost all cases you have a plan whereby your policyholders are participants in the business successes and failures of your operation. You are the holder of many rights, but with them goes a corresponding obligation to make sure that you deserve the trust of the people whom you serve. Your unique contact with the family unit invests your work with a special drama that is not found in any other major business.
>
> How can you even now sit calmly by and see the real worth to the family of your commodity—the dollar—decrease day by day and make no attempt to correct the evil inflationary trend of our times? Your business is the only American industry that has allowed its product to deteriorate materially in value, *done nothing about it,* and still has been able to multiply its sales many times over. As an example, my own policy taken out in 1928 is today probably not worth over 50% of the real purchasing value of the dollars which my wife and I have put into it.
>
> Have you ever considered that it is your obligation and your privilege to help make sure that the social order under which you operate continues to preserve the virtues of a free society? I make no plea for you to rush

[8] Relative inflation is difficult to grasp clearly because the commonest measures, wholesale or retail prices, are usually reported in index figures based on a given date which may be either before or after the most inflationary or deflationary period of a particular country. For example, the United Nations' *Monthly Bulletin of Statistics* uses 1953 as 100. It showed Korea as having a general price index of 381 in June, 1957, and 7 for the year 1950. If the latter figure were taken as 100, the June, 1957, figure would be over 5,000. Applying the same conversion to a 1950 base, the 53 countries reported ranged from about 95 to Korea's over 5,000, with more than 30 countries showing more inflation than the United States at about 114. A study by Donald McDougall (*The World Dollar Problem,* New York: St. Martin's Press, 1957) includes a table ranking some 78 countries by their 1955 prices as a percentage of their 1945 prices. Fifty countries showed a greater increase in retail prices than did the United States.

out and protect some vested interest, or to crusade for some outmoded ideal, but I do suggest that you have a great opportunity through the family to stress the basic community virtues of participation, communication, and cooperation, and reasonable economy in Government.

In Japan, in 1951, I went with a Japanese friend while he cashed an insurance policy he had purchased some years before. Prior to the war, when the yen was worth about 50¢ in U.S. currency, his policy was worth approximately $50,000 in U.S. money. Because of inflation of the yen, the surrendered policy was then worth a little less than $200 U.S. equivalent. The day before the Chinese Reds took over Canton, a friend of mine mailed me a 1-page letter from there. The stamps required to mail it represented the equivalent of $3,300,000 U.S. money, based upon 1936 values of Chinese money. Here was inflation to the vanishing point.

In Greece live some friends for whom I have great admiration and respect. I do not know whether I could personally carry on as they have. Almost all of their assets consisted of bank deposits, and twice in their lifetime the value of every drachma they owned was wiped out by inflation. The money was in the bank; but so far as the value of their savings was concerned, it was beyond their control, and the entries became merely valueless ink spots. And then they had to start all over again.

Even though this study does not go into the intricacies of Russian economics and finance, it is interesting to note that in 1957 by executive decree the savings bonds of the Russian people were, for all practical purposes, confiscated. Now this was not in a capitalistic country, but still there is the hue and cry from the Soviets against the "mistakes" of capitalism!

We have largely taken inflation in this country in our stride, with the exception of some retired elderly people, pensioners, those on fixed incomes, and widows and children. Many of their cases are pathetic, as they try to live on a devalued dollar that hardly purchases for them the bare essentials of living. The average American, however, because of our abundance, because of the efficiency and production of our business, our relatively high wage and employment levels, and the wisdom of our government and monetary agencies, is getting along reasonably well.

But the fact remains that one of the reasons people in many of the countries of the world are afraid of capitalism, is that they fear inflation. Of course, those who own land, material property, and goods have some hedge against inflation. But people soon find that there are not enough goods to purchase and not enough land to go around, and then what happens? In India the efforts to hedge against inflation took a strange turn. It is estimated that if all the money invested in gold and silver bangles, ornaments, and jewels (unless except for the joy of owning them or for decorating the bodies of their women) were turned into valuable cash, there would be enough to pay for planned industrialization and many of the programs that might well start India toward its goal as a new world power.[9] Why has this not been done? Frankly, I think you and I might have acted the same way in an economic society such as theirs. One can save gold and silver ornaments when the psychology of demand continues to make them valuable, even though as bangles or ornaments they are useless as a productive part of a capitalistic society.

We must remember that many countries are still feudalistic

---

[9] "Gold Hoards and the Plan," an editorial in the *Hindu Weekly Review* (September 29, 1958) concludes: "The problem, however, of making productive use of the 100 odd million ounces of gold that is in private hands will still remain. Any sound scheme that can draw out even a fourth of these holdings would make a substantial contribution to our external resources, which, in terms of currency reserves, have reached nearly the rockbottom. Although we may tide over our exchange difficulties during the next two years, we have a formidable problem ahead in financing the Third Plan, whatever its size and form may be."

W. S. Woytinski, in *India, the Awakening Giant* (New York: Harper & Brothers, 1957, p. 4) says:

". . . Along the highways we observed women moving in files, bending over each piece of dung, throwing it in the baskets. And strangely, many of these women wore silver bracelets, silver ringlets on their ankles, gold earrings. The gold and silver hoarded in villages is estimated at many billions of dollars. Gold markets operate in almost every city and are patronized not only by the rich but also by people who live in misery and yet have preserved some crumb of their inheritance."

An estimate of $10 billion in hoarded gold and silver is cited by *Business Week,* July 7, 1958. It also reports recommendations of a Finance Ministry commission for a gold loan and other measures to bring out the hoarded metals.

or just emerging from the evils of feudalism—that the people have never learned how they can participate with others in the benefits of the dynamic accumulation of capital goods—putting capital to work for the continuing improvement of society and its individual members merely by owning certificates of paper called stock which will give them a return on invested capital.

Here is another recent example from India. A group of businessmen had formed and was developing a privately owned insurance corporation. The stock company was rendering effective service and apparently doing a good job, although making large financial gains for the control group. The policyholders, however, became distrustful of that particular private venture for various reasons, chief among which was fear of "its inflationary tendency." Apparently, some of the executives did not choose to wait for "inflation," and a scandal consequently developed out of an unconscionable situation, not unlike the one that Charles Evans Hughes uncovered in the insurance industry in New York State during the early part of this century.

When Americans were faced with such a problem (though on a much larger scale), they made use of their sad experience and moved into the field of mutual insurance companies. As a result, a large number of our life insurance companies today are known as "mutuals," operating under strict government supervision, regulations, and controls, but remaining under a form of private ownership where the insured rather than stockholders own the company. India, however, moved rapidly in the other direction and nationalized the insurance businesss in order, so it was said, to "protect the interests of the policyholders."

It is conceivable that had there been available in India some type of advisory service to explain the American fundamental principles of responsible capitalism, the situation could have been quite different. Rather than nationalizing the insurance companies, the Indians might have converted them into private mutuals, using our available experiences as a precedent and guide. Personally, I do not think it is yet too late. If our insurance companies would quietly and in a friendly way offer their advice and counsel to people overseas, the value of the mutual principle of cooperative ownership in this type of business would be recognized and appreciated and probably given a fair chance.

§5. CAPITALISM SEEN AS MONOPOLISTIC

In the field of human or public relations one recognizes that emotions more than facts create opinions, while an emotion based on a fact may generate an irresistible idea. However, there are in this world a great many emotions, not based upon facts, which are influencing millions of people. In practically all the countries that are reaching for a new age, there is a morbid fear of the "monopolistic tendencies" of capitalism.

It does little good to sit here on this side of the ocean and condemn those who do not believe what we believe, who do not think as we think—to condemn those who say that for their country they do not want capitalism. In doing so, we foolishly express our own hasty emotions, and thus hinder the resolve which we should make to give sober study to the problem. Much of the progress of communism in the developing parts of the world has been caused by the critical attitude which we have taken toward individuals who held an opinion different from our own. If we do nothing but condemn everyone who holds a view contrary to our own as being wrong or dishonest, we are sowing the seeds of our own destruction. Other positive approaches are open to us. Public-relations techniques have advanced to the point where it is possible to meet this challenge by an offensive in the field of ideas.

Recently, there came to the United States a group of professors from India, brought here as guests of the government under the auspices of the American Council on Education. Their time was spent in studying at various American universities and observing our organization, methods, and practices. On their arrival in Washington, the group was interviewed by the press. In the Washington, D.C., *Evening Star* of February 19, 1957, an article was published about Mrs. M. F. Jussawalla, a lecturer on economics at Nizam College of Osmania University at

Hyderabad, India, who was to spend ten weeks at the University of Pennsylvania. The article said:

> She explained she is particularly interested in the American private enterprise system, in monopolies, and in small business. She said it is believed in India that private enterprises lead to monopolies and combinations. India is working toward a socialist pattern of society.

This lady is a brilliant professor and conversationalist. I was privileged to have a lengthy visit with her. I found that her thinking, as quoted in the paper, was correctly presented. She believed, as do most of her contemporaries in the field of economics in South Asia, that capitalism and business are monopolistic in tendency and operation, and that the only possible way for people to have a democratic approach to an economic life is through socialism. As long as Mrs. Jussawalla and her contemporaries believe this—and they are sincere in their convictions—there is no use in our merely arguing the point in words, because words never won an argument. She was intensely interested in the dynamics of social service capitalism as it has evolved in the United States. During her stay here, she studied the various organizational structures of American capitalism from municipal to private small and big business. Mrs. Jussawalla was delighted with the idea that our Sherman Anti-Trust Act had helped materially to curb the monopolistic tendencies of giant corporations. After her return to India she wrote me, "It is true that I am intensely interested in the dynamics of your capitalistic system. . . . I am by now convinced that the Managerial Revolution has turned capitalism in America to democratic ends, so that the critiques from Moscow must feel a couple of generations out of date." The foregoing indicates that it is by a demonstration of what we call "service capitalism" that we have an opportunity for it to be embraced by countries which would benefit from it.

§6. CARTELS FATHER COMMUNISM

We, in this generation, have come to take the Sherman Anti-Trust Act pretty much as a matter of course.[10] It was designed

[10] From the speech made by Herbert Hoover when he represented President Eisenhower at the Brussels World's Fair, July 4, 1958: "We are often depicted

primarily to keep the growing field of business, which was rapidly becoming dominated by large corporations, free from cartelization and practices that were in restraint of trade. It may competently be said that this is truly an American approach to business, large and small.[11] It has been bipartisan, it has been supported since its inception by each president of the United States, and the overwhelming majority of American businessmen have abided by its provisions. In proportion to the size of the American business field, it is amazing to realize the almost universal cooperation that business has given to this principle since the "Age of the Moguls" which it was enacted to terminate.

As Chief Justice Edward Douglass White wrote in a 1911 decision:

All who recall the condition of the country in 1890 will remember that there was everywhere, among the people generally, a deep feeling of unrest. The Nation had been rid of human slavery—fortunately, as all now feel—but the conviction was universal that the country was in real danger from another kind of slavery sought to be fastened on the American people, namely, the slavery that would result from aggregations of capital in the hands of a few individuals and corporations controlling for their own profit and advantage exclusively, the entire business of the country . . .[12]

To really appreciate what the Sherman Anti-Trust Act means, one would only have to visit abroad men who are struggling to establish small and middle-sized businesses. Most of the world is in the grasp of cartels of one type or another. The economic kings of these vested preserves are quick to attack any person or idea that is invading their sacred domain.

---

as living under the control of wicked men who exploit our economic life through gigantic trusts and huge corporations. They are supposed to grind the faces of the poor and to exploit other nations. All this ignores the fact that our laws for nearly seventy years have prohibited the existence of trusts and cartels. In few other nations have the fundamentals of fair and open competition been so zealously maintained."

The application of our antitrust laws to American business operations abroad is presented in a recent book by William L. Fugate, *Foreign Commerce and the Antitrust Laws* (Boston: Little Brown & Co., 1958).

[11] See Blake Clark, "What We Owe to the Trust Busters," *Reader's Digest* (January, 1959).

[12] *Standard Oil Co. v. United States,* 221 U.S. 1, 83 (1911).

I was in Austria, in 1951, shortly after a report of a document by Henry W. Johnstone, entitled *The Restraint of Competition in the Austrian Economy,* was published by the Office of the United States High Commissioner. This document, about the cartelization of business in Austria, created a near-revolution. Never in my experience of traveling in a foreign land have I seen such immediate hatreds and powerful pressures directed toward my country as during those few days that summer. Before Mr. Johnstone left, the publication was withdrawn from circulation. We took a defeat, but the facts remain true, as the author pointed them out, that Austrian business cannot prosper for the greatest good of the many under the restrictions of its cartels.

The conditions described in *The Restraint of Competition in the Austrian Economy* typify many of the problems in other parts of the free world where business tries to find "heaven" in scarcity rather than in productive competition. For this reason several paragraphs of the summary section of Mr. Johnstone's report are here included.

On October 2, 1951, the delegates to the Austrian Trade Union Congress were told by Dr. Stephan Wirlandner, a rising young labor economist, that "in Austria private enterprise exists but no competition." Wirlandner stated further that "free competition plays a role only in the text books of the liberal economists. If one wants to characterize economic relationships in Austria, one must speak of a regulated free enterprise system."

Few would dispute this description of the Austrian economy. The institutions and practices that have developed are clearly directed toward the subversion of competition. To describe the resulting system as one in which "cartels and restrictive business practices" are prevalent is a gross and misleading understatement. The basic principle underlying the structure and functioning of the economy is, in fact, that of the internal solidarity of each of the chief economic classes—the farmers, workers, industrialists and tradesmen. Group cohesiveness is assured by both economic and political associations. Indeed, under the Austrian system the lines between economic and political, private and public, become fuzzy and difficult to draw.

* * * * *

An analysis made by the UN Economic Commission for Europe also emphasized the strangling role of cartels in European trade. As reported by *New York Times* correspondent Michael Hoffman in a despatch on

May 27, 1950, from Geneva, the Commission has found that "Governmental policies of liberalizing trade within Europe are being largely frustrated by private, national, and international agreements in restriction of competition." With regard to Austria, the Commission was quoted as reporting that the system of trade licenses "is one of the most effective devices used by established businesses to prevent competition and discourage new enterprise...."

In pursuit of information for this book, I attended a meeting called by the Green Meadow Foundation in Zurich, Switzerland, in 1956, where some 200 educators and entrepreneurs discussed the effect of cartels upon European business. There were only three or four Americans there as observers, but each of us felt a thrill as speaker after speaker drew attention to the fact that what the world needs is the Sherman Anti-Trust principles put into operation all over the globe. I left that meeting firmly convinced that cartels are basically business colonization, as capitalists and colonizers are linked together in the economically distressed areas of the world. Unless the cartels can be largely removed from the operation of business around the world or effectively curbed in their avaricious power and desire for excessive profits, the defeat of capitalism is much more imminent than is its victory.

There are some encouraging signs that cartel-minded Europe is beginning to realize the dangers for all capitalism if it continues to function economically as it has in the past. Britain has passed some laws that are similar in scope to the Sherman Anti-Trust measures of the United States and the Combine Acts of Canada. Italy is taking a long hard look at the situation, and the French press has exhibited increasing interest in market freedom. West Germany is digging into its cartels in a way that would shock the industrialists of the days of Bismarck. Mild though some of its provisions may seem to American eyes, the German antitrust law, which became effective in January, 1958, marks the first legislation in Continental Europe to fetter the freedom of those business groups which have largely made their own laws.

If these movements can gain momentum, then and then only will the real bulwarks be erected against the Soviet brand of state capitalism. If Europe falls to the Soviet principle, much of the fault will be attributable to the cartel concept of business.

A whole book could be written on the subject of the current attempts to "democratize" business in Europe; but since this study is only of American capitalism, we will leave this subject for subsequent exploration—except to point out that the yeast of dynamic capitalism is acting as a leaven in the dough of human desires and "raising" them from within their own container even as a loaf emerges from its own mixture. But a belief on the part of many that cartels offer a certain security still hampers the development of curbs on their exploitive practices. In the same month that Germany's legislation became effective, the movement toward economic freedom received a setback in Switzerland when a national referendum rejected an "initiative against the abuse of economic power."[13]

The new Asian countries are watching these European developments with deep interest. If Europe can find the way to control the cartel, then Asia may decide to try less socialism. A democracy cannot survive with its business controlled by economic kings making their own rules.

§7. MOTION PICTURES MISREPRESENT AMERICA

An alarming number of my overseas contacts have brought up some adverse criticism of the American-made motion picture, as exported, in its relation to American capitalism. Not one of these people has said that we should not have our movies as we want them; but they do question whether many of the pictures shown abroad have anything but a deleterious effect upon a genuine understanding of American life and enterprise.[14]

More foreigners come in touch with the silver screen than with any other exported communications medium of the American economy. American movies are shown in all the principal cities and reach into remote villages via mobile units which travel circuits much as do our circuses. When this purports to be

[13] For up-to-date information on cartels in Europe, see *Euromarket* (January, 1959), pp. 25, 43.

[14] See Paul M. Stevens, "We Are Exporting Un-Americanism," *Christian Herald* (February, 1958), pp. 18 ff.

American life, the people believe it to be a dramatization of the real thing and forget that it is, perhaps, merely a story such as they themselves have in their folklore, legends, or fiction.

The few pictures they see of the real America—travel stories (such as those presented by Burton Holmes), factual presentations that are descriptive of manufacturing or agricultural processes, or those of home-building or domestic science—are accepted as educational and are widely studied and favorably commented upon.

Unfortunately, we have not struck a balance between the make-believe and the real, between a lurid gangster scene designed for a portion of the American market and the effect it may have upon international relations. Our treatment of the American Indian in the Wild West shows has even drawn criticism from the President of Korea. In 1951, when I was with him, he said that these give an erroneous impression of the real America that he knows and loves.

The motion picture industry itself should do some soul-searching to determine whether it is only out to make temporary profits or whether it should try to help turn the tide of history back toward an appreciation of the real America—not the America currently being presented to millions of uninformed and uneducated yet highly intelligent people. If the motion picture industry would really try to help the America that has made it prosperous, it could do perhaps more than any other private agency, at no cost to itself. To date, many motion pictures portraying life in America are either negative or, at the most, somewhere in the neutral zone, since the bad obliterates the small good occasionally accomplished.

§8. Changes Resisted and Slow

A difficult problem affecting our acceptability abroad is the fact that other peoples are, perhaps, satisfied with their own ways. What we need to do is to have an arsenal of facts ready for those who want them—but not to force information upon anyone who is not ready to receive it.

It took a long time for our ancestors to recognize that the law of life is change. In the Middle Ages, people had become so accustomed to the darkness of ignorance and superstition that when the light of a new discovery was made—whether it had to do with astronomy, medicine, the laws of gravity, or the baking of porcelain—it was immediately suspected of being a trick of the devil or a product of witches or evil spirits.

The people of Asia, Africa, and many other parts of the world have been under the heel of some despot or conqueror for centuries. What we call individual liberty is largely unknown to them; and when they see the exploitive business administration carried on by a great many people who, in the same breath, talk about the glories of democracy, they then suspect both as witches' brew. Because of that, the situation is becoming aggravated rather than mollified.

If there is any one basic mistake that has been made in our desire to help the world, it was at the end of World War II. We had hoped that others would grow and live and dream in our image. We found that they like their own image better—many of them are reluctant, even afraid, to change; it is as simple as that. In the fall-winter season of 1956, the National Geographic Society conducted one of its evening lectures in Washington, D.C. Dr. William G. Campbell spoke about Cambodia, Laos, Vietnam, and Saigon. He was sane and sound in his presentation, and stated that these people, in many cases, claimed, "We do not want to change." It may be hard for the American businessman to understand that many people do not want to change —they would like to stay as they are. This is a psychological barrier that must not be discounted.

An article by Thomas R. McHale illustrates this difficulty.[15] He describes the Philippine family system, which follows a pattern prevalent throughout the Orient, and points out that it is an economic as well as a social unit comprised of several generations and remote degrees of kinship. Under this system all decisions are made in terms of the family; so they are often not

[15] Thomas R. McHale, "The Philippine Cultural Matrix and Economic Development," *Far Eastern Economic Review* (Hong Kong, September 19, 1957), pp. 370–72.

in the best interests of the enterprise the family may be conducting and are sometimes detrimental to an individual who would have a better opportunity to exercise his talents and aid the economy if he moved elsewhere. The Philippines want rapid economic development, but the "values" of the family system are not conducive to quick industrialization. Yet the New Civil Code includes an article which virtually invalidates any custom, practice, or agreement destructive to the family as an institution.

The deliberate manner in which people appraise their own situation in regard to change is well demonstrated in an Extension of Remarks by the late Hon. Lawrence H. Smith in the *Congressional Record* of June 7, 1957. Mr. Smith recounted an incident that occurred during his visit to Cairo and a conversation he had there with the chief of the American ICA mission and an Egyptian scientist:

...On the way out the Egyptian and the American were discussing phases of the work and the progress being made at that time. I listened attentively while these two gentlemen talked and finally the chief of the mission turned to me and he said, "Congressman, you have been very quiet. We have been doing all the talking." My reply was that I had come to look and to listen but then I said, "However, I do have a question. Your conversation has been most interesting. My question is: How long do you think it will take to achieve its objectives?"

Before the American could answer, the Egyptian replied quite promptly and vigorously, "Oh, it'll take about 200 years."

My American friend and the chief of mission was flabbergasted. He turned to the Egyptian and said, "Oh, Doctor, you don't mean that." The doctor replied, "Well, it'll take at least 100 years."

We are not fooling our foreign friends—they are realists. It is time that we quit trying to fool the American taxpayers.

American business has learned in recent years that he who does not keep up with the times is lost. When things have been done the same way for many years, it is a good sign that a change is needed. This is really only a recent discovery. We have now learned the value and method of making changes. Today, American agriculture and industry are the marvels of the world largely because we have accepted the philosophy of change itself—the prime, universal, basic principle of life and progress everywhere, at all times—change that shows so much greater respect for the men who operate the machines than for the marvelous machines which have tremendously increased their productive power.

No government cooperation from this side of the water can indoctrinate people abroad in this fundamental idea of change. It must come to them through their own experience which modifies their own ideas and things. Moreover, the American businessman, the American farm leader, and the educated and professional man have the opportunity to be the catalysts to bring this about in an orderly way rather than by revolution of a dictatorial type. This is one of the fundamentals that can be communicated abroad easily if we will but take the time to work on it from a personal point of view. The job cannot be done by sending droves of people on the government payroll into foreign countries to survey and report, report and survey. It can be done by a small but adequate number of dedicated "souls" with experience, working in other countries with local men of good will who are interested in doing this job.

When one considers the recommendations made to the Congress of the United States for money and men to be spent in information services overseas, and compares this with the scope of what might be done by business itself, with a small fraction of those funds, one is aghast at the lack of understanding of international affairs displayed by men both in and out of government. We must bring ourselves to see clearly the obstacles to the spread of our brand of capitalism. Only by understanding them will we be able to overcome them effectively.

V

GOVERNMENT AGENCIES CANNOT
DO THE JOB ALONE

§1. Two Basic Reasons for Delayed Understanding Abroad

This book is concerned with developing a positive approach to the communication of ideas overseas. It would be derelict on my part not to offer some observations on how some things done in good faith have not only failed to accomplish their purpose of communicating our ideas overseas but, in many cases, have actually boomeranged.

There are two things that are basically delaying the effective communication abroad of the fundamental ideas of modern American capitalism. First, the various government agencies moved in to help governments overseas do things that are basically in the state or socialistic plan of operation rather than in the main pattern we have at home. And when the United States did help private business, particularly in Europe, the general impression was too often left that it helped entrenched cartels rather than assisted the little man to find a way to independence through economic organization on the small corporate business level.

The second big hurdle has been the fact that American businessmen have taken too little interest in these overseas operations. They have erroneously left them to the government. But if the private sector of American business is ever going to get the rest of the world to understand how it has prospered—and contributed to making this a great nation—it is going to have to do the job itself. When businessmen sit by and let the government do it, they can also expect this result: Private enterprise will gradually be pushed out of the scheme of things, except as a manufacturer and supplier of goods to be shipped overseas, often to be disposed of by our governmental agencies to governmental agencies there.

There is no devil in this play. I have not found a Communist crouching behind every bush or contract. I have close friends working in all phases of our overseas operations. They are honest people trying to do a job as they see it and as they have been told to do it.

The basic mistakes are at a high level—they are not among the field operators. If a vote were taken among these people overseas—government representatives as well as private business-men and those who represent foundations—the overwhelming majority of them would say that it is time to take a look at this whole situation with a view to gradually withdrawing from the public sector of our overseas business operations and substituting the private efforts characteristic of modern American business.

If the people of other nations want them and find they can use them, they can and will adopt our corporate organization and practices in their own way and under their own names. Most of the potential for success lies in the attitudes and manner of our future communications. What we are doing now certainly is not teaching others to use our economic system.

§2. Technical Assistance Emphasis on Gifts Believed Wrong Policy

The bulk of the technical assistance program in which we have engaged with high purpose and clear conscience has been handled in such a way that it has delayed and will continue to delay the understanding and acceptance of the fundamental eco-nomic principles by which we operate.

At home we seldom rush around and make big gifts. We found that the way out of the depression was to train young people to work with the Civilian Conservation Corps, the Works Progress Administration, the Public Works Administration, and other agencies. In the days of Woodrow Wilson, we developed the Federal Land Bank Ssytem which during the great Depression was greatly enlarged on a bipartisan basis into the Farm Credit Administration, which included the creation of a central and twelve regional banks for agricultural cooperatives. These banks borrowed capital on the open market and loaned it to cooperatives owned by the farmer-borrowers. Over a period of years the original government capital has been largely repaid, the farmers are self-respecting, now largely own their own cooperative corporations, and in a few years will own all of the capital in the thirteen Banks for Cooperatives. All this has materially strengthened the economic position of American agriculture.

When the benefits of electricity were to be found only in the large cities, the people in the rural areas were not able to keep up with their urban cousins. Unfortunately, private utility capitalism did not make a serious effort to extend the benefits of electrification to American farms. Even as late as 1935 only approximately 10.9 per cent of American farms enjoyed electricity. In the spread of the benefits of modern civilization, we did not rush out with great gifts to these rural areas. Rather, we passed laws setting up the Rural Electrification Administration to loan funds to groups of farmers who established rural electric cooperative corporations to furnish electricity to the farms. The private power companies in a large measure accepted the challenge for new business and together with the REA cooperatives have changed the pattern of American rural life, until, as a result, in a period of twenty-two years, electrification on American farms increased from 10.9 per cent to 94.2 per cent. Nearly four millions of farm homes now enjoy electricity, and the benefited farmers are jointly repaying the loans to the government. In this way we have helped our American farmer to keep his self-respect, even though he was poor and in many cases during the great Depression temporarily insolvent.

We passed laws whereby the returning GI borrowed money to buy homes or start a business. Of course, along with this we do have a certain amount of federal housing where the people pay rent lower than generally available, but these are looked upon only as temporary living quarters until the occupants can increase their income to a stipulated point and move out to housing in the general rental or purchase market. Slum clearance is becoming an increasingly forceful idea in our democratic service capitalistic system.[1]

The fundamental principle of American business, government, and education is centered upon the elementary idea that every American should have the opportunity to be a capitalist, and that it is part of the comprehensive functioning of democratic dynamic capitalism to make this opportunity a real one.

This is a good system and it works, but, unfortunately as a rule, our technical assistance programs have given our overseas friends little opportunity to see these principles in action. The bulk of our help has been in the form of gifts and all too often routed to government-owned and -operated projects. My biggest shock regarding this was in India in 1953 and 1954. I traveled with an Indian government official who had visited the United States and who was a great believer in our system of responsible capitalism. He said several times that the average Indian in authority did not know what American business was, nor how it operated.

He was very complimentary to the United States as to the gifts we have given, but he said that in the long run this was money down the drain. He said, "Our people are not being trained, except in a limited way in the village improvement areas, to understand what you mean by American business." And then the announcement was made in the press that we had made a gift of some $20 million to the nationalized railways. He showed us the paper and made this crisp comment: "When are you people ever going to learn that it doesn't do any good to subsidize inefficiency?"

A new program, which would enable American enterprisers to directly assist countries desiring economic development and which would afford a better opportunity for overseas people to see and learn to participate in North American capitalism in

[1] Charles F. Palmer, "Capitalism and Slums" (Mimeographed article, Harvard Graduate School of Business Administration, November 17, 1958).

action, was proposed by Donald K. David, Chairman, Committee for Economic Development, in a speech at the 50th Anniversary of the Harvard Business School Association on September 5, 1958. In speaking of the type of our government-to-government aid to date, he said:

> This approach is not only ill-adapted to the needs of emerging nations and economies but ill-adapted also to the capacity of our own economic structure to respond effectively to those needs. The continued pursuit of economic development on a predominantly government-to-government basis could well be self-defeating.[2]

When President Harry S. Truman announced the Point Four Program, I immediately became, and still am, one of its most enthusiastic supporters. In 1951 Dr. Henry Bennett, then Director of this program, asked me to become his public-relations consultant and to visit all of the countries in which his organization was operating. I accepted this assignment. Shortly thereafter Dr. Bennett was killed in Teheran in an airplane accident, but at the request of the State Department I went ahead with the study which Dr. Bennett and I had planned of the relationship of the Technical Cooperation Administration to the Latin-American area. This history is included here because to me it is highly important that we get our sights straight and utilize the thinking of the men who really were the pioneers in trying to do something. Dr. Bennett's philosophy was well put in a statement which he prepared and I presented after his death to the Committee on Foreign Affairs of the House of Representatives on June 2, 1953. This deserves to be read and studied by all who think seriously about America's role in international affairs. Unfortunately, it has been largely forgotten. A brief quote is illustrative:

> The program we have described to Congress and to the public is a simple, down-to-earth, self-help program designed primarily to assist other peoples in increasing their food production, bettering their health conditions, and improving their educational systems. It is my view that the cost of this program, which shall be effective only if it is pitched on a

---

[2] Published in book form in Dan H. Fenn, Jr. (ed.), *Management's Mission in a New Society* (New York: McGraw-Hill Book Co., Inc., 1959).

long-term basis, should be enough to finance a broad, dynamic technical cooperation effort, but not to include the large-scale grants-in-aid. This has been my consistent position and conviction and I must be faithful to it.

It is my desire that we press forward as rapidly as possible with all of our programs, but without spending money recklessly. It would be far better for everyone concerned if we turned back unneeded money to the taxpayers rather than waste it on unsound projects.

§3. METHODS OF SURPLUS FOOD DISPOSAL SOMETIMES HARMFUL

In recent years we have in some degree disposed of part of our surplus food and fibers by grants to needy nations, believing they were thus serving as weapons of peace. We have "sold" for local currencies huge quantities of "surplus" food supplies, spending these currencies in the countries concerned. Most of the money thus spent actually turned out to be a grant or gift, though some funds are loaned. It is my observation that in many instances this practice has been a burden to good international relations. On the face of it, this may sound preposterous. The fact remains that we were so interested in disposing of our American agricultural surpluses that we failed to recognize that the people in many countries were primarily interested in producing something for themselves and were not anxious to be pauperized by becoming the recipients of such gifts, no matter how camouflaged by the use of the terms "local currencies," and so on.

Monsignor L. G. Ligutti, the official Permanent Observer for the Holy See with the Food and Agricultural Organization of the United Nations, commented in a recent letter to the author:

Much American surplus food is being distributed in Spain. It's a great work of charity, but I am afraid it is creating in Spain, as elsewhere, a whole group of paupers, and that such result (unwittingly created) is actually harmful to any nation because it debases human personality. A way must be found to give food and clothing to people as a reward for work done. Except in cases of disaster or extreme urgent need, a handout is not a sign of Christian love. We ruin characters when we fill stomachs. I have been told by very responsible people that U.S. government regulations demand handouts. On the other hand, Congressmen I have talked with insist that such was and is not the intent of the law. It is my earnest conviction that if we cannot figure out a way of distributing surplus food abroad (or at home) without creating a race of paupers, it is better to dump the food into the ocean. "Them is strong words"—but—"them is my sentiments."

We have shipped rice into Korea, at a time when the Koreans actually did not need high-priced rice, but would have better used other low-cost cereals.[3] Thoughtful Koreans, with the politeness of the East, have told me that they just cannot understand this type of capitalistic effort. Right or wrong, they believe that it represents an attempt aimed at keeping the rice-grower in the United States supplied with a large production quota rather than any sincere desire on the part of the American people to help Korea better its domestic position. This belief is representative of the thinking of others as expressed to me in many conversations. As an American, I know that our intentions have been highly altruistic as well as materialistic, but in the long run it is what people think that counts, and here we find mirrored the thinking of many people from many lands. Others think otherwise. I am presenting the middle view.

This book does not pretend to be a treatise upon foreign aid or assistance programs except insofar as they have a bearing upon the acceleration or deceleration of others' understanding of our methods of business enterprise. The whole matter of foreign aid should be re-examined to determine whether an attempt at temporary alleviation of an agricultural or industrial surplus here in America is perhaps inadvertently interfering with the long-range good that might be realized from following through on the principles enunciated in the Point Four Program.

The fundamental concept of the use of capital for the benefit of man, as well as for the fair profit of those who own it, is an idea that must be spread by an enabling movement and not a

[3] Because of our domestic price support policy, rice from the U.S. is generally higher priced than that produced elsewhere and also above the cost of other grains, notably barley. It is also interesting to note that in mid-1958 when poor growing conditions in parts of Asia indicated an impending world rice shortage, the FAO reported there had not yet been any appreciable rise in Asian prices, primarily because of Burma's policy of cutting allocations to each foreign customer rather than raising prices.

gratuity program. This may sound like a strange statement. People as a whole do not really appreciate, understand, or benefit by what we do *for* them gratuitously—it is what we do *with* them that counts. Even going overseas and building new dams or roads or laboratories—in this particular battle for the minds of men— does not bring the same benefits as do the things we enable them to do for themselves, directly or through organizations such as the Food and Agriculture Organization of United Nations of which their governments are members. We must encourage them on their home ground to engage in new socio-economic organizations and practices to help themselves.

§4. U.S. Business Abroad Thwarted by Conflicting Government Rules

It has been my general observation that an appreciable number of American business operators abroad are really trying to make progress in a practical, business way, but the effect of their demonstrations of our type of enterprise is often undermined by the diametrically different approach to problems made by representatives of the continuing Point Four groups of the U.S. government. Two different sets of rules, often conflicting, cause the difficulty. The businessmen operates on the basis of "rules of the game" as he knows them. The government man is honest, but follows the rules laid down by his administrative officers as they interpret the acts of Congress. Congress has gone into Point Four with the best of motives and intentions, but has done so with the idea that almost any problem can be solved by merely writing a check. This may work as a palliative, but it does not cure the cause of the ailment.

Credit and risk capital with modest returns is widely needed. The Export-Import Bank is typically American—firm, yet fair, and adventurous. Set up under the laws of Congress, it has been more successful in trying to export the fundamental principles upon which American business operates than has any other segment of our government operations. Personnel of the Export-Import Bank recognized from the beginning that in the long run their most effective role is to stimulate local industry. While they have made many loans to governments, they have done their best to make certain that private entrepreneurs commence operations in their shadow so that ultimately the government operation might cease and private groups carry on.

Their operations reflect the truth noted in this quotation from a digest of the Hoover Commission Reports:

> The genius of the private enterprise system is that it generates initiative, ingenuity, inventiveness, and unparalleled productivity. With the normal rigidities that are a part of Government, obviously, the same forces that produce excellent results in private industry do not develop to the same degree in Government business enterprises.[4]

Looking at it from the outside, it has seemed that recently there have been pressures on the Export-Import Bank to participate in loans for which the principal justification seems to be for political or military purposes. A case in point is the ICA loan to Iceland, for which the Export-Import Bank acts as agent. This loan apparently was intended to set up some kind of a counterplay for the protection of the people of Iceland. I doubt seriously that in the long run this type of approach will work. Nor do I fully understand how oil companies from NATO countries could in good conscience distribute Russian gasoline in Iceland, even though the foreign exchange situation decreed it.[5]

[4] Citizens Committee for the Hoover Reports, *Digests and Analyses of the Nineteen Hoover Commission Reports* (Washington, D.C.: privately printed, 1956), p. 113.

[5] George Williamson, "Iceland's Eruption: Once-Placid People Find Industrializing In a Hurry Can Cause Some Convulsions," *The Wall Street Journal* (April 23, 1957):

"Even now, all the Esso pumps in Iceland are filled with oil from Baku, U.S.S.R. American car importers have to compete with Russia's Moskvitch and Zim. 'Russia has become very important to us,' says one fish exporter, 'more important than many of us like.'

"American aid is designed to stem Iceland's eastward drift, and maybe it, or other considerations, will. At least Iceland's foreign minister recently said in a radio talk that 'Iceland intends to renounce a dangerous and illusory neutrality' and went on to profess allegiance to the West.

"Whatever the political future, Iceland's present economic woes show that trying to grow up into a modern industrial state in a hurry can be painful indeed. Perhaps few Icelanders would want to go back to the not-so-distant cow-bartering days. But they are far from happy with the convulsions of civilization."

§5. ACTIVITIES OF U.S. INFORMATION AGENCY OFTEN BOOMERANG

The U.S. Information Agency is of particular interest to me because it operates in a field with which I have long been concerned. For many years I have conducted a weekly radio program—"World Views"—carried by several stations in the United States. When overseas, I have often visited the USIA offices and utilized their equipment in preparing broadcasts to be forwarded to the United States. The people there have always received me with the utmost courtesy and consideration.

Mrs. Miller and I have visited many of its overseas libraries in Asia and Latin-America. We have been favorably impressed with them. I remember with particular interest one in Rangoon, Burma, where I spent considerable time talking with patrons who happened to come in. I found that the books, as a whole, were well selected; personnel was attentive; and the people who came had an evident desire to learn. I have, however, also seen the reverse.

I shall never forget an experience in New Delhi, India. Some Indians asked me to please go to the Information Agency to see why certain large pictures were on display in the windows showing graduation ceremonies at West Point. These were beautiful blown-up pictures that might have been of exceptional interest to the families of the young men concerned, or to the couples who, in some of the pictures, were being portrayed in marriage ceremonies. The Indians felt, however, that these indications of military development were very much out of place in the capital city of New Delhi. Right or wrong, that's how they felt.

The *New York Mirror* of August 30, 1957, in a Bell Syndicate dispatch from Istanbul, Turkey, by Constantine Brown reports:

Turkey is one of the relatively rare countries where American prestige is fairly high and Americans, whether in uniform or not, still receive the red carpet treatment. There have been only a few incidents between the native population and our GIs.

Radio stations in the USSR and Bulgaria continually blare out against

"American imperialism" and warn the Turks that they are rapidly becoming a "Yankee colony," but this makes no impression.

There are few radio sets—by our standards—in this country. But every village has a loud-speaker in the local cafes where the peasants gather every afternoon to listen to news, music, and propaganda. Despite their pro-American feelings, I am told, they prefer the programs from the Iron Curtain countries to those of the Voice of America. The Turks say the Voice (two hours a day) is drab, uninspiring and sometimes outright stupid.

The masterminds in Washington do not seem to realize that the simple Turkish folk are not interested in such topics as the lives of great Americans, or in mild, academic criticism of the enemies on their borders. Nor do they care for Turkish music originating in New York when they have better here.

The short-wave broadcasts of the Reds, with continuous programs for six to eight hours a day, are far more to the taste of the average Turk who at the same time apparently fully recognize the Communist propaganda line, such as when the Reds accuse America of attempting to bankrupt Turkey "in order to take it over with greater ease."

While these instances might be regarded as minor matters, or just due to poor judgment, I do have one basic criticism of the whole U.S. Information Agency. The fundamental mistake is not in the Agency itself but in the laws under which it operates and in the huge appropriations given it over a period of years. This opinion is based on long hours of study and conversation with USIA men from practically every part of the world. I have been fortunate, also, in having a rewarding, friendly relationship with all USIA Directors since its inception.

When Director Theodore Streibert left, I wrote him a letter in which, among other things, I stated that he had been assigned to do the toughest and most impossible job given any one man in Washington. I think that holds true for whoever might become head of the U.S. Information Agency, until the Congress of the United States definitely makes it clear that it does not expect the Agency to promote the fundamental principles of American business overseas. This cannot be done by a government organization.

On numerous occasions, I have told members of Congress my thesis that Information Agency techniques abroad should be reserved to explanations of the fundamentals of American political democracy and the operations of civil life. Our efforts to communicate the fundamentals of constitutional democracy abroad should be directly under the jurisdiction of the State Department through the U.S. Information Agency. It is my opinion that the USIA technique is good when showing the American heritage of democracy: why we revolted against colonialism; why we believe in the freedom and equality of man; why certain cultures and educational systems have developed with us; and why we believe in the separation of church and state. All of these subjects are in the field of government, and people abroad can understand why our government is involved in them. It is entirely proper that our government announce to the world that we believe in the private free enterprise system. But it is just as ridiculous for the Congress to expect the USIA or any similar governmental agency to promote the fundamentals of our mid-twentieth-century capitalism as it would be to entrust the government with the promulgation of any particular religious faith. It just will not work!

When our government attempts, through its Information Agency, to explain the merits of American business, American service capitalism, and the private enterprise system, its efforts are immediately regarded by people overseas as definite propaganda in its worst sense, and not as an acceptable effort to communicate useful ideas to them. This statement may seem to be extreme, but it is what many people think, and that is what counts. Let's face the facts!

There is a verse in the New Testament that says "Render therefore unto Caesar the things which are Caesar's; and unto God the things that are God's." If we could follow this same idea in deciding what is the field of government and what is the field of private enterprise in disseminating information overseas, we should have gone 90 per cent of the way toward bringing the world to accept and understand the great discovery we have made that capital can both return a fair profit to its owners and provide a service to mankind. But government cannot do this.

Businessmen are beginning to alert themselves to the situation in an increasing number of cases. A most encouraging example is this report, by Walter H. Waggoner, from Amsterdam, in *The New York Times*, August 11, 1957:

> Amsterdam, Aug. 8—The American business community in the Netherlands has agreed to pay for continuing the United States library here.
> The library has been closed since July 26 as a result of a deep cut in the budget for the United States Information Agency. The library will reopen Sept. 1. It will be operated by the Netherlands American Institute, with volunteer help from the American Women's Club. Contributions from twenty subsidiaries of United States business concerns will finance it.
> The Netherlands American Institute is an organization of Dutch and American citizens dedicated to the advancement of cultural relations.
>
>   *   *   *   *   *
>
> A policy-making committee will consist of a board member of the institute, a representative of the American business community, and an official from the Dutch Ministry of Education, Arts and Science....

The United Press International, Associated Press, and many other agencies owned and operated as private profit business or as nonprofit cooperative newsgathering agencies, are well equipped to distribute news about our enterprise system at a fraction of the cost we have been paying for an abortive attempt to do something that couldn't be done. If these professional agencies could do a better job, understanding would move ahead rapidly. Under the present government program it takes two steps backward for every step forward.

Independent pioneer action was undertaken in December, 1957, by a Rio de Janeiro English language newspaper, the *Brazil Herald*, which published a series of seven articles by Paul Vanorden Shaw under the title, "The Democratic Capitalism of the United States." These portrayed the nature and the development of our new kind of capitalism. Mr. Shaw gave many facts and figures, but I shall quote two of his conclusions:

> The U.S. has passed through an epoch-making revolution that has transformed its old classical capitalism into a democratic or Peoples' Capitalism that has gone far beyond Socialism and anything Marx ever dreamed of in raising the standard of living of a whole people.... The

fact that the capitalist transformation occurred without bloodshed or revolution is ample proof that Americans believe in and rely on democratic process to right wrong.

One result of the *Brazil Herald*'s step in publishing these articles was an invitation to Mr. Shaw to write for Brazil's oldest daily, *O Jornal Do Comercio,* in order that his material on American capitalism might reach the Rio public.

We Americans too often have reached the sad point where, when we see a job that needs to be done, we expect the government to do it rather than go out and do it overselves. No better illustration of the fallacy of turning more and more power over to government is available in any place than in this example of negative results from expecting the United States government to be a promoter of the ideas of the American capitalistic system. Time is running against us, or as we lawyers say, "Time is of the essence." It would be an invaluable service to the nation if the various press agencies should study this problem to determine what they should and can do, because it is only by the communication of ideas to men that we can stem the tide of present-day Soviet imperialism.

In this connection I should like to refer to Kent Cooper's *The Right to Know.*[6] I have long been familiar with the historical reasons why the Associated Press was primarily formed—to gather world news for its own members rather than use the offerings of "news" from press cartels or governmental propaganda departments—but it is nowhere so clearly stated as in the above-mentioned book. Since reading it, I recommend that anyone really interested in understanding the "why" of international affairs should do likewise. When the reader has completed its pages, he will remember forever that Kent Cooper, former Executive Director of the Associated Press, has shown that the road to dictatorship is paved by government-produced propaganda, while the road to democracy is through the products of private press agencies.

[6] Kent Cooper, *The Right to Know* (New York: Farrar, Straus & Cudahy, Inc., 1956).

These three paragraphs from the concluding chapter of *The Right to Know* tell the story as based upon the lifetime experience of its author, one of the greatest Americans of our times:

> The American government was the last in the world even partly to copy others in the matter of withholding news and engaging in news propaganda. It should be the first to abandon both practices and return to recognition of the people's Right to Know which made our country strong. If we do, it will bring new vistas out of the fog. And if we do, who knows but that others will follow us!
>
> *   *   *   *   *
>
> The plea of all peoples should be that their governments stand aside from this activity and first of all treat their own nationals honestly by not withholding news from them until their plans are either frustrated or successful or until their chief figures can profitably sell as memoirs documentary accounts of the government's business, some of which need never have been more than temporarily withheld, if withheld at all.
>
> If peace really is the goal, let truthful mutual news exchange bring acquaintance and understanding, peoples to peoples. Governmental efforts, through spraying self-centered news propaganda on a world long since sick and heedless of that method when applied internationally, never will do it.[7]

§6.   OVERSEAS VISITORS FAIL TO LEARN ABOUT PRIVATE ENTERPRISE VALUES

We have been working in the United States to bring to this country foreign representatives, exchange students, business leaders, and others—up to several thousand people each year. These programs head the list of all effective government-sponsored activities in foreign relations.

Most fortunate are the international visitors brought here by the Department of State's International Educational Exchange Service and the International Cooperation Administration. This group is offered a week of orientation to the United States at the Washington International Center, a project of the American Council on Education, operated under contract with the federal government.

[7] From *The Right to Know*, by Kent Cooper, pp. 314, 316. Copyright, 1956, by Kent Cooper. Used by permission of the publisher, Farrar, Straus & Cudahy, Inc.

The Center program is effectively backstopped by the volunteer services of several hundred men and women who among other things offer home hospitality. It is through this *volunteer* participation that visitors become acquainted with the typical American way of life. Probably two aspects stand out—the American attitude toward work and the American custom of ordinary citizens organizing together to solve community problems by direct action.

The Center program may vary from one day (largely for teams) to a full, five-day week. A series of talks is given by specialists in their fields on the physical and economic geography of the United States, social changes in U.S. history, U.S. government and politics, religious life in the United States (presented by a panel of Protestant, Roman Catholic, and Jewish speakers), economic trends, the contemporary challenge to education, U.S. foreign policy and its formulation, the place of minorities in the United States, with special emphasis on the present status of civil liberties and race relations (given by a faculty member of Howard University).

Visitors are taken on tours of the city—its schools, hospitals, parks, housing developments, and the like; another regular tour is to visit the Capitol, Supreme Court, and Library of Congress, and sometimes the National Gallery; other tours are offered to city elementary and high schools with classroom visits and participation in assembly programs. Each weekend, a trip to historic landmarks is offered, to the Lincoln and Jefferson Memorials, the Arlington National Cemetery, Mount Vernon, and historic Alexandria.

The Center continues its interest in its visitors, who are welcomed back again for brief visits at the end of the international guest's trip to America. A quarterly newsletter, devoted to news of Center "alumni," is sent to every person who has participated in any part of the Center program; this is based on a continuing correspondence with former visitors. The newsletter is mailed currently to more than 20,000 former visitors in 96 countries.

This experience in Washington has led to the organization of similar services in many communities along the same lines. In

February, 1958, an "Interim Council for Community Services to International Visitors" was formed in Washington by representatives from 16 cities. Avenues for expanding such services are being explored by this group, with a view to establishing a national service bureau to foster this development.

Fine as these things are, there are some basic faults in most of the foreign visitor programs. Too many of these "student visitors" are instructed in our technical methods of production, in making goods, in the standards of manufacture, in the rudiments of retailing, and the like. Only an occasional person goes home with any firsthand knowledge of the actual spiritual and moral values involved in the functioning of American business. It seems almost as though the people to whom these "student visitors" are sent are afraid to tell them of the fundamentals of what we call private enterprise or the responsibility of business to the community. A few of them do; but, as a whole, this area has been neglected in student contacts and training.

One method for the development of a better knowledge of American capitalism overseas is to make certain that all these "student visitors" are given an opportunity to study firsthand, and at the decision-making level, the workings of American business —the profit and nonprofit corporations, the development and functioning of trade associations, the junior chambers of commerce, and the multitude of other factors that are fundamental to America as we know it—far more so than the actual turning out of a thousand pens per hour or the making of powdered gelatin. Techniques and technical know-how are important, but they lack the leaven that has raised America to her present superior economic position.

We neglect another opportunity regarding guests from abroad —the follow-through. Unfathomable to me is why we, in America, have been slow to recognize the fact that overseas visitors and those we meet abroad are as anxious to keep us as contacts as we would be under similar conditions. Only the exceptional person who has been in this country or who has met visitors overseas is likely to receive any more than a few perfunctory letters from Americans he has met.

One practical and simple method of exporting the fundamentals of American capitalism would be for persons in authority in the various companies, universities, trade associations, and organizations that have contact with this flow of people from overseas to obtain their home addresses and write them sincere letters upon their return home. They should then be put on the permanent mailing list for the company publications, or trade association magazines, so that they will have continuing ties with American business. This is so important it is hard to comprehend why such a follow-through has not been more generally practiced.

One of the strongest criticisms I have heard about our failure to follow through has to do with the development of literacy. This has been particularly true in some of the areas where our mission schools have educated thousands of young people. Most of them have become literate to the point where they can read and write their own language and perhaps some English. But, whether they live in urban or rural areas, they then have such a dearth of material or contacts with the free world that they fall easy victims to the mass of information given them by the people on the other side of the Iron Curtain. I have visited communities abroad where almost the only visible printed information on the community came from the Soviet press. This is something so fundamental that it seems strange we have been so negligent.

There are some interesting exceptions which "prove the rule."

In 1952, in South America, I met six young men who had been in the United States on one mission or another in conjunction with educational activities. Of the six, three had received letters from people they had met here. They were more or less in constant contact and received a trade paper or two. The result: these three Latin-Americans were basically pro-North America in their concepts.

The other three had come here, had an exciting time, and then returned home, but had no further contact with the United States. Thereafter, they had become so frustrated and disillusioned that they and we would have been far better off in the long run if they had never made the trip. They were the real leaders of Communist thought in the communities in which they lived, and they had nothing good to say about what we call North American philosophy. Friendship, like flowers, dies unless cultivated.

§7. PEOPLE-TO-PEOPLE CONTACTS MOST EFFECTIVE

The technique of transmitting information from people to people is as old as man. The printed word, the drawing, the picture, and other means of communication all have their places; but in the long run, it is the face-to-face or person-to-person contact that is most effective.

Where the concept of the United States operating abroad on a face-to-face basis actually began is hard to tell; but today it is of increasing importance. The first person I know of to advocate publicly this policy, together with the concept of the "peoples' capitalism," was Murray Lincoln, president of CARE and of the Nationwide Mutual Insurance Company. In 1951 he encouraged me to make a trip around the world to study how information might best be sent from people to people. The strength of his convictions led him and his directors in 1951 to open a radio chain with headquarters in Columbus, Ohio, which is known as the People's Broadcasting Corporation. The objective of this system is to transmit information, particularly on subjects designed to improve national and international conditions, with various individuals participating in this objective. It has been my privilege since its inception to have a program, "World Views," on this network. The results of Mr. Lincoln's experiments and investigation have been fantastic. Visitors from overseas and Americans who know of his many efforts are practically unanimous in their belief that he is doing very worthwhile work.

The movement received tremendous impetus in September, 1956, when President Eisenhower announced his "People-to-People" program idea—a voluntary nongovernment-sponsored information service.

The important part of this whole concept is that information flows best directly from people to people, not from people to government and then to people. There are many phases of this particular program. It is being worked on a front covering some forty different activities and professions in America. It is the first large-sized serious attempt on the part of an American group to talk to the people of the rest of the world in the language that all men and women can understand—through human beings simply as individuals. Most of the People-to-People programs fall in the field of the professions, the arts, the sciences, and so forth, all of which are extremely important. The central organization has recently been dissolved because the various groups are now able to carry on independently.

American businessmen should recognize that through these particular programs they have an opportunity to perform a service for posterity by perpetuating the type of life under which they have found optimum conditions for growth and almost unhindered development. It isn't going to do American business much good to accumulate unlimited millions of dollars and have the type of government and opportunity under which it has grown suddenly change and disappear, as has happened during the past few years in many areas of the world. Are we justified in a feeling of smug complacency that it can't happen here? Each of us must work on a "person-to-person" basis as he has the opportunity. We cannot sit back and let the government agencies do it.

VI

WE MUST REDEDICATE OURSELVES
TO CAPITALIST PRINCIPLES

§1. Private Business Better Qualified than Government To Sell Capitalism Abroad

The problem of communicating and instilling overseas the fundamentals of American capitalism has for the past several years received the attention of many leaders of thought in the United States and Canada. However, there has been too little action taken without subsidy even by groups and organizations that have proved in America that they are able to capture an idea and put it to work. There have been some pioneer leaders in this regard whose ideas might well be emulated and made available for use in overseas operations.

In this connection, there is quoted an excerpt from the 38th Annual Report, 1954, of the National Industrial Conference Board, Inc.:

In line with what Mr. Erwin D. Canham, Editor of the *Christian Science Monitor,* said at our Cincinnati Meeting a year ago, we believe that the most effective way of strengthening the free world is to open the channels of communication between the business communities of the various nations. Thus through the mutual exchange of ideas and experiences the business leaders of these countries may draw closer together in their thinking, in their understanding of one another and of their common problems, and in the formulation of world policies for international trade. And on this basis of mutual understanding they may work together more effectively for the peace and prosperity of the whole world.

But as Mr. Canham indicated, what is needed to accomplish this is "a privately organized clearing-house"—just such a clearing-house, it would appear, as THE CONFERENCE BOARD has been for American industry. We feel, therefore, that because of our philosophy, our tradition, and our experience—and because for the past twenty-five years we have had a group of distinguished Foreign Correspondents in the leading commercial countries of the world—the Board has a deep obligation to carry forward this vital work as soon as possible.[1]

If the idea of the National Industrial Conference Board, Inc., could be adapted to use by other areas in the world on a local, regional, and international basis, it would probably come closer to leading the way for the successful implantation of fundamentals of American capitalist ideas abroad than any other one thing heretofore tried. The National Industrial Conference Board defines itself as:

... the oldest research and educational institution for cooperative study of the economic and administrative problems of American business by economists and businessmen. It was founded in 1916 by associations representing twelve branches of industry. Its founders believed that the American voluntary competitive economy, founded on private property and individual liberty, is the one best suited to promote enduring human welfare, and that impartial fact finding and education will keep that system sound and healthy. These principles have been the basis of all the activities of The Conference Board for thirty-eight years.[2]

No attempt should be made to foist our system upon other parts of the world, but the fundamental rock-bottom principles upon which it is operated are as sound in India, Japan, Italy, and the Latin-American states, as they are in North America; and they have proved that industry can voluntarily help itself.

The thing that baffles the man from overseas is the fact that instead of transferring this idea to the world for us through voluntary, private efforts, and encouraging others to act accordingly, we have all too often depended upon the subsidy or the

---

[1] National Industrial Conference Board, 38th Annual Report, 1954 (New York: The Board, 1954), p. 17.
[2] *Ibid.*, p. v.

direct action of government itself. This is not what free governments were designed to do.

We can no longer afford to leave all of the work abroad to government. This cannot be overemphasized. We have seen in the previous section of this book that, even with the best of intentions and selected personnel, the government has to overcome a multitude of public-opinion and public-relations hurdles in developing its work abroad, which would not stand in the way of private industry. As a member of the American Society of International Law I have met many diplomats in many lands of many countries. No matter how friendly they personally are, the function of their office is not primarily to make friends.[3]

President Eisenhower, with great vision and clarity, has defined the place of the private American who is traveling abroad in a letter which is being placed in each passport.[4] Secretary

[3] See the partial transcript of an exchange between Secretary of State John Foster Dulles and Representative Winfield K. Denton at a hearing of the House Appropriations Committee, *The New York Times* (August 11, 1957).

[4] The letter reads as follows:

THE WHITE HOUSE
Washington
July 12, 1957

Dear Fellow Citizen:

You have been issued a valued credential—the Passport of the United States. It requests that, in the countries you intend to visit, there be provided you, as an American citizen, safe passage, lawful aid and protection in case of need. As the holder of this passport, you will be the guest of our neighbors and friends in the world family of nations.

Year after year, increasing numbers of our citizens travel to foreign countries. In most of these lands there exist a reservoir of good will for the United States and a knowledge of what we stand for. In some areas, our country and its aspirations are less well understood. To all the world varied peoples of these many countries, you, the bearer of an American passport, represent the United States of America.

As you travel abroad, the respect you show for foreign laws and customs, your courteous regard for other ways of life, and your speech and manner help to mold the reputation of our country. Thus, you represent us all in bringing assurance to the people you meet that the United States is a friendly nation and one dedicated to the search for world peace and to the promotion of the well-being and security of the community of nations.

Sincerely,
/s/   Dwight D. Eisenhower

Dulles and the President have well stated the position of the government servant and the individual and the place of each as an emissary of America.

When we go abroad—whether it is for the government, for business, or as tourists—we must remember that we are the guests of sovereign powers and are not at home where people are accustomed to our actions. It would be well if we would ask ourselves what impression would be made by a foreigner in our home town who did the same things we do abroad. Would Aunt Mary or Grandpa enjoy having a non-English-speaking stranger rush up and take a picture of either of them, without even the formality of an introduction? Would Uncle Joe be pleased to hear foreigners making loud remarks about his best new sport shirt? . . . and so on ad infinitum.

Either all my informants from around the world are wrong or we must change our approach. Either we must help people to help themselves by providing them with ideas directly from our own people individually and collectively; or we must abdicate and recognize that we do not have the faith in voluntary, private action that we claim to have. Time after time foreigners have said to me, in one way or another: "You ought to be proud to be an American; no country on the face of the earth ever made such a serious attempt to help others to help themselves." But almost invariably, the discussion would end with something like this: "But money cannot do it alone, and we believe that you are rapidly losing the initiative because you have abdicated and let the government do it. It just won't work."

I am proud to be an American, and to be part of this generation where America is trying to help other people to help themselves to a higher standard of living. As Arnold J. Toynbee has written:

The Twentieth century will be chiefly remembered by future generations not as an era of political conflicts or technical inventions, but as an age in which human society dared to think of the welfare of the whole human race as a practical objective.[5]

[5] Arnold J. Toynbee, as quoted by the Honorable Lester B. Pearson in his Nobel Peace Prize lecture in Oslo, December 11, 1957.

§2. THE COMMUNIST APPEAL

If we are to work effectively, both as individuals and within organizations, for the spread of American capitalism, we must understand our competitors. We must look squarely at the appeal of the Communists to the minds of men.

Dr. Marshall Knappen, Professor of Political Science at the University of Michigan, has been of inestimable help to me in this book. His own book, *An Introduction to American Foreign Policy,* is worth studying in its entirety by anyone interested in the subject of international relations. One especially pertinent paragraph from the book is quoted:

> *The Moral Appeal of Communism.* Communism and the Soviet regime which supports it have one great source of strength which is not readily connected with any of the great political motives previously mentioned. This is its moral appeal. However fallible their ideology, however crude their manners and methods, however low their standards of living, Communists are generally more devoted to their principles than they are to material gain or even their personal safety. They are hard-working opponents and critics of many of the weaknesses of modern industrial society and the political economies of the underdeveloped areas from which it derives so many of its raw materials. As a scholar and economist their spiritual father Karl Marx made many mistakes, but as an indignant critic of unregulated capitalism he achieved a position of moral leadership which his followers have never entirely lost. In those parts of the industrialized Western world where effective measures have not been taken to correct the abuses he decried the Communist party still has a strong following ... In the underdeveloped areas where the problems of poverty, illiteracy, and diseases are not always attacked as vigorously as they might be the Communists gain many followers, particularly among the younger and better educated elements, by calling a spade a spade and preaching the need of immediate and drastic change.[6]

The Communist organizer carefully selects those upon whom he will lavish his attention. We sometimes think that poor conditions breed Communists—they do not. Mere hunger and cold will not make a comrade. Millions of hungry people are not desperate; they are reconciled to their condition by inertia or

[6] Marshall Knappen, *An Introduction to American Foreign Policy* (New York: Harper & Bros., 1956), p. 70.

culture or lack of hope. However, in all groups there is always a minor number of "constructive thinkers." One finds these in schools, in business, in mobs, in the jungle, and in the city streets. These natural leaders whom the rank and file will follow are found by processes easily learned by anyone interested in mass psychology. The Communists are past-masters in learning how to separate these few from the "flock." Once the selection has been made, the approach begins.

The Communist appeal has a strange siren effect upon people. The approach to the "prospect" is made in different ways, but basically the technique is the same. His known frustrations and economic ills are studied and cataloged. Then the dedicated Communist approaches and having sympathized with his victim's unfortunate position points out that these troubles are the result of either the malfeasance or nonfeasance of capitalism. Hunger, disease, illiteracy, lack of opportunity, poor housing, and scant clothing would not have been his lot had capitalism not drawn off resources that rightfully belonged to him. We all like sympathy and also to have a "whipping boy." When the "prospect" has been well indoctrinated with this theory as to his pitiful position, then the "carrot" is offered. Join the Communist movement and "all these things will be added unto you." In the workers' paradise you will have the fruits of your labor and not the "crumbs from the table" of the capitalist. The poor man feels that he has nothing to lose, listens, and often becomes a crusader for the new life. The Communist instills *hope* in his breast, and this is the chief appeal and sales device. In the party he will find all.

If the person approached is of a higher class economically or by education, the approach is varied to the extent that he is confronted with an opportunity to help his "brother" to a better life. All men have a latent desire to help others, especially if it costs them little. In this case the final solution is to come with the liquidation of the capitalists, while the convert himself survives. So he can help others, save his own skin, and take delight in the elimination of a "capitalist" whom he has come to look upon as a devil.

This is the appeal of communism—not complicated. The promoters of world communism are rational hard-hitting salesmen of an idea. They make a market survey of their sales areas and then proceed with startling success.[7]

§3. ACTS, NOT WORDS, WILL COUNTER COMMUNISM

Reviewing all of my many interviews of the past years, I have been impressed by one thing that people overseas think about us. They consider that we overtalk and underact. They are amazed that we spend so much time and enthusiasm in attacking, by speeches and writing, the fundamental principles of Soviet communism, but then as individuals do very little about it. They also bring out the fact that in many cases they have asked Americans to define communism and have found it almost impossible to get even a coherent answer from the average American as to what this enemy is that he talks so much about.

Research must be translated into action. The American people need to be alerted to the two basic phases of communism: its alleged efforts to improve the lot of the common man; and its behind-the-scenes, cruel, uncompromising dictatorship of one political party. Then business—itself the chief objective of the Communist army of ideas—must take action to make certain that it is able to defend itself.

Business cannot force anyone to be its friend. Unfortunately, we have consciously tried to do so in dealing with too many people in other parts of the world, particularly where they were of a different color, race, or religion. We can be friends only by being truly friendly. American business has in its hands the knowledge and the ability to make friends by working with other nationals in accepting common business ideals with a little give-and-take. Regardless of many other considerations, the entire recorded history of man demonstrates that the innate desire of

[7] For an account of Communist propaganda activities in 1955, prepared by the Office of Research and Intelligence of the United States Information Agency, see Evron M. Kirkpatrick (ed.) *Target: The World* (New York: The Macmillan Co., 1956).

men everywhere has been to trade with one another—to do business. Therein lies the common desire which can be used as a common denominator to cement the diverse peoples of the world. On such a foundation, American business should plan its superstructure for action.

It is interesting to note that the Bolsheviks, who control the Russian orbit, like Hitler who dominated the German scene, put the handwriting on the wall for all to read. They are against capitalism first, last, and all the time and are perfectly willing so to tell the world. They say they will win only as capitalism is destroyed—and the cold fact is that they are winning.

We rant and rave and curse them without ever taking the trouble to discover what promotes their success. Business has been content too long merely to "lay them out" with words. The representatives of organized labor, on the other hand, have gone abroad and have fought in the trenches of the battle of ideas. Too often they have been fighting alone, because there was not an immediate profit in sight for the business concerned.

These may sound like harsh statements, and they are; but in a public relations diagnosis such as this, we should not mince words. If we find cancer, let us say so and not call it a lump.

§4. THE DOLLARS-AND-CENTS APPROACH IS NOT ENOUGH

The greatest prime mover of human emotions in all the world is hope. Remove hope from a man, and he becomes as spiritless as the dead ashes of a spent fire in a cold room. Give him hope, and he soars to the zenith in a warm sunshine of shimmering light. Responsible capitalism holds out to man hope for something better for himself and posterity, and the opportunity to realize it in this world.

If we are going to help others to understand this, we must present it to them in an inspirational way as well as in straight, cold, dollars-and-cents materialistic terms. Of course, a business must make a profit, and a cooperative must operate at cost for the profit of its patrons, or else they go bankrupt. All the world likes a fair profit for the individual, and the non-Communist world approves of a fair profit for corporate entities. When America is accused of being profit-minded, it is being accused merely of an eternal, common trait inseparable from human beings. Unfortunately, we have thought and talked too much abroad about profits and dollars and not enough about the spiritual values man gains from proper use of capital in economic production and distribution of goods and services.

The *Christian Science Monitor* of January 26, 1957, in an article by Leslie Warren entitled "Brazil's Hostility Toward U.S. Rises," says:

... Another factor is that United States motives are suspect. Since it is a capitalistic nation, even the most altruistic acts are suspected of being motivated by the desire for profit. American business, against whom the bulk of anti-American propaganda is directed, does little or nothing directly to counter it.

This statement confirms my own observations in Latin-America that this is one of the most dangerous situations confronting American business. If one analyzes this *Christian Science Monitor* report, he finds that we are really losing the battle through default by business, whose duty it is to interpret its own operations to those in the areas where it operates. This is the crux of my thesis. Our system of capitalism can most effectively be explained by those who are using it, know it from experience, and know of its value to man as an individual. Otherwise, our modern capitalism will be completely misunderstood by people abroad whose only prior experience has been with the "exploitive capitalism" of the nineteenth century, with local moneylenders, and capitalists who have never learned the value of responsibility to the public in the use of capital, or with those relatively few American companies that are still inclined to follow the easy trail of mere exploitation.

Capitalism as a responsible tool for civilized man to gain a higher standard of living is unique and too little understood overseas. If we cannot get an understanding of our type of capitalism from the thoughtful leaders of the neutral and free world, the end is not too far distant for our particular system of civilization. One shudders to consider this possibility, because twentieth-century capitalism has made it possible for those of us who have been fortunate enough to be born here in this era to live and flourish in a golden age of a material culture without sacrifice of other cultural values.

The Communists have missionaries for their materialistic state concept of life, and to date they are succeeding. We have been too smug and content, as individuals, to think that we were on the right side and that ultimately we would win. Perhaps we will in the centuries ahead. We have felt that communism would sink of its own weight. We forget, sometimes, that time is of the essence. We are in a new world, and the sooner we recognize this, the better. We need "Johnny Appleseeds of business"—quite a few around the world.[8]

When Mrs. Miller and I were in Taipei, China, in 1954, we were told by Dr. Mah Linn, head of the Joint Commission on Rural Reconstruction, a story that is applicable here. While it concerns agriculture, the moral of it can be taken to heart by American business. During the war days, Henry Wallace, who had been Secretary of Agriculture, went to China on a government mission. On his trip he wanted to take some presents to the Chinese.

Knowing that he had neither the baggage space nor the means to take great quantities of goods, he studied what he might take that would be of greatest benefit to the Chinese people and yet within the restricted weight allowance. Being a plant scientist, he came up with the idea that the region where he was going (in the interior of China, near Chungking) was a natural optimum area for the growing of honeydew melons. So he filled his pockets, his suitcases, and his briefcase with honeydew seeds. As he went from meeting to meeting and place to place, and

[8] I presented this same idea to the 10th National Conference of the Public Relations Society of America where I said in part: "The modern Dynamic Capitalism of the mid-twentieth century in North America with its concept 'He profits most who serves best,' is as different from the old 'exploitive capitalism' as is a chicken from the egg from which it was hatched. Our service capitalism is changing business into something about which people can enthuse. The Marxist is an evangelist. We need evangelists of Dynamic Capitalism. The threat to our society is not so much against Government, as against the creature of Government—corporate business."

shook hands with people, he left a few honeydew seeds in their hands. And they were planted. Dr. Mah Linn told us that they grew and grew and that millions and millions of honeydew melons later became part of their regular diet. When the Nationalists fled to Taipei one of the things that Dr. Linn and his associates hated to leave the most was the "Wallace," the name they had given to that honeydew melon.[9]

There are certain advantages in the Communist promotional organization over our approach in reaching the minds of men. Their dictatorial educational and propaganda setup is organized and on the job all the time and is ever ready to act quickly in any emergency at any time. We have reason to believe that its far-flung moves are planned and geared to fit particular countries. Its missionaries are pretrained in the languages and even in the dialects of the countries to which they are sent. Its material is printed, ready for translation into any major language of the earth. It is adapted to meet the desires, customs, prejudices, and even the religious beliefs of the people to whom it is being sent. It is probably the best organized and most intensely emotional propaganda system in the world today.

The battle of the twentieth century is not for political loyalty alone; it is a competition to fulfill men's hopes for a better economic life—something new in war. As emphasized repeatedly in this book, we have left it very largely to the government, not realizing that this is the battle of all our people who go abroad and particularly of American business. In the Sino-Soviet bloc the economic, the military, and the political are all different fronts of the same war. The Communists can move on all fronts at once. We, however, having reserved certain powers for the free individual, sometimes forget that each of us has a corresponding responsibility within a responsible society.

[9] A Johnny Appleseed reaching behind the iron curtain is Mr. Roswell Garst who developed a fine type of hybrid corn and marketed it in Rumania. *The New York Times* of September 26, 1957, described his project with the following headline:

"IOWA CORN BREEDER SOWS SEEDS OF AMITY
FOR U.S. IN RUMANIA
"Grower's Business Venture Is More Successful Than 'Cold War' Diplomacy"

§5. How Missionaries Have Promoted Understanding

Really the only Americans in the Orient who have won the minds of men are the missionaries, who took back to other areas their religion which had been anciently received from Asia. While the missionary did not convert the world, he did make converts who are today suffering like the martyrs of ancient Rome under the persecution of the Communists. Mao Tse-tung has stated that over 800,000 Chinese had to be liquidated as anti-Communists—many of them Christians. A visit to the streets and slums of Hong Kong is illustrative. Here, the cream of the crop of missionary effort in China, graduates of missionary colleges both Protestant and Roman Catholic, are eking out a mere existence, carrying night soil, weaving and anything but begging, hoping some day to be able to carry on again with comparative freedom.

Why are these men in Hong Kong? Because they chose to leave Red China rather than renounce their religion and the men from whom they have learned it in order to accept positions of educational and governmental authority in that land. Freedom? Yes, they have it, for they have escaped. But because of the lack of business opportunity they are in dire need.

Moslems, Hindus, Buddhists, Parsees, Shintoists, and atheists in Asia and Africa have told me that the revolution in the minds of men in their respective parts of the world was due to the teachings of the Christian missionary. While only a small minority of the people accepted and followed the faith of these crusaders, the fact remains that they opened the door for rising expectations. And it is an interesting fact, also, that the only sizable group of people in these areas who are basically supporting the principles of democracy are those who learned them from a missionary.

The world-famous Commonwealth Club of California, whose motto is "Get the Facts," had scheduled Dr. John Earl Baker to address them on August 2, 1957. Dr. Baker had served in China for thirty-six years as Red Cross Famine Director, and Railway and Finance Adviser to the Chinese Government. Unfortunately, he died on July 27, but the club was so desirous of getting his message that the manuscript he had expected to deliver was read by another member. The address pointed out that resentment is created by American "high living" abroad, and then added the following significant observations as to the dedication needed by Americans going overseas:

—We cannot order from Sears Roebuck the thousands of people to represent us abroad. We must train them.

—We must start with devoted, consecrated characters. The Communists in China recruited college men not on the basis of salaries paid or privileges to be won, but as an opportunity to sacrifice comfort, fortune and even life itself for the good of the country.

—The young manhood of this country would likewise respond to a call for sacrificial effort. Our missionary boards recruited on that basis for years.

—The rich will probably always be envied by the poor, but even the very rich can so mind their manners that they will receive the friendship of the poor—without buying it.[10]

§6. MODERN CAPITALISM HAS A MISSION OVERSEAS

I know of no cases, and I have heard of none, where men have chosen to fight or to leave home, traditions, and business because of a belief in and a devotion to the system of private corporate enterprise such as we have. I do know of dozens who have fled from behind the Iron Curtain because of a faith in God which they had learned from missionaries. While the two are not the same, man does move by emotional motivation. Too often our business leaders have been too proud to admit that they can learn anything from the missionary. The men and women I have interviewed concerning things abroad have pointed out that the businessmen, and too often the men in government, have smiled or sneered at the missionary. Even though the men overseas, the nationals of the country involved, did not accept the faith of the missionary, they accepted his friendship, his integrity, and his dedication.

[10] *The Commonwealth* (August 12, 1957), pp. 206–7.

Indonesia has tried democracy but is now considering leaving it for many reasons—some political, some religious, some military, and some as the result of pressures from Asia to the north. But one of the reasons that is of concern to us here is the fact that Indonesians have had tragic experiences in contact with some American business.

In 1956 I visited the superintendent of one of the major American operations in Indonesia, and he told me:

We deserve what we're getting. We have always looked upon these people as second class, third class, or no class at all. It was only in 1955 that my company has allowed us to even mix in living quarters, or permitted social exchange with those in our compounds or company premises who are Indonesians.

William H. Whyte, Jr., of *Fortune* magazine, some years ago wrote a series of articles called "Is Anybody Listening?" which had to do with the public-relations approach of American business to its employees in their communities.[11] Mr. Whyte summed up the series to the effect that there were literally hundreds of millions of dollars being poured down rat holes in pursuit of a phantom called "public relations." Little study, consideration, or appreciation was given to the mental attitude of the people to whom an approach was desired. His conclusion was that the money was largely lost.

My conclusion about the present methods used overseas by business and government is similar to that of Mr. Whyte.

In recalling pertinent points, I must refer to discussions with justices of the Supreme Courts of India, the Sudan, Japan, Nationalist China, and Korea. Each one of these men individually told me that the concept of freedom under law in the United States has been largely the motivation for the development of the desire of freedom in their countries. Nearly all mentioned the fact that the Fourteen Points of Woodrow Wilson was the stimulus that set off the present nationalistic urge. Nearly all said that prior to this the ground had been cultivated and the seeds sown by the missionaries. These justices, without excep-

---

[11] Published in book form as *Is Anybody Listening?* (New York: Simon & Schuster, Inc., 1952).

tions, told me that the type of business, private enterprise, and service capital, such as we have in the United States, is so largely unknown in their part of the world that it is classed with "exploitive capitalism," which to their peoples is synonymous with hated colonialism.

A member of the high court of the Sudan in substance told me: "If American business could get the world to understand the revolution it has brought into the material lives of men and women, comparable to that of a revolution against colonialism, it can sow the seeds of peace, harmony, and prosperity in the world as a whole."

I inquired whether this sort of revolution would work, since the people in these lands have small resources, limited political knowledge, and a large proportion of illiteracy.

His answer in substance, was: "They are men, with desires, spirits and souls. They will not build big companies such as your General Motors, your General Electric; but they are going to have to start where they are, and the fundamental principle that you have learned of the use of capital for service through corporate organization as well as for profit is as applicable to the man with a few coins as it is to the man with a million. Your American cooperatives are capitalistic in form and are designed to help the small landholder, the small industrialist, the laboring man, to make money his servant as well as the servant of the rich. Generally your trade associations do not deal in big money, but they do help their member to serve better."

He went on and on in this vein, and he is right. We have, within our hands, the key to unlock the door to the golden opportunity of the future. Unfortunately, the key is unused in most cases, and we are letting the government, with the best of intentions, fumble for the keyhole with an instrument too large and too heavy and inadequately adapted to fit the lock.

Economic power, used for social justice, with government as a referee and umpire, is the optimum material condition of man. With business trying to serve as well as to get, we can combine greater freedom of conscience with an even higher level of material well-being. The present-day American and Scandinavian systems of capitalism are approaching nearer to this optimum condition than has ever happened before in the history of business and enterprise. The other extreme in the world is the Soviet government as the source of both political and economic power. And it makes a religion of its precepts without otherworldliness as an aspect of its religion.

Forty years ago, American business had a few spokesmen at home who stressed the service motivation. Today there is hardly a business meeting without an inspirational session. There was a time when business tried to get the edge and worked for special favors—that was the accepted thing. Today this attitude is found less and less. The great trade associations are creating a better climate of business. Of course, mistakes are made; and there is still power politics, with labor unions, big companies, and small companies failing to recognize the duty they owe to mankind. But as a whole, business realizes that the customer must be taken into its confidence, and that competitors can exchange knowledge for mutual benefit. This conception can be exported and it will be welcome. In much of the world it will be unique. If exported it will take root and thrive as did the "Wallace" melons.

§7. Our Economic Ideals Are for Export, Too

As far as I know, every one of the many countries born, or reborn, since World War II—India, Pakistan, Burma, Indonesia, Ghana, and the several countries in the Near East—has, without exception, done two things. First, they have copied so far as seemed possible the principles of the Constitution of the United States; and second, they have adapted to this framework a "socialist" form of government with varying degrees of control over the economic life of the nation.

A striking example occurred in 1957 when the old Gold Coast of Africa became Ghana, a member of the now loose and flexible Commonwealth of friendly nations. The United States government, in common with all the major and many of the minor governments of the earth, welcomed the new country into the family of nations. Its birth and christening were attended by Vice-President Richard M. Nixon of our country, who presented gifts to the newborn nation in the form of a library and a Steuben glass vase depicting the Four Freedoms of the Press, Assembly, Religion, and Speech. He was well received; the gifts were accepted, together with a plane and automobiles and other gifts from Soviet Russia. A news dispatch was printed in the *Boston Daily Globe,* March 6, 1957, relating to Ghana:

Nkrumah, a bachelor who was educated at the schools in England and the United States, describes himself as a Marxist Socialist. He is the youngest government head in the Commonwealth. Nkrumah told the assembly he would take over the cabinet posts of defense and external affairs, in addition to serving as prime minister.

Note that the "George Washington" of the new country of Ghana describes himself as a "Marxist Socialist." Here is a man, educated in America, who publicly makes this announcement. It isn't going to do us any good to criticize his attitude and say he should or should not do this. The truth is that he has done it, and that we want and need the friendship of this new country. The economic pattern which will finally evolve in his country remains to be seen.

We cannot say we do not like state interference with the functions of private enterprise. Our own economy is not the capitalism of the nineteenth century. The basic thinking for us was presented ably by James B. Conant, then president of Harvard, and more recently our Ambassador to Germany. Certainly he is not a Socialist or Marxist, but a realist, who saw that corporate capitalistic democracy changes with time in its relationships with individuals and business, in order that it might forever guarantee the thing from which and for which it has been built, namely, human liberty. His article, "Wanted: American Radicals," as printed in the May, 1943, issue of the *Atlantic Monthly* should be required reading for every person studying for a career in business or government. It is a prophetic message. Whether one agrees or disagrees with Dr. Conant, he happens to have "called the turns." He sounded a call for "American radicals" whose attitudes would reflect such ancestors as Jefferson, Emerson, Thoreau, and Whitman, and who would be the political link between the past and future of democratic America.

The American radical would: apply the doctrine of equality of opportunity, not of rewards; prevent inherited privilege by effective inheritance and gift taxes and the breaking up of trusts and estates; provide universal educational opportunity at all levels; decentralize power, though ready to invoke the federal government if necessary to maintain real freedom of the masses; and be sensitive to such "old-fashioned" subjects as individual rights as opposed to the police power of the state.

The demobilization of millions of men would be considered by the American radical as a God-given moment for reintroducing the American concept of a fluid society. Thus he would have federally financed agencies set up to see that the returning soldier was retrained and placed in the kind of employment for which his talents were suited. Lending agencies might be created to enable competent veterans to start small businesses.

In the cultural field the American radical would think in terms of every man and woman. He would want reforms in education. He would be "both unkind and unjust" to this century's methods of advertising and sales policies, seeing the "half-truths with which our eyes and ears are saturated" as "one of the most insidious maladies of the age."

Somewhat similar are some of the ideas recently expressed by Prime Minister Nehru, though his political party has from its inception been committed to an undefined socialism:

INDIVIDUAL FREEDOM
NEHRU'S CONCEPT OF SOCIALISM

Prime Minister Nehru expounding his idea of socialism has said that he did not at all prefer State controlling everything because he attached great value to individual freedom.

*   *   *   *   *

Mr. Nehru stated, "I do not want State socialism of that extreme kind in which the State is all powerful and governs practically all activities. The State is very powerful politically. If you are going to make it very powerful economically also it would become a mere conglomeration of authority.

"I should, therefore like decentralisation of economic power. We cannot, of course, decentralise iron and steel and locomotives and such other big industries but you can have small units of industries as far as possible on a co-operative basis with State control in a general way. I am not at all dogmatic about it. We have to learn from practical experience and proceed in our own way."[12]

The fact is that state enterprises in India are not as productive as some which are privately owned and operated.[13] The Union of Burma, too, has had disappointing experience with concerns which it initially nationalized. Said U Nu in June, 1957, in a speech on the new Burma four-year plan:

... In order to step up production in the economic field, the operation of all industrial and mining enterprises, except certain key projects, should not be entrusted solely to those who are only interested in getting salaries. They should be entrusted also to those who have profit motives.

If the Government continues to operate these enterprises, the salary-earners in charge of operations will go to their jobs as if going to picnics, without achieving results. ... The result will be just squandering public funds.

From practical experience, I no longer like to see the Government's finger in all sorts of economic pies. If it is allowed to go on unchecked, then due to lack of proper supervision and efficient management, the state enterprises will sooner or later only line the pockets of thieves and pilferers. ... In the circumstances, from now on, the Government will only concentrate on key economic projects.

As a second step, with a view to Union solidarity, facilities must be given to the people of the country—and especially to Government servants and workers in industrial factories—to buy shares in these enterprises. Such participation will encourage their interest in the stability of the Union. ...[14]

As these and other underdeveloped countries, become industrialized, they are adapting to the results of their experience. Yet, to date, they are fundamentally socialistic in principle. Their future direction depends to a large degree on whether they become aware that a type of capitalism can evolve which preserves the drives of individual freedom and yet serves society.

[12] *The Hindu Weekly Review* (May 26, 1958), p. 2.
[13] See: Cameron Hawley, "India Faces the Facts of Life," *Saturday Evening Post* (September 14, 1957), pp. 44 ff.
[14] Reprinted in "The Public Weal," excerpts from speeches by the Honorable U Nu, *The Atlantic Monthly* (February, 1958), p. 106, and reproduced by permission from Intercultural Publications, Inc.

VII

BUSINESS ABROAD MUST BECOME AWARE OF PUBLIC RELATIONS TECHNIQUES

§1. BUSINESSMEN CAN TURN THE TIDE OF HISTORY—IF

We revere the memories of Patrick Henry, Alexander Hamilton, Thomas Jefferson, George Washington, Benjamin Franklin, Robert Morris, and others. They envisioned a future on this continent for man to attain the highest living standard and freedom of mind and speech that had ever come to him. It is easy for us to read about these men as being so important and contributing so much to our country.

But do we ever stop to realize that, as individuals, we have basically similar obligations to our present system of political and economic democracy? If we leave it all to the government and the missionary, if we decide to "let George do it," the system will deteriorate and ultimately collapse. The main principle of American responsible service capitalism is the assumption that the person who "has" will assume a responsibility over and beyond the actual making of fair profits.

Our concept of capitalism cannot possibly be exported abroad and understood by people so that they can use it to revolutionize their lives in the direction of economic democracy unless we as individuals accept our responsibility to do something about it.

People in other countries welcome as a friend the American businessman who comes not with an order book but with an idea and an ideal. The youth of the world who hunger for education would sit at the feet of the elders of American business. Businessmen might well turn the tide of history if a few hundred dedicated men would go abroad on a people-to-people basis—without a price, without subsidy from government, to help people there understand the rules of life and business which we have learned.

Near Salonika, Greece, I met an American businessman, a retired insurance executive from St. Louis, who had chosen to live there on his retirement income, devoting his life to helping the Greek people understand the philosophy of private enterprise and responsible capitalism.

He was doing a good job; I could see widening circles of influence and understanding going out into the areas of Macedonia. Here was one man, dedicated to the purpose that the Greek people might understand the basic economic principles that had made America great.

Just a few years ago, Morris Sayre, former President of the National Association of Manufacturers, was also one of the most constructive forces in the building of a better rural America. He was convinced that this was the way by which the American dream could be made a reality in much of the world. He went abroad on a Commission to study how American business could help the rest of the world to help itself and unfortunately died prematurely in Asia in the pursuit of his goal. It is to be hoped he did not die in vain.

We are at a crucial point in world history. The future, as far as we are concerned, is in the hands of the individual American, who has demanded that he enjoy a right to enter business for himself, who has proved that he can make it work here at home, but who unfortunately has failed to venture abroad and transmit this idea effectively to others or cause it to be done.

However, before we as individuals, as corporate executives, or as representatives of the government attempt to "go to far places" and transmit the concept of life which we enjoy we must learn to understand other people and their reasons for doing things as they do. We must learn, when abroad, not to look

upon residents there as foreigners, but to realize that we ourselves are the foreigners. We must remember that the effects
of our actions have world-wide implications, just because we
happen to be Americans. An editorial from *The Financial Post*
of Toronto, Canada, of August 10, 1957, is applicable to all of
us and illustrative of how trouble can befall when we go off
"half cocked":

Americans who wonder why they're not always loved or "understood"
in Asia should take a look at the case of Maxwell Henry Gluck, the U.S.
chain-store magnate who recently gave the whole world a belly laugh.

Mr. Gluck subscribed "$20,000 to $30,000" to the Republican campaign fund in the 1956 election. Custom says that so generous a patron
should have as a reward, if he wants it, some government post with not
too much hard labor attached but "a little social prestige." So Mr. Gluck
was named U. S. ambassador to Ceylon.

But the Senate has a right to investigate the qualifications of these
presidential appointees. Answering questions on the stand, like a
wretched schoolboy who hasn't done his homework, poor Gluck didn't
know the Ceylon Prime Minister's name, "couldn't pronounce" the
names of India's Prime Minister and on other questions was equally
flummoxed. His grade would be a non-passing D-minus.

This was perhaps hilariously funny, but not for Gluck and definitely
not for the Ceylonese. For them Gluck is an insult; and their alert press
didn't fail to say so.

When government tries to explain and defend capitalism,
there is a backfire of thinking on the part of the people who
listen. Their thinking is: "Well, if capitalism is of the people
and is the people's way of doing business, why is it that capitalism is not explained by *private individuals*? Why is it that the
government has to enter into it?" Then, unfortunately—and this
is tragic in many cases—the overseas United States government
representatives, with good intentions and perhaps the best training in their own fields, prove to be utterly useless in their efforts
to explain the principles of business, and the principles by which
industry operates.

Unless business can prove that it has something to offer be-
sides profits, the tide of "social democracy" will engulf our feeble
attempts on behalf of the world's "economic democracy." The
tragedy is that we in the United States have discovered and are

applying the socio-economic laws whereby capitalism can serve both a social and economic purpose, but we have not always been able to transmit these to others. We seem able to interpret the laws of science which we discover, but not the ones concerning human relations.

Foreigners with whom I have discussed this situation agree that our capitalistic system is not wrong, but that our fault when presenting its concepts abroad lies largely in our mass approach.

A few businessmen, using a personalized approach, who are truly dedicated to helping others understand our methods and how they might be adapted to use by people with different social, religious, and historical backgrounds, would undoubtedly meet much greater success.

To individually interpret the American philosophy to others is not an easy task. *The Evening Star*, Washington, D.C., July 19, 1957, reporting on discussions between President Eisenhower and Marshal Zhukov, says:

The President confessed at his news conference yesterday that during a long argument with Soviet Marshal Zhukov after the war he was "hard put" to defend the proposition that democracy is a more ideal system than communism.

The President's difficulties confirm my own experience that the trained Communist is extremely skillful in presenting his beliefs.

The Canadian efforts have been much more productive of effective results than have ours, even though Parliament has never seen fit to create an organization similar to the U.S. Information Agency for news dissemination. Canada has less than two score total personnel in its overseas government news service. However, it has built a splendid reputation in many places where we have failed to do so regardless of our best intentions and the expenditures of millions of dollars for "propaganda." One secret of the Canadian success is perhaps that Canada is a smaller nation and a part of the Commonwealth. But over and above that is the fact that, as a whole, its businessmen going overseas are better briefed on how to be "foreigners" themselves rather than looking upon others as "foreigners."

One of the most thought-provoking current books is *The Next Hundred Years*, written by three California Institute of Technology experts. It is worth reading in its entirety, but one paragraph is included here because the last sentence puts in capsule form the real dilemma of the businessman and, through him, of free society itself:

> We have seen that, in principle, man can, if he wills it, create a world where people can lead lives of abundance and creativity within the framework of a free society. It is apparent that there will be many difficulties; there will be many dangers. But it seems reasonably clear what men must do in order that the path may be negotiated. It remains to be seen whether he will recognize these problems in time and proceed to create a still higher level of integration, or will permit his civilization at its present state of development to disintegrate, perhaps never to reappear. The future of industrial society *revolves around the question whether man can learn to live with man.*[1]

§2. WE ARE ENGAGED IN A PUBLIC RELATIONS BATTLE

By their very operations abroad North American business concerns have an opportunity to demonstrate and communicate the values of our enterprise system, which could very quickly be lost through expropriation.

One of the most inspiring interviews that I had in the whole preparation of this book was a few hours spent with John M. Begg, Deputy Director, Office of Private Cooperation, U.S. Information Agency, who told about some of the splendid results that had been obtained by private business taking overseas the fundamentals of private enterprise—not just for their own profit, but for the benefit of others.

I asked Mr. Begg to add some of his own observations to this section and he sent me a reprint of an article in *Advertising Age* of January 4, 1954, with the comment that these statements expressed his view then and now. On the next page are excerpts from his statements as printed.

[1] Harrison Brown, James Bonner, and John Weir, *The Next Hundred Years* (New York: The Viking Press, Inc., 1957), pp. 153–54.

Public relations in the U.S. proceeds on the axiom that no industry or business sensitive to public or official attitudes can remain outside of or indifferent to the community in which it operates. How much more applicable is this in the case of American business operating in a foreign country. Pressures exist which no U.S. concern ever faced domestically—political and economic nationalism, nascent local industries, dollar imbalances, the spread of Marxist thinking, communist-guided trade unionism, incessant anti-American and anti-capitalist propaganda. Enterprises overseas can be wiped out by simple decrees; their actions restricted or paralyzed, their profits restrained, their properties impounded.

No action by business can guarantee that any of these things will not happen. But certain actions by business can help create an atmosphere and attitude within a country that will mitigate against arbitrary or unreasonable fiat. These actions fall within the sphere of public relations.

Either American business effectively demonstrates that where it operates it gives as well as takes, that it is an integral part of the community in which it does business, or it faces the possibility of ultimate rejection. Its future, over the long pull, is shaky.

This simply is a restatement, in different geographic context, of a fact that American industry domestically has long recognized—that successful operation depends in large measure on continuing public recognition, public acceptance, public good will.

Only a fraction of what is required for an effective public relations effort domestically is needed overseas, particularly in view of the more limited possibilities and media outlets. But it is needed on a broad basis—vertically through the various elements of an enterprise—advertising, employee relations, etc.; horizontally through as many separate businesses as can be gotten together.

Communists are spending millions every year to undermine and, whenever possible, to destroy American business operations abroad.[2] Their methods, based on years of experience, are shrewd, mostly under cover of front organizations, and, too frequently, effective. Particularly effective are their efforts to use nationalist groups to carry the ball for them. The Communists provide the ball in the form of pamphlets, rumors, infiltrators, and every other means at their disposal. Material expropriation of American business is their ultimate goal.

[2] See, for instance, *Communism in Latin America: A Vision Report.* Prepared by the Editors of *Vision*, December, 1958.

In this deadly game American business unfortunately has no organized team of its own. But every American business, large or small, could contribute to a voluntary effort (or to a properly organized effort like the Transportation Association of America activity domestically) to clarify the thinking of men in distant parts of the world regarding service capitalism.

Every company operating overseas, by sending abroad only personnel who have been trained in the fundamentals of American capitalism and are capable of communicating them, has the opportunity to further the acceptance of these concepts by men and women in other parts of the world to use in their own way, in their own business and at their own discretion. A few experiments have been made in this direction—seminars of company personnel at home and abroad have been highly successful.

§3. BIG BUSINESS CAN PROMOTE UNDERSTANDING OF CAPITALISM ABROAD

It cannot be denied that big business has several strikes against it in appealing to the minds of the masses of the world. This is no indictment of big business. Certainly I have enjoyed the fruits of big business, as has the generation of which I am a part. I was born in an age and community where the horse and cart was the accepted mode of travel, and where a mule furnished the power for cultivating the land. We had no electric lights, and only the most primitive plumbing and other necessities of rural living. Conveniences as we now know them existed only in the dreams of the Jules Vernes. However, in my lifetime, I have seen the whole countryside change to the point where today practically everyone in the United States participates in the benefits that industry has made available for the wide mass of people. Big business in its operations overseas can foster a similar development among the underprivileged peoples of the world, for the size of its activities offer it an opportunity not open to an individual or to small business.

Using small corporate subsidiaries or affiliates as feeders for large processing, fabricating, or distributing organizations is one of the effective methods that has developed in the sphere of responsible capitalism in North America. Unfortunately, this idea of integrated corporate organization for efficient production is too little used abroad. However, there have been some examples worth observing and these might well be emulated in other parts of the world.

Sears Roebuck and Co. has received a great deal of acclaim for opening up its stores in Latin-America and making it possible for the people south of the border to gain the benefits of mass distribution of products which formerly were available only to the wealthy few or the economically elite. Sears Roebuck stores are good examples of the type of American capitalism we should export. They manifest the benefits gained from long research in the integrated fields of manufacture, transportation, retailing, and public relations. But there is another angle worth mentioning.

When Sears went into these countries, it was naturally presumed by most of the people there that they would import most of their stock from the United States. However, Donald Nelson, General Wood, and those who planned Sears' policies felt that, in the long run, the company would do the finest possible job for the areas in which it was going to engage in trade if it made it possible for the people there to participate in the development of the Sears plan and begin manufacturing the products Sears would sell.

Having learned by long experience to help people to help themselves in industrial development in rural areas and small towns in the United States, Sears acted similarly in Latin-America and, by advice, counsel, and financial advances, helped a multitude of small organizations to begin the local manufacture and assembly of products for sale by Sears and other stores.[3] The people in these countries can definitely understand this type of operation, which gives them a sense of profitable participation,

[3] This policy had been initiated and proved its worth in Mexico, whose peso had sharply dropped in value to such an extent that Mexico placed an embargo on all imports within a year after Sears opened its first store on the Latin-American mainland. See Sears, Roebuck de Mexico, a case study published in 1953 by the National Planning Association, New York, for an appraisal of the benefits of the Sears' operations to Mexico.

dignified responsibility, and individual proprietorship. This is a successful exportation of the ideas, patterns, and local benefits of American service capitalism.

Without preaching the glories of America, Sears, by actual demonstration of how service capitalism is organized and how it works, has been able to perform miracles in good will and good public relations, to the benefit of itself, the people to the south, the United States, and "civilized" business everywhere. The Sears type of operation, however, cannot cover all the areas of business abroad which need development of the service corporate type.

§4. STORY OF AMERICAN SMALL BUSINESS MUST BE TOLD

In 1952 and 1953, when my study of public relations in Latin-America for the Technical Cooperation Administration of the State Department was made, I came to the very definite conclusion that the role of small business in the American economy was almost completely misunderstood by the people south of the Rio Grande. They had had little direct experience with it—they knew very little about it, and the efforts there of our government in trying to explain America had very largely omitted this phase.

In the resulting report I recommended that the work of Dr. Wilford White, Chief, Managerial Assistance Division, Small Business Administration, should be made known overseas. It was suggested that the work should be enlarged and made the basis of a special report to be widely disseminated to show what might be done by the United States government in Latin-America in advising small business.

The United States government is, of necessity, going to do a certain amount of educational work abroad. Government also has important contacts with overseas business people who come here. The overseas businessman, or the overseas student or government official who comes here to study America, should be routed in such a way that he will gain the benefit of the experience of the Small Business Administration of the United States government. It is unimportant whether the man goes home and establishes a small business. At any rate, he does go back recognizing that American responsible capitalism has within it a highly competitive and respected place for small business.

Multiplied millions of dollars are being spent overseas by the United States government in a serious attempt to check by one form of economic means or another the devastating onslaught that challenges world democracy. A most fruitful expenditure would be to enlarge the activities of the Small Business Administration to the point where it could make available to countries concerned, on a governmental basis, the advisory facilities it has available to aid small businesses. It has now become an established domestic policy of our government to encourage and substantially help small business to operate. This is not by gifts or grants, but rather by helping to create for it a favorable business atmosphere and political climate, by making available knowledge of technology, sources of supply, and markets, and by putting up needed loans. All of this is practically unknown in those parts of the world where we are making an attempt to have people understand our type and manner of business. Even in the United States we are only beginning to awaken to the importance of small business:

Today we are witnessing a revival of interest in small business as the hard core of the American free enterprise system. The publicity of huge corporations proclaims their dependence upon the myriad of small independently operated enterprises scattered throughout the land. Small business as an economic institution is as old as the Jamestown settlement and as American as the Washington Monument. It is the father of the corporate system rather than being its dependent. Strong healthy small businesses not only provide the beginnings for large enterprise, but they also perform certain functions which are vital to our way of life. Some of these functions are:

1. Helping free enterprise to remain competitive and free.
2. Decentralizing economic and employment opportunity.
3. Providing a high degree of stability and opportunity for the evolution of new ideas.
4. Meeting local needs and situations which cannot be otherwise served.

5. Constituting, in many instances, the final link in the chain of production and distribution.[4]

In 1953 and 1954 I was in India, with two other Americans and two Scandinavians, working with the Indian government to develop a plan for small industries. At that time, C. Leigh Stevens, a member of our team, presented to the Indian government, as part of the report, a recommendation that a small industry board, patterned very much after the smaller U.S. War Plants Production Board during World War II, be established. Mr. Stevens had been a consultant to that organization and was very familiar with it.

I shall never forget the astonishment with which members of the Indian Cabinet received Mr. Stevens' suggestion, and their desire to take immediate action toward using it as a basic part of India's development of its private sector of business.[5] In subsequent conversations, several members of the Cabinet said they had no knowledge that the United States had ever done anything of this sort. They were under the impression that what "Uncle Sam" had done was to eliminate small business and help big business get bigger. This one recommendation of Mr. Stevens went a long way in that particular cabinet to convince them that the United States was interesed in small business. Mr. Stevens had emphasized in his presentation that basically small business was the bulwark of a capitalistic society and that as such it should be encouraged by all legal means to help itself to success. The plan is now working, as can be seen from this report from the *Hindu Weekly Review,* October 6, 1958:

The report of the Small Industries Corporation for 1957–58 mentions a rise in the tempo of its activities. This is as it should be, though one would feel that in the circumstances of our country a much larger expansion of the Corporation's activities is called for. A significant aspect of the Corporation's work has been to secure orders from the Government for articles which can be supplied by small-scale units.

[4] *Management Training for Small Business* (Washington, D.C.: Government Printing Office, 1958), p. 1.

[5] As compared to the first five-year plan, India's second five-year plan multiplied by over six hundred times the funds to be budgeted for the development of village and small industries. See W. S. Woytinski, *India, The Awakening Giant* (New York: Harper & Bros., 1957), p. 194.

§5. The Marvelous Machete—Small Business in Action

I have come back from many trips into the tropics with re-newed respect for a particular small business in Collinsville, Connecticut, which is doing a successful public relations job for capitalism in underdeveloped areas. The Collins Company has sold a highly satisfactory product at a reasonable price in the far reaches of the earth, making loyal customers for itself while adding friends for the capitalist system under which it operates as a corporation. By good business practices, this company has perhaps promoted more lasting good will than multiplied millions of dollars in gifts from government to government have done.

If even ten other small manufacturers in the United States would begin to produce goods designed to fill the needs of a nonmotorized technology, many of the shadows on the wall of international affairs would disappear. Hundreds of persons inter-viewed during the preparation of this book have stressed the need for this type of action in world trade.

Joe P. Faulkner wrote the story of The Collins Company for the July, 1957, issue of *Coronet*. With the permission of *Coronet*, it is included here in its entirety, not only for its own message, but for its lesson in how to communicate abroad the fundamentals of American capitalism.

THE MARVELOUS MACHETE

by Joe P. Faulkner

A South American was traveling along a jungle trail near his native village not long ago. With him were his young wife, their three small children—and ever-present Senor Machete.

At a turn in the pathway, the man suddenly halted his family by stretching his arms out horizontally. No word was spoken. The young mother simply stopped and clutched the youngsters to her side.

Drawing the keen-edged machete from his belt, the father stealthily approached a mottled shadow he had detected draped about a banyan tree at the trail's edge—a full-grown boa constrictor. At a distance he consid-ered respectful, the man stopped and began swinging the long, glistening blade of Senor Machete back and forth before the snake's beady eyes. Soon the mesmerized boa was swaying its triangular head and part of its body in unison with the knife. Quickly the man flicked the blade outward and downward, and the snake's severed head dropped harmlessly into the jungle underbrush.

Snake-killing is only one of the countless roles played by Senor Machete (pronounced by Webster "Mah-chay-tay") in the tropics and subtropics, where it is considered the most important instrument yet devised by man. From the time a boy is strong enough to lift one, he is given a machete, educated to its multiple uses and taught to regard it as a second right hand.

All native workers in about one-third of the world's countries carry machetes, and pocket whetstones to keep them sharp. Marriages are considered beyond the pale until the couple has in its hope chest a pair of machetes as passports to survival, independence, success.

With this sword-like steel blade the native hacks down palm trees and bamboo to build his home, slaughters cattle for food, battles through the jungle's leafy tentacles to get to his job. There he uses it to slice banana stalks, milk rubber trees, chop sugar cane, or tap the sapodilla evergreens for chicle.

At home he depends on the same thin blade to help peel potatoes, husk coconuts. At the table he carves the meat and slices the cake with it.

If friends drop by, there's a game in the yard—throwing machetes at targets. And the following morning the omnipresent knife gives its owner a quick, clean shave.

Over 80 per cent of the world's supply of machetes is turned out in Collinsville, Connecticut, 15 miles northwest of Hartford, by the Collins Company. This $4,000,000 firm is comparatively unknown in this country, but is famous throughout Latin, Central and South America and parts of Africa and India. Collins manufactures more than 400 varying types of machetes.

They are made from strips of steel, heated, stamped into blades, tapered, cooled, tempered, immersed in molten lead, quenched with oil and hot water and squeezed between hot cast-iron plates. The secret lies in carrying out each step in the process to the proper fraction of a second.

Machetes vary in length from nine inches to three feet. Straight ones are used for dress occasions. Most are razor-sharp at the tip. Some are blunted.

In Costa Rica and Puerto Rico the blades must be painted flaming red. Nicaraguans insist upon down-swept blades. Some Brazilians want upward curved blades. Rubber plantation workers demand scimitar-shaped blades. Colombians in the interior order machetes with blades sharply curved; their countrymen along the coast prefer only slightly curved blades.

Handles of a tough acetate plastic are now used instead of the English horns which had a tendency to split. To sooth the vanity of some purchasers, handles are fashioned into the shapes of heads of elephants, cocks, eagles and intricately twisted wire designs. Multiplicity of shapes also is designed to meet demands of certain crops, as well as to satisfy personal preferences.

When a native wants a machete, he goes into a trading post and merely asks for "un Collins." Those who cannot pronounce the name simply wave a bended arm and clenched fist, gesturing the Collins trademark of a clenched fist rising out of a crown and holding a hammer.

Although special and elaborate types are more expensive, the average machete costs from 75¢ to $2. It lasts from six to eight months of "constant use," and is used right down to the last quarter inch of the blade.

In 1934, German manufacturers tried to flood Cuba with inferior machetes illegally bearing the Collins trademark. The traditionally shrewd Yankee traders had one of the German counterfeits sent to Collinsville. After examination, the company had a trunkful of tin machetes made, an agent took them to Cuba, rounded up natives, went to a German outlet and bought one of the competitive knives. He placed it on a table, point down, drew a Collins machete and with a mighty blow sliced the German product in two. He then opened the trunk and threw the tin machetes to the natives, crying, "If you want inferior machetes, you don't have to buy them . . . we'll give them to you free!"

The natives laughed the Hitler regime machetes right back to the Rhine.

U.S. Army details rely on machetes about a foot and a half long to scythe through tropical bramble. During World War II, Japs infiltrated New Guinea and the natives asked permission to "go get them." Not with guns. With machetes. The Army gave the natives one machete for each Jap they made into a memory. It cost Uncle Sam 1,000 machetes, but it ended the Jap infiltration.

Personal conflicts as well as international battles are frequently settled with the help of Senor Machete. But most important, it can be safely said that the fascinating Senor has been largely responsible for opening up the tropical world to trade and commerce, and that he can be depended upon to keep it open.

§6. Businessmen Should Participate in Community Improvement Abroad

Businessmen abroad have many opportunities to develop good public relations. However, they should recognize that feudalistic approaches to local community problems and community suppliers are harmful and must be dropped. Their effort must be to help communities develop their own system of supply and exchange of goods, even though the company might thereby somewhat temporarily reduce its profits. "Live and let live" is and always will be sound economics. To be patronized, business must patronize.

Unfortunately, this type of activity has not always been recognized abroad. Local capitalists have often lived a restricted life, have spent their money in building palaces and hunting preserves, depositing money in foreign lands, and doing a multitude of things which have little to do with improving the community or assisting it to a higher standard of living. One of the problems around the world is to get people who are engaged in business to take time out to participate in community and state affairs. The brand of responsible capitalism which we enjoy in North America is fast becoming community conscious. If Americans engaged in international business would demonstrate what we have learned is the proper thing to do, they will do a job in the exporting of the American concept that could not be done by any government or by any number of philanthropic agencies. The fact that a busy executive participates in community improvement on his own time receives wide acclaim and is never without appreciation.

In 1949, when I was in Thailand, one of the finest examples of this that I have seen was brought to my attention, during visits with the Minister of Education, the Prime Minister, and Prince Wan (who more recently has been President of the United Nations Assembly). Each of these men told me the story of Captain Seth Blakeman, a pilot for Pan American Airlines, who came to Bangkok from San Francisco on quite regular occasions, and who, in California, had been Scoutmaster of several local Boy Scout Troops.

Boy Scouts in Thailand were using the German goose-step, and the Scout organization was looked upon mostly as a training ground for noncommissioned officers in the army. The basic principles of scouting—helping to make individual, self-reliant citizens, and promoting the dignity of man—were very largely ignored. Capt. Blakeman took his leave time to help organize a troop of scouts in Bangkok, based upon what he had seen operate so successfully in California. He met with the leaders of the Scout organization in Thailand, and, singlehanded, so ably demonstrated the value of this type of community organization that when I was there later I found the whole Scout system was being converted to the kind of operation that they had learned by experience to be so valuable. One private citizen, with an idea and a sense of service, feeling responsible for doing something in his hour on earth, did more in the circumstances than dozens of official government information officers, writers, and press-release artists could possibly have done. The three high officials mentioned above told me that it was the finest demonstration of American good will they had ever witnessed. The Thai people liked it.

If this one Scoutmaster could take time to do that job and thereby change the whole concept of a social organization in a nation, there is very little excuse for the rest of us not to take time out to do the things which lie before us in the way of good citizenship and the promotion of world understanding of America.

§7. COMPANY TOWNS
A HANDICAP

Too often, the large extracting companies operating overseas —mining, oil, timber, fishing—suffer from the "company town" complex. They do not act merely as employers of labor and developers of industry, leaving the community to its own way of living. The community hall is built by the foreign patron from overseas, rather than from community funds saved from wages high enough so that people can do it themselves. If this picture were changed, one of the fundamental attacks against American overseas business would be removed. This would take a lot of planning. It would be impossible to rush into it overnight. However, over the years, it was done in America.[6] Had it not been, America probably would have had much more of a welfare-state complex than it has today. Actually, by ceasing to be the overlord of the community, the company saved its own neck,

---

[6] See Joseph P. Blank, "Good-By to the Company Town," *Reader's Digest* (January, 1959). Condensed from *American Business* (September, 1958).

forestalling regulatory or competing action by the State at the demand of the people.

In nearly every part of the world, the so-called company service organization adds to the political unrest of the area involved. I know that several companies will immediately write and say: "Prove it insofar as we are concerned." I make the flat, cold statement in reply that the Number One public-relations problem confronting American-owned mining, oil, timber, and similar businesses abroad is the need to divorce itself from "the company town." This will go a long way toward solving its other problems.

On May 10, 1957, at a meeting of the Canadian Public Relations Society at the Seigniory Club in Quebec, E. H. Eberts, Assistant Vice-President of the Aluminum Company of Canada, Ltd., made a most illuminating talk on the development by the Aluminum Company of Canada of the towns of Arvida in the Province of Quebec and Kitimat in British Columbia. The Arvida area originally consisted of scattered farms and woodlands; and when the company built the aluminum facilities there, it erected at the same time home and service facilities for its increasing personnel. Some of these were sold to the employees but most were retained by the company. Mr. Eberts said:

> In 1948 we suspended our house selling programme pending a complete reassessment of the situation including an investigation of the possibility of having one or more institutional lenders provide first mortgage money. We finally worked out a scheme whereby the purchaser was required to make a minimum down-payment of 15% of the purchase price, an institutional investor put up 60% of the purchase price on a first mortgage, and Alcan took the second mortgage for the balance of 25%. Over 900 houses have been sold under this scheme since July, 1954.
>
> The decision to offer the majority of our houses for sale was chiefly motivated by our conviction that property owners are happier and consequently more stable and reliable employees; the Company's desire to avoid the multiple headaches which are involved when an employer is also the landlord; and our policy already referred to of making Arvida a normal community in every sense of the word.

Some indication of the reality of problems inherent in company towns is revealed by the name by which the Arvida employees commonly referred to the company—The Octopus! And this was in spite of the fact that wages and living conditions were much better than in surrounding areas.

In 1951 the Aluminum Company began the development of Kitimat in British Columbia. This was really a "beachhead" operation as there were no inhabitants in the entire area except for the small Indian village across the bay. In describing the development at Kitimat, Mr. Eberts said:

> As a result of our experience in Arvida, we decided that if at all possible we would avoid owning any permanent residential property in Kitimat. In other words, we planned to have Kitimat start off somewhat ahead of the point to which Arvida had evolved in the past 31 years.
>
> Of course, it was necessary to build a certain number of temporary houses for construction purposes, most of which are still in use. However, my remarks here are directed to our policy with respect to permanent housing.
>
> In order to make it possible for our employees to acquire houses in Kitimat, we have made arrangements with various housing contractors to erect a large number of houses for sale by them directly to the purchasers. We have facilitated this operation by clearing the land and by making a house purchase assistance plan available.

The experience of the Aluminum Company of Canada with these two towns, both in their own home country, should be carefully studied by any company either owning or contemplating the building of a Company's town, particularly in a foreign country.

§8. BUSINESS UNFORTUNATE IN AFFILIATING WITH VESTED POWER

Overseas American business, unfortunately, too often has allied itself with the vested power in the country in which it operates and has thereby estranged itself from liberal thinkers in that particular country. In discussing this with many Americans who have operated this way, they have told me there is nothing else they can do, which is true if they want only immediate profits. But, in terms of the long-run gain for themselves individually, for their companies, for the countries in which they operate, and for the world as a whole, they had better take a second look. My overseas contacts are almost unanimous in saying that business, by thus operating, proves to the indigenous population that it is nothing more than a cold, heartless structure dedicated to exploitation. Far better for business to withdraw from those areas than to be there in open alliance with the political or economic dictators whom the people themselves fear and openly or secretly desire to throw out.

I admit that many of the criticisms enumerated in this report are hard to face and that perhaps my informants are somewhat harsh. But the fact remains that we are confronted by grim realities; we are playing for keeps with others who are out to win the loyalties of men by alluring representations of "freedom" and a higher standard of living. It was vividly brought out in the recent development of the new country of Ghana in Africa that the ideals of the American Revolution constituted the basis of a similar vision and dream which these people hoped to realize in their new political life; but at the same time they were so disillusioned with capitalistic quasi-monopoly practices that the economic system of that new nation was designed to operate on Marxist socialistic principles. Some companies are trying to cooperate with the new government and are laying a framework for future respect for the "private sector." Mobil Oil Ghana, Ltd., of Ghana, as a "christening" present to the nation, gave a "chair" in business administration to the University College, which is located at Legon Hill, Accra. This position is now filled by James Lipscomb, one of my former students at the Harvard Business School, and I am justly proud.

§9. We Can Learn from the Scandinavians

I have already mentioned my visit to India, with two other Americans and two Swedes, in connection with the development of small industries. At the suggestion of C. Leigh Stevens, our American group asked a Swedish representative, Sven Hagberg, to be chairman. Rarely does a team of consultants from a foreign country have better acceptance in another land than do Scandinavians, and much of the success of our operation was due to the fact that we had a Swedish chairman.

The Scandinavian concept of a moderate profit for profit-entity businesses, of the economic gain of patrons through their nonprofit cooperative business corporations, and of the dynamic interplay of these two forms of private capitalism with each other and with government businesses and services is better understood and appreciated than is modern American capitalism.[7] The Scandinavian economy, which is based upon a philosophy of abundance rather than cartel-imposed scarcity, is more like that of the United States and Canada than that of the other European countries. While the cooperatives do less than 20 per cent of the total business, they have done so much to keep consumer prices in line with reasonable profits that they have been widly publicized. The Scandinavian plan of medical care has worked for a generation, and while it is in the form of "socialized medicine," it has never received the attacks upon it from the United States that did the British.

In Asia the Scandinavian concept is appreciated by leaders more than is the American largely because the few Scandinavians they have met represented smaller concerns and cooperatives. There is little difference fundamentally between the Scandinavian concept and our North American. We have on a much bigger scale found the "middle road." But theirs is understood and ours is not. Unfortunately many of our business leaders here fail to recognize that the middle road of Scandinavia has an appeal that we might have if they correctly interpreted our present-day capitalism.

Even if Scandinavia were united, and not divided into small nations, it would be too small, the national and private resources too limited, to do the whole job. But we can learn some important lessons from them in developing our own public-relations programs on a larger scale.

[7] On my return from India in 1954 I was correctly quoted in a CDN dispatch from Rome by *The Boston Daily Globe* on August 20, 1954, as follows:

"India is slowly swinging around to the Swedish form of small industry, Miller thinks, in which groups of consumers—not workers themselves—own the means of production.

"'Nehru himself,' he says, 'seems to be a socialist not in the Marxist but in the Scandinavian sense. He appears to favor broad distribution of small productive ownership.'"

VIII

INDIVIDUALS CAN MAKE
THEIR MARK

§1. PERSONAL CONTACTS BY DEDICATED
INDIVIDUALS VITAL

Parts of this book may seem visionary and impossible of accomplishment through the individual efforts of people. However, if the free competitive private enterprise system, as we know it, is to be made of use for people in parts of the world that are not now enjoying its benefits, it can actually be implanted in their minds only by the personal contact of inspired and dedicated individuals. No one man can do the job—the world is large, but that fact alone need not scare us. There are numerous persons dedicated to an idea who are natural multipliers. As an example of this, Marx, Engels, and their original followers certainly did a job. They found converts who became proselyters. At first the motion seemed slow, but then it accelerated like a boulder rolling down a mountainside.

A look at our own country and how we have been influenced by individuals is revealing. At the turn of the twentieth century American agriculture was in a deplorable condition. Our forests were being denuded; our mines were being exhausted, with very little consideration for any form of conservation or of full utilization. Oil, a new product, was looked upon as something that might ring up an immediate profit, and natural gas was allowed to escape. It was taken for granted that the farmer was a poor man, a second-class economic citizen. The "country hick" was a joke of many. We had just had "Sockless Jerry" in Congress. The Populist movement was still current. The great Grange movement had spent its early force, and the Farmers Union was coming up out of Oklahoma and Texas. They were all trying to do something, and each accomplished its own purpose in its own way.

The sparkplug, you may call him, who actually got America started toward the type of conservation we now have, was an Irishman who never became an American citizen, Sir Horace Plunkett. He went for a short visit to Wyoming for personal reasons; then became appalled by the waste of our natural resources and lack of understanding by agricultural people of the things they could do by cooperating among themselves. The years spent in Wyoming gave him an insight into the problems of American rural life.

His soul was torn by the wretchedness of the American farmer, and he began to talk—not to thousands, but to the right few, to the natural leaders. Although a foreigner, he became a valued adviser to President Theodore Roosevelt, who adopted his slogan "Better farming—Better business—Better agriculture." Out of his ideas came the Country Life Commission, which was the forerunner of a changed public opinion in the United States that made possible the conservation of land and forests and laid a basis for later growth of the U.S. Forest Service, the National Parks Service, and cooperative American agriculture.[1]

[1] The following is quoted from Margaret Digby, *Horace Plunkett, An Anglo-American Irishman* (Oxford: Basil Blackwell, 1949):

"Theodore Roosevelt's appreciation of all he owed to Plunkett was deep and freely expressed. No man understood the President's rural policy so well or, next to Pinchot, had given him more help. As his term of office drew to a close, he decided to make a more formal recognition of his debt to Plunkett through the British Ambassador.

"'You have, I know, followed with keen interest the work of the Country Life Commission, which has pointed the way as I think to a better handling of country problems and a more satisfying life on the farm. But I do not know how far you are acquainted with the origin of the movement in the United States. Of course I have been interested for many years in farm life, and especially in the tasks and troubles of the women on the farm. But my

From this grew the American Institute of Cooperation, the great educational effort of American agricultural people to develop the use of a nonprofit corporate entity as a service organization to make farm people self-sufficient. Plunkett's enthusiasm and practical approach complemented the work of Seamon A. Knapp, a Texan, who developed the Extension Service which has made it possible for farm people to utilize the knowledge of the Experimental Stations and the laboratories; thus, through their own effort, with only small expense on the part of government in furnishing necessary information, making themselves more self-sufficient.

Still later Frank Evans of Salt Lake City, Utah (formerly general counsel of the American Farm Bureau), and his wife, both lawyers, spent more than two years of devoted personal service without hope of compensation to produce in 1935 the first volume of *The Law of Cooperative Marketing*. This soon became the bible for the cooperative corporate organization of American agriculture.

All this great expansion of ideas came largely as the result of one man dedicated to a cause, who found others in America who would work with him. He later returned to Ireland where he died. Today in London there is a small foundation known as the Horace Plunkett Foundation, carrying on some of his work.

---

interest did not reach the point of action until I began to follow what was being accomplished through the farmers' co-operative movement in Ireland. My old friend Horace Plunkett, whom I saw on his periodical journeys to America, kept me informed of the Irish agricultural situation and of the movement for better living on the farms of Ireland. We Americans owe much to Ireland and to Plunkett in the work we have been trying to do in the United States, and before I leave the Presidency I want to acknowledge our debt and to send through you, my thanks for the help we have had, and not only my thanks but the thanks of every man who knows what has been done and sees the need and sure results of this great movement to help the men and women who feed the nation and stand at the foundation of its greatness and its progress.

" 'Sincerely yours,

" 'Theodore Roosevelt' "

The judgment of Plunkett's friends is worth quoting. Gifford Pinchot wrote: "Some of these days it will be known that you are the man who stirred up the whole movement in America."

The moral of this story is that much of the leadership that we now hold in the rural areas of the world was substantially implanted by this one man, an Irishman with no large appropriation available to him, and his single devotion to the strength of a beneficent idea.

In 1949, in the city of Lucknow, India, it was my privilege to hold a public-relations seminar for a group of businessmen and educators. This was done at the request of a friend, Dr. N. K. Sidhanta, who was then Dean of the School of Economics at the University of Lucknow, and now is Vice-Chancellor of the great University of Calcutta, the largest university in the world. In preparing the present book I had the benefit of three days with Dr. Sidhanta in Boston, and we went over many of my conclusions. He told me that the American businessman, as an outside consultant, who both answers and asks questions with a view to social justice, would perhaps be the most welcome contribution from America to the development of the new India.

Businessmen in their operations in the undeveloped areas of the world have tended, unfortunately, to insulate themselves from the people. There is no one particularly to blame for this—it is merely because we have not studied the situation. I do not believe that over 2 per cent of the people of the countries involved with whom I have discussed this problem have failed to mention in one way or another the fact that too many Americans who come to their area tend to build a compartment for themselves and nestle into it. There are too few exceptions to this rule.

§2. REPRESENTATIVES FOR CAPITALISM THE PRIME NEED

Robert A. Whitney, President of the National Sales Executives Club, is quoted in the *Denver Post* of March 27, 1957, as having stressed the vital role of sales in the long-range progress of capitalism, and the need we have now in America for 450,000 new salespersons. Probably no one knows these facts better than Mr. Whitney. In a few sentences he has distilled the basic philosophy of what is needed overseas as well as at home.

In the Indian Small Industries Report referred to elsewhere, it fell to my lot to write the section on marketing and distribution. The following quotation taken from that document illustrates the vital role of selling brought home by Mr. Whitney:

. . . We found numerous examples of successful enterprises developing new markets and making a good living while performing a service to an otherwise market-wise neglected people. An example; in one small city we met a shirt salesman. He was a retired civil servant who had become frustrated trying to live on his pension and also the idleness did not appeal to him. He had made an arrangement with a shirting sales organisation to provide him with a continuing supply of good medium quality shirting material. He had then hired an unemployed tailor and provided him with patterns for six sizes of shirts. He also made up a sales kit containing sample shirts together with samples of cloth in various colours. He then started a house to house sales campaign for shirts. He timed his visits to call when the family were assembled for meals. Net result in two years he had taken enough orders that he now has three tailors and repeat orders enough to make a good living. All from a market in one of the poorest areas in India.

Progress depends very largely upon the ingenuity of salesmanship; and what is true in material things is also true in the dissemination of ideas. Even as the retired Indian civil servant found he could serve unrecognized needs, representatives of our North American capitalism could uncover a yearning for what it has to offer, despite the negative attitude in many parts of the world toward capitalism as it has been practiced there.

If we only had salesmen of the ideas of present-day American capitalism who would go out without order books in their pockets and merely sell its fundamental concepts, we should be in a position to feel that the fortresses of democracy are being buttressed rather than undermined by the termites of frustration and despair. Could this not be equal to or more important than the business at hand of selling a few yards of cloth, a few kegs of nails, or some pharmaceutical products?

A hundred men imbued and dedicated as was Horace Plunkett, with the idea of helping to make this a better world in their particular fields, through the development of responsible corporate capitalism and local private enterprise, could change the history of mankind. Neither this figure nor this conclusion is stated without substantial basis for judgment. It is proposed only after careful consideration and after years of study and after conversations with hundreds of people who are close to the world situation.

§3.   Businessmen Are the Best "Ambassadors"

Any American businessman abroad can be of great service around the world by making use of his opportunity to introduce a better concept of North American capitalism. Practically all of the people of the world are inquiring for the facts as to economic prospects within their areas. Such facts, when properly researched and reported, are not looked upon as just another propaganda document, but rather, are carefully studied and in many cases are implemented. Unfortunately, however, too many of these reports have, of necessity, been made by government people who were not actually familiar with the development of American business. In my travels, nevertheless, I have met a few of our businessmen who have taken to heart the matter of helping the man abroad understand the fundamentals by which America gains its stature in production and distribution.

One such is C. Leigh Stevens, with whom I traveled several times in the Far East. Mr. Stevens is a Management Consultant who recognizes the need abroad for the type of knowledge he has acquired during a lifetime of work in the United States. For the past several years, he has devoted a fair share of his time, without pay, to helping to make it possible for other people to understand the fundamentals of American production and distribution. His pet theme is that before you can divide the goods, you must produce them[2]—perhaps the best answer that has come from anyone to refute the socialistic approach. Mr. Stevens, with no order book in his pocket and nothing but his conscience to guide him, has been heeded by men from Prime Ministers and Presidents to owners of small shops. This type of advice is

2 See "The Industrial Process—Its Implementation," from *Report on Small Industries in India*, Ministry of Commerce & Industry (New Delhi: Government of India, 1954), chap. vi.

welcome, is wanted, and is one of the most effective ways by which the concept of American capitalistic enterprise can be taken to many parts of the world where it is so badly needed.

The church missionaries, as previously stated, are the principal persons who have actually made an impression on the minds of the people in developing countries. How do they do it? Not only do they have a message, but they are also a living demonstration of devoted service. This does not imply disrespect for the person who goes abroad for the government. But, as noted before, he has several strikes against him. He must maintain a certain economic and social standing; he usually travels in a fine car; and he has to take part in the normal government functions of diplomacy with its parties and other conventionalities, which unavoidably separate him from the people with whom he might work. Some serious action about this problem could lead to better results.

The wandering businessman is in an entirely different category. There is a subconscious respect for him apparent in cases which have come to my attention. One example is a Quaker business adviser, Horace Alexander, a Briton, whom I met in India at conferences with men in business, politics, and education. He had spent several years there as an adviser to anyone who wanted to understand the basic fundamentals that make business democracy work.

Queried as to just how he operated, he replied:

. . . I do not consider my personal function goes beyond that of the student who tries to listen to all sides, to understand what is going on, and then to act in some sense as an interpreter to any who may care to listen. . . .

Horace Alexander is one of the businessmen pioneers in presenting to many in Asia a realistic concept of modern private enterprise.

If this book does no more than induce a dozen retired American executives of medium or smaller companies, or men who have been in trade associations, to go overseas and donate their time to the crusade to make this a better world, it will have accomplished the beginning of my purpose.

The representative of the "big business" corporation has a number of disadvantages. Certain executives of giant corporations that have really tried to do a good job find the obstacles difficult to understand. But the fact remains that the executive or representative of "big business" has a stigma against him that is hard to overcome. The size of his company makes him suspect. The "Age of the Moguls" is still the picture the average foreigner has of big business in America.

The small-business entrepreneur has much more chance of helping people in other lands to understand the fundamentals of the use of dynamic capitalism for the betterment of business conditions than has any representative of a large business organization. The small businessman is one who has not more than a few hundred employees. He has watched his business grow and develop. He has paid for his research with the sweat of his brow. His business is not just a profession, but a way of life. A man of this type can do an inestimable service if he can go abroad and help people there to learn by his experience. He does not need to transfer a plant abroad; by precept and example he can let people know that he has gone through fundamental experiences not unlike their own.

A few years ago there was organized in the United States the Young Presidents' Association. This organization of younger leaders successful in industry has, from its beginning, been voluntary, operated without government aid or assistance, and has in many respects brought to the forefront in America the thinking of a progressive group of young men who were not afraid to face the facts of life in business, from both a material and spiritual point of view. This organization, by example, has done much to better the social climate in the business field.

If the younger business executives of the world today, who will be the industrial leaders of tomorrow, could be brought to accept and implement the philosophy of the Young Presidents' Association, a great step away from socialized government ownership and toward private business enterprise would be effected.

Reference will be made later to the work of the Junior Chamber of Commerce. This organization has found an idea that works. One of the chief reasons for its success overseas is the fact that it consists of young men. Time and again in my conferences in the preparation of this book it has been brought to my attention by leaders from overseas that we make a serious mistake in ascribing validity according to age. While the venerated man abroad is recognized for his accumulated wisdom and experience, the fact remains that the groups today that are successfully enticing the minds of men away from the philosophies which we believe to be sound, are spearheaded by comparatively young men. It is interesting in this regard to think of the Buddha, Mohammed, and the Christ, who established their thoughts in the minds of men when they were in their fertile youth and not in their senile dotage. Our chances of success will be greatest if we are able to capture the imagination and thinking of youth and young men before hardening of the arteries crystallizes their philosophy of life and business.

§4. ORGANIZED LABOR HAS SET A GOOD EXAMPLE

There is one thing I have found undisputed, apparently universal in its application. Representatives of our organized labor have done a better job of explaining our economic system abroad than have the representatives of American business. George Meany, President of the AFL-CIO, wrote:

Collective bargaining, we have learned, can exist only in the environment of political freedom. Where there is no individual liberty, there is no free trade-union movement either. Every dictator, from left to right, as a first step in the consolidation of power has sought to destroy free trade unions. And so we are dedicated to freedom, not only political but also economic, through a system of private enterprise. We believe in the American profit system. We believe in free competition. The American private-enterprise system, despite some defects, has achieved far greater results for wage earners than any other social system in history.[3]

The trade unionist, who is willing to work with business and who has not been in favor of government ownership, is in much of the world the real bulwark in stopping the growth of Soviet

[3] George Meany, "What Labor Means by 'More'," *Fortune* (March, 1955), p. 92.

communism. If American business would study the ways by which the American trade union movement has encouraged the trade union people in other nations, with a view to doing a similar task with its own counterparts, it could perhaps save the situation.[4] Even before the close of World War II, representatives of the organized labor groups in the United States went to Europe to contact labor leaders there. The trade unions in Europe had become more and more a part of the socialist—not Communist—movement and had in many cases made the labor drive a part of a particular "controlled" political party. This was especially true in Britain where the old Liberal Party gradually gave way to a new and vigorous Labour Party. American labor had long felt that it should work within the framework of existing parties and also that it was not in favor of the socialization of industry. It felt and feels that its "place under the sun" was found when its members contracted with capitalistic businesses and were not dependent upon the state for employment through government-owned business. As John L. Lewis, head of the United Mine Workers of America, told me in 1945, when discussing the Soviets, "You can't strike against the government."

This idea from our side of the sea about labor being in favor of capitalism was a shock to the labor of Europe. Our labor people were subjected to questions and often to ridicule. They were accused of selling out to the vested interests. But they stuck to their guns and by encouraging the travel in this continent of teams of labor people from Europe to see for themselves they began the movement that is gradually taking root in Europe—that labor thrives best under a controlled and prosperous capitalism. This program, largely the brain child of Clinton Golden, formerly Vice-President of the United Steelworkers of America, is probably the most effective "long range missile" yet devised to counterattack the theory of the Marxists. West Germany and Britain are examples of the effective work of the labor strategists.

[4] Some facts concerning the international labor organizations to which our unions belong, their fight against the organization by which the Communists try to control and subvert the world's labor movement and the support our unions give to free trade unions, particularly in underdeveloped countries, are given in *The American Workers' Fact Book*, U.S. Department of Labor (Washington, D.C.: Government Printing Office, 1956), pp. 385–94.

When the labor leaders of these countries saw the truth of the situation, they gradually changed their beliefs and have begun the new experiment in working with capital, even to the extent of encouraging the purchase of shares of stock by their members.

Unfortunately, the capitalist has not sold his theory to fellow-capitalists as has labor to its counterparts. There are some exceptions, but as a rule European capitalists have not seen the "light of the new day" in service capitalism. Had business done as good a job in selling its "new model" as has labor in selling its "accessories," the day of the cartel would be numbered. Progress is being made and the "cartel mind" is being "educated," but the lack of follow-through by business has delayed the change to the new concept of capitalism a generation, and perhaps for centuries if the Communists take over—and they will surely do so by default unless business wakes up.

It is strange to observe that there have been many cases where trade union representatives from America have done an effective job in convincing people overseas that private enterprise is the way to prosperity, that labor working with capital and management and government can help man to help himself to a higher standard of living. But in at least one instance which came to my attention, the work they had done had been undermined by an American business company going overseas with a cartel heart. American business must take a lesson from the work of organized labor. Individuals and companies must all help in the task of selling the free-enterprise system abroad.

§5. Soul-Searching Here Necessary Before Others Will Accept Our Message

Before we can help the people of the earth to understand the fundamental principles of the twentieth-century American use of capital, we have to do some soul-searching ourselves. I do not know how to express this any better than by saying that primarily we must learn to practice modesty. Americans have unconsciously developed an infallibility complex; we feel we have all the answers. Perhaps we do so far as our own affairs are concerned, but even that is debatable. Too often we have warned other people: "You can't do that; it won't work." Maybe it will in their case, which may have a different racial, traditional, educational, business, or psychological background.

Socrates and his disciples taught by asking questions. This was to make people think. In our approach to people overseas, particularly those who are rapidly emerging or are trying to emerge from poverty, ignorance, despair, and colonialism, this appoach is infinitely better than a dogmatic lecture telling them how we do things.[5] We must help them to think out their problems, and find their own answers. Admonition is no substitute for education. This whole approach is one of good public relations.

In 1946 I wrote a brochure[6] on the same general subject as this book, and in commenting upon it Edward F. Johnson, then General Counsel of the Standard Oil Company of New Jersey, wrote me as follows:

.... industrial management itself must be aware of corporate obligations to society and be vigilant in meeting them squarely. Otherwise I fear government controls will be tightened and eventually private enterprise as we now know it will disappear.

Mr. Johnson well stated the case for the need of service capitalism if capitalism itself is to survive; and world events have proved the statemanship of his outlook.

W. P. J. O'Meara, Assistant Under Secretary of State of Canada, is very often referred to as the "father confessor" of Canadian business. His official duties for a quarter-century have put him into constant touch with all phases of Canadian business both at home and abroad. The American and Canadian Bars and the Commission on Uniform Laws in both the United States and Canada look to him perhaps more than to any other one individual for advice concerning the adjustment of the corporate person to the environment of the natural person. By request he has given

---

[5] This approach is fundamental to "A Proposed Program for Communicating North American Capitalism" which was independently developed by Dean William S. Barnes of the Harvard Law School and is herein included in Chapter XII.

[6] Raymond W. Miller, *Keepers of the Corporate Conscience* (Washington, D.C.: Public Relations Research Associates, Inc., 1946).

several lectures to the Seminar on Public Relations at the Harvard Graduate School of Business Administration. At his May 1, 1957, appearance he concluded his presentation entitled "Companies are Peculiar Creatures" with the following "meaty" paragraphs that might well be framed and placed on the wall of every corporate directors' room in the world where private enterprise corporations still survive.

Because of the magnificent material success of corporate free enterprise in our North American democracies, we face a tremendous opportunity, presented by an inspiring challenge, that of Noblesse Oblige—To whom much has been given, of him much is expected.

Now the laborer is worthy of his hire. The company is entitled to its profit. But each must render its tithe of service to the community, for it derives much from its fellows of opportunity, of protection, of the almost endless list of blessings available to all who will participate industriously and honestly in the business of serving their fellows in our modern democracies.

We, who already in our lifetime have fought and won two world wars in order that freedom might not perish from our midst, are again at war. We are besieged by Communism, tireless and ingenious, vigorous and unscrupulous, avowed enemy of democracy. A favorite weapon in this war of ideals is the charge that we are capitalistic despots. In jealous rage these foes attack our system of corporate free enterprise with every weapon of speech and print. Pitilessly and vindictively, they turn their searchlights upon our manner of doing business. Our failures are magnified, our successes are distorted or ridiculed. We must show cause for the faith that is in us or its practice cannot persist.

Material prosperity is ours, yet we are beset by strikes, by cartels, by constantly rising prices, for all of which the Communist enemy blames our corporations. We cannot evade that challenge; we must face it squarely and, proving it false, fling it back in the teeth of our traducers.

I submit to you that there is but one way to achieve that goal. Let each of us bend his best efforts, ceaselessly, vigorously, unfalteringly and unselfishly to exert his influence on the corporations of which he is a shareholder or with which he does business, to the end that these juridic persons may join us natural persons in the battle, that they may so practice the Golden Rule in business that their worth will shine forth more brilliantly than even the searchlights of the enemy.

We have the means at hand to clothe our corporations in a mantle of justice, honesty, benevolence, to adorn those bodies corporate that already have produced a magnificent harvest of material benefits.

Man cannot live unto himself alone. The corporate form of business cannot survive on profits alone. Many companies, large and small, already are proving that the greatest of virtues, Charity, which is love of one's fellow man, can be practiced by the corporate entity as successfully as by the individuals who comprise it.

I offer you a sure shield and a wondrous weapon in the cold war raging at this moment at our very doors. Yes, peculiar creatures though companies are, for them as for all of us human creatures, as that shield and that weapon I offer you the practice of the sublime principle which our forefathers exemplified when they wrested this continent from the wilderness—"He profits most who serves best!"

§6. Needed: "Economic Statesmen" from Business

Beardsley Ruml, noted economist, speaking at the graduation ceremony of the Jewelry Store Management and Merchandising Course at New York University, September 21, 1956, made this significant statement: "The test of a business should be, does it make its money honestly?" This is a definition applicable to American capitalism—not that all of it practices this great principle, but basically it is striving upward toward this optimum position.

Business can, by self-analysis, search its own soul as to whether it is within or without this circle. If without, it has no right to call itself real American capitalism. That name should be a hallmark of integrity. If within, then it can, in good faith, know that it is helping to create a world at home and abroad where the seeds sown by the Marxists will fall on "stony ground" and where the efforts of those who believe in man will enable us to brand imperialistic communism as a subtle fraud on the rights of man. With business on such a level, it need not fear the admonition to consider the "beam in its own eye." Workers in the field of public relations know that it does no good to gloss over evils; rather they should be eradicated and there will be a new growth "of the tree that bears fruit."

Probably no writer probes deeper into the American scene than Max Lerner, Professor of American Civilization at Brandeis University. In the July, 1957, issue of *Pageant* he said:

The urgent need of mankind today, and of America as part of mankind, is not more technology but more social intelligence. And we will develop that intelligence if we become a great culture, not a magnified ant-hill of technicians and conformers. The aim of education, as it has been put, is not to develop "technically accomplished zombies," but men and women who know something about both the tragedy and the promise of the human condition.

The world has accepted two American products as being of great value: our concept of government, which is desired by many men in every land and which has few detractors, and our quality mass-produced goods, which are appreciated and desired. However, our concept of economic progress through social justice in a democratic political framework is not understood. This is due largely to the fact that one group of the custodians of this philosophy—the American businessman—is too busy or too inarticulate to take the time to explain it.

Professor E. D. MacPhee, Dean of the Faculty of Commerce and Business Administration, The University of British Columbia, most succinctly stated the need for "economic statesmen" in an article entitled "The Conscience of Business":

. . . Perhaps the large modern corporations, if led by socially-minded men, will set the code for industry. If these corporations have the other type of leadership, society will give its support to the political body in any effort the state may make to protect society. That is why the future freedom of business is so largely in the hands of the leaders of corporations. If business wants more self-control, it must train economic statesmen. This seems to me to be the issue, and it is on the performance of such leaders that society will decide which group will continue to be the "conscience of business."[7]

An economic statesman from business is Charles P. McCormick, Chairman of the Board of McCormick & Company of Baltimore, spice merchants, who has developed the "multiple management program" for spreading the base of management among an increasing number of junior executives.

In his book, *The Power of People*,[8] Mr. McCormick states:

. . . Our most successful approach, therefore, to the fight against communism in the United States is the positive approach. The only real way

[7] E. D. MacPhee, "The Conscience of Business," *The Canadian Banker* (Spring, 1957), p. 35.

[8] Charles P. McCormick, *The Power of People* (New York: Harper & Bros., 1949).

to stamp out the threat of communism is through developing an enlightened and publicly accepted free enterprise system. That statement implies two tasks for all of us. Management and labor and government must be close partners in co-operation on this subject.

First, we must research our practices of capitalism, review them analytically, bring them up to date, and arrive at the enlightened capitalism which I believe is that which holds a responsibility for the welfare of people on a par with the responsibility for making a profit.

Secondly, having made sure we are right in our practices of enlightened capitalism, we still have ahead of us the task of gaining widespread public acceptance. People must be told what we are doing, and why they benefit from it.

Each of these tasks is useless without the other. The public cannot be fooled into accepting something which isn't right, and even that which is right is still partially ineffective unless the people know it to be right and accept it accordingly.

Both at home and abroad, we need more business leaders of this caliber—men who believe wholeheartedly in the principles of modern service capitalism, understand the obstacles that stand in its way, and are ready to do something to overcome them.

IX

"LITTLE THINGS" THAT HINDER
WORLD UNDERSTANDING

§1. The Importance of "Little Things"

Big things invariably come from little starts. Some years ago, Keith McHugh, then Vice-president of the American Telephone and Telegraph Company, gave a talk entitled, "How Big Are the Little Things in the Telephone Business?"[1] His conclusions were that they were really the important things out of which the misunderstandings of great corporations arise.

In two of the Asian powers most friendly to the free world, there were, in 1957, distressing occurrences involving the killing of Asians by Americans. Leaving out all the legal matters, these situations have proved the thesis that emotion is the ruling passion of man rather than facts per se. Most of the flames of demonstrations were fed by "little acts" of Americans that had nothing to do with the killings themselves.

On its "Worldgram" page of June 21, 1957, the *United States News & World Report* wrote of one of these situations which is typical of international troubles stemming from thoughtless statements and acts.

Most Americans in Japan are aghast at the overtones of racism aroused by the Girard case. The Japanese press had previously leaned over

[1] A talk given at the Bell System Public Relations Conference, July, 1947.

backward to present the American side of the controversy. But Japan's papers are inflamed now by statements made by Louis Girard, elder brother of the GI who has been accused of shooting and killing a Japanese woman on a firing range.

Louis, in a telephone call to his brother, now in U.S. military custody near Tokyo, said his brother had become a "national hero." Embittered Japanese ask how the killing of the mother of five children, even if the shooting was accidental or while the soldier was on duty, could possibly make him a hero.

An American attorney then poured fuel on the flames by saying that he intended to find out who "threw Girard to the dogs."

These statements have convinced many Japanese that some Americans consider them inferior people. Japan's newspapers are filled with letters from readers that disclose how deep the resentment goes.

A Japanese housewife writes: "I myself believe the United States is a country where human rights are highly respected. But I cannot help thinking that American justice is often influenced by racial prejudice."

A law professor says: "Just as in the case of the Taipei riots, the trouble here seems due to ignorance and racial prejudice of a segment of the American people. If the place had been Europe, no American would have shot at a Caucasian housewife for picking up shells."

An American Negro GI, in his letter, says: "The so-called excitement emanating from Congress and the American public is but reflective of a hysteria based on a feeling of racial superiority by American Caucasians . . ."

In the other case, riots resulted when a U.S. Army sergeant in Taiwan was acquitted in his trial for the killing of a Chinese "Peeping Tom." As *The New York Times* of May 28, 1957, reported:

When an army panel of five sergeants and three colonels announced the verdict of "not guilty," the widow of the victim wept. About 150 Americans in the courtroom, many of them friends of Sergeant Reynolds, applauded. Chinese spectators, numbering about sixty-five, were outraged by this display in the widow's presence.

Remember that the riots in Taipei and the Japanese situation were precipitated, not by the unfortunate killings but by the earlier and follow-up words and deeds of other Americans. Just as in these cases governmental trouble came from the unthinking acts of individuals, so do larger international problems often multiply, as they did in the Suez situation, because of similar acts on the part of business, individuals, and governments. For the purpose of this book it can be added that the "little" acts of Americans are equally important to the acceptability of American capitalism.

§2. OPPORTUNITY FOR ADVANCEMENT NOT GIVEN LOCAL CITIZENS BY U.S. BUSINESS ABROAD

American business prides itself upon being able to develop leaders from within its own organizations. Perhaps no other one thing adds more to the morale of a developing business in America than the feeling throughout the organization that the man or woman who becomes part of it is afforded an opportunity to ascend the ladder of advancement as the company expands.

This has not been true, unfortunately, except in rare instances, in the operation of American-owned companies overseas. True, there is a slow improvement today—but time is running out. Only when our businessmen recognize they must work to build good will in overseas operations by installing executive training programs for local employees, comparable to those carried on at home, will lasting good will result.

The fact that "natives" in many overseas countries are used as laborers and only a paltry few are given more important posts in some American business operations has a detrimental effect upon morale. This affects not only the company concerned, but also the long-range understanding of, and friendship for, Americans in these areas. A change in this situation can be brought about so readily and easily that it seems strange that its importance has not been more widely recognized heretofore—its own internal value in the organization as well as its effect upon international relations. As individuals, however, we quite often have much better hindsight than foresight. Let us not blame anyone, but admit that this is a mistake that should be rectified as rapidly as possible.

Incidentally, a plan like this cannot be put into operation merely by pressing a button or dictating a letter at headquarters. It is going to take the sincere and watchful interest of the managements of business corporations. The international situation is so tense today that top executives in American companies operating overseas should take it as one of their first orders of business to investigate this situation firsthand and begin to generate a feeling in their organizations that opportunity, on all rungs of the ladder, is available to all employees.

"Big business" of all nationalities is so far removed from the experience of most people of the lesser developed parts of the world that it is largely ineffective in the battle of ideas save to its own employees, and too often there, because of absentee control, it is able to develop loyalty only upon the basis of pleasant experiences with the company. Tibor Mende of France, former editor of the Economic Section of the Paris Edition of the *New York Herald Tribune*, says in a most thought-provoking book entitled *South-East Asia between Two Worlds*:

. . . When my motor-boat stopped at the BPM's [Batavian Petroleum Company] elaborate jetty, I was received by an official of the Company. We walked around for hours among the gigantic and complicated machines, cooling towers and storage tanks. We visited the modern, well-equipped workshop where the apprentices were trained in elementary technology. Then I was led along to the stone-built barracks where about a third of the refinery's workers lived and I saw the hospital, cinema and assembly hall built for them by the Company. Finally, rather exhausted by the heat, we entered the cool corridors of the principal administrative building. The manager, a surprisingly young Dutchman, gave me the facts with a competence as cool as his refreshingly air-conditioned and very elegantly furnished office.

BPM alone employed some eleven thousand, and the livelihood of about four times as many—or well over a third of Palembang's population—depended on it. The American company in the neighborhood had about an equal number on its payroll. But in all Indonesia, BPM employees numbered nearly twenty-five thousand. Of the six thousand working there, in the Pladju refinery, nearly a thousand were Europeans. Yet only 170 Indonesians had obtained salaried positions. The rest were weekly wage-earners, making 200 rupees or a little more (approx. $10 a week). According to the manager their pay was better than the earnings of Palembang employees in any other trade. Was there any effort made to train Indonesians for better-paid jobs? Well, twenty were sent each year to the Bandung technical high school in Java, at the Company's expense. My question whether any were sent abroad was dismissed with polite impatience. As for the country itself, it derived three benefits from its oil: royalties, taxes and export duties. When I referred to the water-kampongs, across the river, I was silenced by a gesture towards the workers' barracks, visible through the manager's window. Had I not seen their splendid new assembly hall, the cinema and the hospital? The Company was doing its best. If two-thirds of the workers had to live across the river, that was on account of lack of funds. Still, he admitted with a resigned shrug of his shoulders, there were strikes; often for silly reasons. The trade union leaders were coming back from Moscow and Peking congresses with new ideas and they were causing the trouble. And their offices displayed large pictures of Mao and Stalin. . . . After that we went to the European employees' bar and drank whisky on the terrace opposite the water-kampongs.[2]

The water-kampongs, closely spaced huts on stilts along the marshy edge of the river, suggest a great underlying blight and deterrent to new, needed economic organizations and operations in Asia, the Middle East, Africa, and parts of Europe, namely, that of overpopulation. The purpose and scope of this volume precludes a detailed analysis of this significant factor. Suffice it to say, it is a prime cause of the half-education which in turn provides a seedbed of intense material wants and credulity among the masses. This condition makes the Communist promises of a better standard of living alluring—with little or no thought among the common people of the cruel dictatorship which they will suffer by falling within the Soviet orbit.

During the past twenty-five to fifty years, domestic American industry has learned and put into practice more enlightened principles of human relations in business than in its entire earlier history. While mistakes are still being made, the fact remains that the average American company today is trying to do a good job in public and human relations within and without its own organization. In the history of all economic development, there is nothing to compare with this change in the attitude of American business within the past generation. America has found the way, and it has a duty to communicate the methods by which it has learned to blend the material needs and the spiritual aspirations of man.

[2] Tibor Mende, *South-East Asia Between Two Worlds* (New York: The Library Publishers, 1955), p. 32.

Too often, in our development to this technological age, people themselves have become the problem, as we have overcome one by one what seemed like insurmountable technical problems. From an engineering and professional point of view, today most production, construction, distribution, and transportation problems can readily be solved. But the tragedy lurks in the handling of the human equation, especially overseas. The human-relations problems have become proportionately more and more important. Unless the technological change accompanying economic development abroad is paralleled by better practice of human and public relations, it will continue to sow within itself the seeds of its own destruction.

§3.   "COME HERE, GEORGE!" AND THE
      "UNCONSCIOUS ARROGANCE OF
      CONSCIOUS WEALTH"

Some years ago, the Reverend Clarence E. Wise, a Methodist pastor in Washington, D.C., told me that, although he had never been abroad, he had always been tremendously interested in the problems of people overseas. Over a period of years he had studied and examined the reports of missionaries and the observations of travelers and had come to the conclusion that most of the problems, particularly in the Middle East, could be summed up in the attitude of mind expressed in the phrase, "Come here, George!"

That phrase, he said—or a similar summons, "Boy!", commonly used by the European or American in addressing nationals in the areas concerned—gave these people a feeling of inferiority and resentment that sooner or later would develop into a movement to expel the light-skinned people from that area. Dr. Wise's idea has haunted me ever since; and on many a trip to the Far East I have remembered his statement and have come to the conclusion that he was right. On April 13, 1957, *The New York Times* carried a story which is, to my mind, not only proof positive of the truth of his original conclusion, but presents for American business and professional travelers a key to the closet in which are locked the solutions to international problems.

PSYCHOLOGY USE IN ALGERIA URGED

Robert Lacoste Tells French Aides to Respect Moslem Dignity—Cites Right of Dissent

As a first step toward improving basic relations with the 8,500,000 Moslems in Algeria, M. Lacoste urged the 1,000,000 Frenchmen there to stop addressing them with the second-person-singular form reserved for intimates or inferiors.

Such grammatical discrimination offends educated Moslems and epitomizes a contemptuous attitude common to a majority of French settlers in Algeria.

Most of these problems are so simple to solve that they escape our attention as our thinking grows more and more complex.

I earnestly recommend that the observation of Dr. Wise and the recommendations of M. Lacoste be taken to heart by all who have anything to do with international operations of business or government. Until this apparently contemptuous attitude is corrected I can see no hope for solving the problems of the Middle East, Asia, Africa, or even our own internal racial tension.

DeForest Anthony, Small Business adviser to the Quartermaster General, and a man who has spent many years in studying human-relations problems in business and industrial relationships has summed up in a few brief words the essence of the problem confronting the American businessman overseas. It should be memorized by everyone who is at all interested in human relations. He pointed out to me how easily executives fall into the trap of "the unconscious arrogance of conscious wealth."

He first told me this several years ago. As I traveled into the highways and byways of India, Pakistan, Burma, Indonesia, Japan, Korea, and other countries in subsequent years, I became more and more impressed with the truth of his observation, not only as it applied to others but as it applied to me. I had a ticket that would take me home, money and checks in my pocket that would buy for me the best there was if I wanted it. While I could become concerned about the problems confronting these people, unconsciously I was not a part of them. I think that this observation of Mr. Anthony's had more to do with my evaluation of the real situation facing the American as he tries to help the world than any other single incident.

It might be well, in regard to each action we take in dealing with others, whether as a nation or as individuals, to remember the fundamental truth given to the world by the humble Man of Galilee, who himself was an Asian and not a European: "Do unto others as you would that they should do unto you." He was in the class to whom the phrase of our generation, "Come here, George!" would have been addressed.

§4. White Man Must Treat Other Races as Equals

In order to appreciate the basis for the development of capitalism in much of the world, it is well to take a look at Japan. Along in the 1870's Japan opened her doors to the rest of the world. By so doing she proved many things. The chief item, so far as the world is concerned, is that science draws no color lines. In one generation Japan emerged from the dreamy past and became scientifically minded. Reams could be written on this subject. Japan's present position in the forefront of research and application in such fields as optics, the agricultural sciences, and electronics is well known. One of the tragic attitudes of the European-American part of the world has been an unconscious belief that the marvels of modern science were restricted to those who had white skin. Yet in 1957 the achievements of two Asians received world-wide attention when two Chinese-born scientists, Chen Ning Yang and Tsung Dao Lee won the Nobel prize in physics.

In 1920, Lothrop Stoddard wrote a book, *The Rising Tide of Color Against White World-Supremacy*.[3] It received momentary consideration and then was largely forgotten. Today, it can be found only in a few libraries and secondhand bookstores. But in this particular book the author stated, among other things, that if the white race entered into another interracial war, its day of

---

[3] Lothrop Stoddard, *The Rising Tide of Color Against White World-Supremacy* (New York: Charles Scribner's Sons, 1920).

supremacy in the world was over. He also pointed out that when the white race imported nonwhites to fight its battles against white men in Europe, in World War I, it had probably put a noose around its own neck. Unfortunately, very little studied attention was paid to this book. Much of what Stoddard said is perhaps unscientific, but the fact remains that his prophecies must not be ignored, for part of the chameleon-hued Communists' propaganda throughout Asia and Africa is to cultivate ill will toward the occidental white race.

In Cairo, a young Egyptian told me in the summer of 1956 in substance: "You know that I am pro-American; you know that I believe in the type of American business that I saw and studied in America, but I want to tell you something. When Col. Nasser, upon the advice of his attorneys and advisers, seized the Canal, in line with what we believed to be our legal rights, he still had some people in Egypt who were critical of his actions and did not have a firm belief in the wisdom of his judgment. But one act by the Europeans, with the approval of your people, solidified Egypt as nothing else has ever done."

I said, "What was that?"

He said, "The statement made that the ships could not operate except with European pilots. That was a slap in the face. It's the same thing that your business organizations have insisted upon in their operations with the people of the Near East for a hundred years; and it's going to stop!" My mild-mannered friend raised his voice and the light of the new Asia and the new Africa shone in his eyes. The debacle of armed intervention by England, France, and Israel in this atomic age demonstrated better than anything I could say that the prophecy of my Egyptian friend will come true. Needless to say, the Egyptian administration has operated the canal ably, with ships passing through in record-breaking numbers.

Yes; American business, if we are going to export the fundamental principles of North American service capitalism and enterprise, we must recognize that the people with whom we deal have minds and intellect comparable to our own; that only the desire for heaven on earth as well as hereafter gave the

occidental nations a head start in the freedom of thought resulting in scientific inventions and superior corporate organization.
This knowledge can be shared—others can use it, whether it
be in science, engineering, banking, or business—it's all the same.
The day of the white man's supremacy because of his know-how
in civil and military operations is past. He had better plan to be
an equal, because there are forces in the world today that, if
allowed to run their courses, will make him a slave. One of the
greatest of the Soviet psychological successes has been to convince
millions of nonwhites that under the Communist era to come
there will be complete racial equality. Whether our children of
future generations will be free men or slaves may depend very
largely not only on whether our military might exceeds or equals
that of Russia, but on whether the American businessman coop-
erates in exporting equalitarian service capitalism throughout
the world. This is a cold, hard statement made only after due
deliberation, based upon many years of almost constant study of
successes and failures in the communication of ideas between
peoples of different races, religions, vocations, and education.

§5. THE INDIAN-AMERICAN—
    AN OVERLOOKED OPPORTUNITY

Right on this continent is an example of capitalism's failure
in its philosophy of economic opportunity for all. This is a failure
with world-wide implications in the field of winning the minds
of the world's population to our ideas. A few years ago, the
Prime Minister of a leading Asian country asked me a question
which I could not answer as I would have liked. He asked:
"How do you Americans expect to help my people, when you
can't help the Indians in your own country solve their problems?"

Unfortunately, the Prime Minister is right. We have for
years, with all good intentions, given the Indians millions of
dollars in gifts and charity, but we have not helped them to solve
their own problems. We have not seen to it that the Indian-
American had the same economic opportunity as do the rest of

our citizens—the opportunity to support himself by the sweat of his brow.[4]

On the credit side, I have learned recently of the new and original planning being done in the Indian field which looks as if it might hold real hope for the First Americans for the first time. Perhaps some day I can give the Prime Minister the answer I would like—that the Indian is no different from any other American and that his economic status is on a par with all other sections of our society. Under the present Commissioner of Indian Affairs, Glenn L. Emmons, a New Mexico country banker, economic opportunity is being brought to the reservation areas and those Indians that want to leave are being relocated in industrial centers and trained to perform industrial jobs requiring special skills. Many of our younger Indians, particularly those who have had experience in our armed services, are convinced that their people would be the gainers if they left the protected tribal atmosphere for one where they would be dependent on their own efforts.

Several industries have recently located branch plants on or near reservations and have employed Indians. The results have been remarkable. An outstanding example of this success is to be found in Rolla, North Dakota, where the United States government has installed machinery in a community-built plant supervised by the Bulova Watch Company to make jewel bearings—an item essential to our national defense.

Jewel bearings are tiny bits of synthetic sapphire with a zero coefficient of expansion. They are so small that it takes 20,000 of them to fill a thimble. They must be perfectly shaped so as to fit into recesses in the mechanisms of watches, precision instruments, vital control devices, and the like. Each jewel requires 32 different machining operations, some to tolerances of 1/200,000ths of an inch. At this plant 77 per cent of the

---

[4] This is not to be confused with the problem of internal segregation of the Negro and other minority groups. The political amalgamation of these groups and community acceptance of the realities of the racial problem are a subject for another treatise. Suffice it to say here that our unsolved racial problems are perhaps our Number One political problem in the stream of world thought.

employees are Chippewa Indians who have never had previous factory experience; almost all of them had never operated a machine of any type prior to this employment. Many of them had never performed any work other than that of an agricultural nature. Since 1952 these Indians have performed with less than one-half the national rate of absenteeism and turnover.

Perhaps the greatest accomplishment of this project in Rolla has been the proof to all that man was created to work and to be self-sufficient. The Indians employed are a changed people since this project came into being—they take pride in their homes and their families; they take pride in themselves. They no longer live on charity and government handouts; rather, they live by the sweat of their own brows and the dexterity of their own hands. Where there was a shack before, there is a home now; where there was a broken family before, there is a closer relationship now. Some officials in North Dakota have given full credit for a drop of almost 60 per cent in juvenile delinquency on the Chippewa reservation to the fact that the Indians are employed.

Perhaps the history of our earlier dealings with these First Americans has given good grounds for the widespread belief voiced by one European and quoted in *U.S. News & World Report* of June 21, 1957:

> This is the way some of the French in Algeria react—
>
> A young woman: "We should do with the Arabs what the Americans did with the redskins—kill half of them and put the other half on the reservation."

If we can act to correct this situation, we shall have removed one of the obstacles to understanding with men of other races.

§6. AMERICANS OF ALL RACES SHOULD TELL OUR STORY

The color problem is a difficult and baffling one in our own country. How are we to accomplish the integration into the community and business life of people who are not of the same color or ethnic background as the majority? This problem will be a serious one for years to come. Over fifteen million of those with non-European background are from African ancestors. In addition, there are several thousand from Asia, and some 400,000 American Indians. We also have a great many American citizens whose language and cultural ties are with the countries south of the border. Many of us fail to recognize that in the United States today we have a population that is more heterogeneous than that of any other so-called "white" country in the world. It appears certain that, as we work out our problems here at home, our success will not only help toward our own salvation, but will also have a favorable effect on people overseas.

The more business appreciates and utilizes the abilities of individuals within the various ethnic groups that constitute the population of America, the better American capitalism will be understood and the more readily accepted overseas. Several years ago, this was dramatically brought to my attention in Thailand while meeting with a group of middle-income people. As an American, I was told something which is most interesting: that a former president of Union Pacific was a descendant of one of the Siamese twins[5] who emigrated to the United States from Thailand in the nineteenth century. That fact, in large degree, has been a basis for much of the lasting friendship between Thailand and the United States. The directors of the Union Pacific, who elected him president because of his ability, probably had no thought of international affairs—but in one land a long way from Ogden, Omaha, and Los Angeles responsible and thinking leaders of a nation now feel a comradeship for America because of it.

Too little thought has been given to how representatives of these various groups might serve in transmitting the American idea in any but military relations. However, during the war, the Japanese-American, or Nisei, was widely used and his heroic exploits are a part of the finest in U.S. military history and tradition. The Indian-American, with his strange language and customs, was employed to transmit messages which defied codebreaking because they were not in code but rather in his tribal tongue.

[5] See "Chang-Eng's American Heritage," *Life* (August 11, 1952).

In 1949, on my first trip to the undeveloped parts of the world, I came to the conclusion that the Americans of non-European stock could do an excellent job of public relations abroad. In my Public Relations Audit made to the State Department in 1953, based upon studies made during previous years, I stressed this as much as any other phase of the report. So far as I know, no objection was ever raised to this recommendation.

Only a few people who are closely associated with the development of information as to ethnic origins of the populations of the earth are familiar with the fact that south of the Rio Grande, in the great Latin-American part of the world, the population is increasing at such a rate that it will perhaps double within the lifetime of those born today. There are now as many people in Latin-America as there are in North America. The North American Indian is a small percentage of the general population here; but when one goes into Latin-America the situation is often reversed, and the largest percentage of any one race is made up of people of Indian stock. Many of the problems having to do with the development of a better world for us in the near future concern our relationships with the people to the south. If American business can begin to use in its operations there men and women of different ethnic groups recruited in America who are qualified, educated, and have the native ability to carry on, they will provide a living demonstration of the fact that America is not a restrictive country which still practices colonialism toward its Indian Americans.

Today one is encouraged by the number of members of the nonwhite races that are operating overseas for the United States government. The record of their success is extremely high and their ability well demonstrated. They represent probably one of the finest possible forms of public relations for the United States government overseas. The private sector of America, however, has been slow to recognize the public-relations value of incorporating in its overseas efforts men of a racial stock unlike that of the normally accepted and known American of European descent.

A few years ago, the Food and Agriculture Organization of the United Nations sent a woman of Sioux-Indian stock from the United States into Latin-America as a Home Demonstration

Adviser. I have never met her, but on inquiring in Latin-America regarding relationships between the people there and here I was told about her presence and fine work. The local people were greatly impressed. She was an American citizen, educated and capable; and the fact that she had been hired by an international agency to come there as an adviser on their local problems proved to this particular group of people that America was a land of opportunity.

During the time I have been gathering the material for this book, I have probably been asked more questions concerning the lack of opportunity for nonwhite American citizens of minority stock in working for companies overseas than on any other one point. A limited inquiry to American companies concerning the reason for this dearth of opportunity for these people was made, and it appears that no one planned it that way. Rather, it is one of those things that people have not considered. There are a few exceptions. Some companies have sent people of non-European ancestral heritage overseas and have had extremely good results.

Business should consider assigning to overseas work qualified people from within its own organization who are of various racial stocks. The opportunity is unlimited. As an example, it so happens that the great problems of colonialism still existing in the world are practically all centered in Asia, the islands of the sea, and Africa. The missionaries of the churches, the International Cooperation Administration of the United States Government, and the military have found that our Negroes perform a dual service in these distant areas. One is the job for which they are sent; second, and vitally important, is the fact that they are a living demonstration to the people there that America is solving its own internal problems. Other Americans of non-European stock have made equally important contributions.

X

THE PROBLEM OF EDUCATION

§1. The Hazards of the Wrong Kind of Education

During the past centuries the most useful organ of man—his brain—has been largely neglected and undeveloped. The intellect of the common man has been unexposed to the processes of education and training. Today in every country of the world there is increased emphasis upon literacy, education, and practical instruction. Americans have been pioneers in this worldwide movement, including such great leaders as Frank Laubach and Jimmy Yen, with their "every one teach one" program that has helped millions to read and write elementary words. Every developing nation is feeling the impact of the trained educator sent out by mission boards, the Fulbright Program, the Colombo Plan, or other means. Great progress is being made in the mechanics of education. At the same time there is a serious problem with regard to the proper understanding of modern capitalism.

To take one example, in much of the world many of the textbooks in arithmetic and reading and on up into economics are based upon a highly critical attitude toward capitalism. Take, for instance, this report from Japan:

Though the Ministry of Education is supposed to pass on all textbooks, those who really do the selecting are members of the powerful

(500,000 teachers) Japan Teachers' Union, which is dominated by Marxists. Each year Japan's publishers woo the teachers at "hot spring parties," and the teachers see to it that Marxist texts get adopted by their schools. One such text, *Model Junior High School Study*, [which] was edited by the author of the story that inspired the anti-American film *Hiroshima*, is nothing but a propaganda tract against capitalism and Western imperialism.[1]

Here is another illustration of the infiltration of ideas into education. The story was told to me by a friend who was in the country at the time it happened:

A certain University has three schools: the Schools of Agronomy, Law, and Medicine. The latter two are virtually nonexistent. There are about 400 students. The University is about two hundred years old and has been a cultural center, not only of its own country, but for neighboring lands.

An eminent American visited the School of Agronomy recently. Upon entering the institution, he noticed that the laboratories and equipment were in a serious state of disrepair and had been sorely neglected. He was there during the normal school period during the day, but saw no classes in session. The students were lounging around, and no formal instruction was taking place.

He had personal knowledge of many hundreds of volumes of textbooks on soil and the plant sciences having been sent to the School, but when he went into the library he found none of these appeared on the shelves. Instead, the literature was mostly by Marx, Lenin, Engels, and other Communist leaders.

Upon questioning some of the students, he found that they did not have classes during the day, only at night and then only to study Marxism. Upon further investigation he found the faculty was largely Communist-dominated, that the student body was practically all Communist or at least heavily penetrated by Communists, and that the head of the student organization had made several trips behind the Iron Curtain for further indoctrination.

This kind of upsurge of the Marxist philosophy during the past twenty-five years has been accelerated as the result of the

[1] *Time* (August 26, 1957), p. 36.

teaching of the late Professor Harold J. Laski of the London School of Economics, and the dissemination of his ideas in far places of the globe by his former students who, in many cases, became ardent Marxists. The influence of this teaching cannot be discounted. The tragedy is that North American capitalism with its great potential benefit to mankind has not, to date, developed enough disciples even to counteract the teachings of the followers of Laski, much less to go beyond and *crusade* for economic democracy.

Much of the teaching in new countries is done by enthusiastic dedicated local people who have not had much real training in the field of education. The natural thing for them to do is to teach from their own or their community experience—and this experience reflects a fear of capitalism usually inflamed by recollections of colonialism and fanned by the extractions of the local moneylender. Many believe that this educational situation is the most explosive of any facing the survival of modern service capitalism.

Coupled with this is the frustration of those who get an academic education and then have no suitable job. From personal observation in Calcutta in 1949, I know of 2,500 college graduates who applied for a total of twenty tractor-driving jobs. The advertisement for the tractor job said, among other things, that the driver must be able to read and understand the directions for driving, written in English; none of the applicants previously had ever driven a tractor.

A story from the June 1, 1957, edition of *The New York Times* is inserted here because it really states the whole situation in a few paragraphs:

Idle Graduates Aid Reds in India

> Joblessness Among Educated Is Called Factor in Nehru Party's Loss of Kerala
>
> > by Henry R. Lieberman
> > Special to *The New York Times*
>
> Trivandrum, India, May 29—
>
> *   *   *   *   *
>
> Widespread unemployment among Kerala's educated young people helped the Indian Communists achieve their ballot-box victory. Many

unemployed high school and college graduates voted for the Communists and persuaded others to do so.

The "educated unemployed" problem is worse here than in a number of other places in India.

Trivandrum, capital of Kerala, shows considerable evidence of past enlightened rule in the form of schools, an art museum, public library and a general appreciation for education. The former Maharaja of Travancore, who ruled here before the disappearance of the Princely States after India became independent in 1947, had a reputation as a patron of arts.

Today, however, there are far more high school and college graduates that can be absorbed by the Government, the chief employer of the man who can handle words and figures. Hassan Marikar, a tall personable Moslem who runs an auto agency here, observed there were too many clerks and not enough skilled mechanics and welders.

While Kerala boasts a relatively high literacy rate of 56 per cent, it is plagued by heavy densities of population, inadequate food production and little industry to absorb its unemployed.

The chief secretary of the State Government, N.E.S. Raghavachari, a civil servant, noted that 15,000 applicants responded some time ago to an advertisement for high school graduates to fill 100 jobs.

"Forty-two per cent of the people who get out of high school and college are unemployed," said Prof. Joseph Mundassery, new Communist Minister of Education.

The impact of American education has had a tremendous effect upon the minds of many of the men and women who are creating the new world in Asia, South America and Africa. There are few leaders of the newer countries of the earth who have not been largely influenced by American education, most of it from the missionary-supported schools. It was through the stirring of the hopes and desires of the uneducated yet intelligent young people of these lands that the spark of new ideas of a better world was ignited. But there has not been enough follow through and the leaders who were trained by North Americans in many cases are plagued by the disciples of Laski.

Just one more story: One of the leaders in present-day Red China was educated in a mission school. Sometime ago he met his former American professor at an international congress. The professor asked the Red leader how he, who had been educated in Christian philosophy and tradition, could now espouse communism. The reply was: "Christianity is a very good thing, but it is too slow." Maybe American business leaders can find some deep-flowing thoughts underlying that remark.

§2. WE MUST BREAK DOWN
ACADEMIC BARRIERS

The major part of my world travel has been in areas that are in the earlier stages of economic development. During these years, as Public Relations Consultant to the Director General of the Food and Agriculture Organization of the United Nations, I visited over 75 universities in Asia, Europe, Africa, and Latin-America. On each occasion I talked with students, faculty, and very often with the nonacademic personnel that maintained the services of the institution. The university community represents a group that is in many respects apart from the rest of the country. Most of the universities of those parts of the world are of the type that was in existence in North America before the coming of the Land-Grant College, which was due to the recognition by Abraham Lincoln of the fact that colleges and universities could teach the liberal arts and sciences along with courses for improving agricultural production, for using proper machinery, and for modern farm merchandising methods.

The matters of greatest interest to the young people with whom I talked on these various occasions abroad dealt with education in America, and the close relationship between the ordinary lay businessman and the university. I well remember visiting twenty-seven Asian universities and colleges in 1949. In each session there was a question-and-answer period. The questions exhibited the alarm with which the young people received my statement that many an educated man could also get some grease on his hands and not lose dignity or "face." It is by emphasizing this principle that we can counteract some of the intellectual influence of the Marxists.

Probably no greater revolution ever came to the educational world than that embodied in the development of the American Land-Grant College concept. This revolution consisted not only in the practical down-to-earth, how-to-do-it skills that were taught the young men from industry and farms, but also in a marked change in attitude toward these skills from the chilly aloofness of the earlier scholars. Down through the centuries the scholar had been, and still is in most of the world, looked upon as a person apart from the rest of the people. Aristocracy and democracy are strangers isolated by the social attitudes of earlier higher education. Today in America they are friends in cooperation.

The major trend in humanizing corporate business so that, as an inanimate being, it could live with animate beings in peace and harmony, was accelerated by the establishment of the Graduate School of Business Administration at Harvard, which was the first of its kind in the world.[2] From the beginning, in 1908, its aim was to enlist, train, and guide future executives in becoming actively interested in man as a person, not merely as a statistic. This development was contemporaneous with the advent of the production line and all the human-relations problems that accompanied it.[3]

A small segment of businessmen and capitalists helped by employing the graduates of the School and by making business "secrets" available in the form of case studies. Elton Mayo, who a little later became a professor at the Business School, developed the theory that man adapted himself to automation through group action and responsibility coupled with participation. From his studies in the Hawthorne plant came the stream of thought that has emerged as real public relations. Public relations as pageantry and "gilding the lily" is but little removed from the days of the "king's jesters." Public relations dedicated to business responsibility within a responsible society is a direct descendant of the Mayo thinking. His vision was that unless the economic slide rule were set to the social Golden Rule, chaos in industry would result and the fruits of a capitalistic economy would be sacrificed.

The business schools of America thus began to evangelize and professionalize the type of work that had nearly always been

[2] William Lawrence, *Memories of a Happy Life* (Boston: Houghton Mifflin Co., 1926), pp. 416–20.

[3] Melvin T. Copeland, *And Mark An Era* (Boston: Little, Brown & Co., 1958).

previously characterized by craft and cunning, exclusiveness, and monopoly, and effectively aided it in developing a social conscience. One elder business statesman in commenting about the contents of some teaching material used at a business school said, "I see. Men used to make money; now you teach them to make it honestly." Although the Harvard Graduate School of Business Administration pioneered in this field, its work has been subsequently paralleled by many other great educational institutions with the same objectives.[4]

North American capitalism has been largely nourished by the business schools of this type that have sprung up in nearly every state and province of the United States and Canada. Few are over fifty years of age, and their birth coincided with the end of the "Age of the Moguls" and the present reversed trend of thinking. They have acted as bellwethers in leading the unorganized flocks of businessmen out of the valley of danger into the fold of safety. It is my considered belief that the tensions and strains between the excesses of business and attempts by the public to defend itself would have landed our whole economic system in the ash can had it not been for the timely appearance of the modern business school, with its clarion call for regeneration and adaptation in harmony with twentieth-century conditions.

Some of our business schools are doing a praiseworthy, pioneering job in various parts of the world trying to develop an attitude of business responsibility within a developing society. There have been experiments going on in Turkey, the Philippines, India, and various other countries. These experiments have tended to shake the type of thinking that previously prevailed in these areas. The export of American know-how through these business schools to men abroad will be regarded in the years ahead as the beginning of a great new epic. Time is running out, however, and there are only a few people being reached by these leaders. Further, unfortunately, the majority

---

[4] J. B. McGeachy, in the Toronto *Financial Post* (September 13, 1958), points out: "It is impossible to imagine the old-time robber barons flocking to Harvard for learned opinions about their duties and mistakes. But to do just that 2,000 modern professionals in the art and science of management came to a conference at the university's business school."

of these contacts are limited to executives in some vested place of authority, and perhaps to some governmental employees, who do not wish to change a social structure that operates to their benefit.

This type of work needs to be greatly expanded and expedited. It should be carefully scrutinized to make certain that the concept of the responsibility of business to its employees, and to the community as a whole, is not only accepted but is shown to be the best possible way by which large masses of products can be produced and sold in the public interest. It is this lesson that the people of the new countries will be eager to learn if it is properly presented.

§3. Schools of Business and Public Administration Can Help

Just as the philosophy of the Harvard Business School became continental in scope, the beneficial results of the present North American business-school idea can be obtained by institutions and businesses in any country in the world. The Salk vaccine shots for polio are as effective with a boy in China, Ghana, or Brazil as with one in the United States. So it is with the injection of better business principles into the veins of commerce and trade in any land. If the world is to be permanently safe from exploitive capitalism and its evil camp followers, it will be through practicing business principles of honesty and integrity coupled with scientific management and efficiency.

A few pilot experiments are being made in many parts of the world. The principles and methods developed here during the past fifty years are being tried out in business education there. The harvest is plentiful but the laborers are few. Many countries do not have a business school to begin with (remember, neither did we fifty years ago); often a business school overseas is an institution teaching only the formal keeping of books and the typing of the thoughts of others. This is all-important, but it is not the dynamic dose that will purify the bloodstream of business. While abroad in 1949, I spoke to nearly every known collegiate business school institution in an area containing over five-hundred million people and, significantly, I made less than ten appearances.

Within the past ten years the trend has been changing, and today there are many business schools trying to start where before there were none. Teams of American professors have been holding Management Schools of Executive Training Seminars in many areas with universal success. However, the ground has hardly been broken.

The North American cannot do more than offer his assisting services. The work must be done essentially by local teachers, who themselves must first be trained. There have been some amazingly satisfactory results from initial cooperative work between overseas institutions and local visiting professors. One of these is in Milan, Italy, and another in Taipei, Taiwan. If dynamic capitalism is to survive in the world as a whole, this training of business leaders in business responsibility coupled with new techniques must be greatly expanded.

In America, the graduate schools of business and public administration have a unique service to perform on two fronts. They can train students to fill positions of responsibility and at the same time help them become oriented to the world of change into which they are entering, both at home and abroad. A few business schools have been experimenting for several years with executive programs. These have been almost uniformly successful in alerting business executives to the responsibilities of leadership. More recently schools of public administration have been doing the same in regard to executives in business and government.

Two current operations are pioneering in new fields. At The American University in Washington, D.C., the School of Business Administration is endeavoring to raise the resources to establish a permanent conference on Business-Government Relationships. Dean Nathan Baily describes the new venture as follows:

An important part of the answer to "Can Capitalism Compete?" will be provided by the ability of business and government, two of the major factors in our society, to work together "for the common good." The entire world watches what is said and done in Washington, D.C. Both omission and commission have their impact on the reactions to our form of government and to our business system by people everywhere.

It therefore becomes essential, for success both at home and abroad, for business executives and government officials to learn to know each other better, agree on an equitable division of duties and responsibilities, better understand each other's problems, and cooperate more effectively.

Despite recent improvements, we are far from such a situation today. The past twenty-six years have brought wide and fundamental changes in the functions and operations of all governments, at all levels. Without question, the greatest of these has been in the direction, philosophy, concept and policies of the Federal Government. No part of our society has felt the impact of these changes more than the business community. Unfortunately, however, the majority of business people do not understand government—its climate, its benchmarks, its operations, its limitations, or its strong points.

The situation is little better with most government personnel. They do not understand business, the dynamic nature of business institutions, the creativity of our private enterprise system, or the needs which must be met if business is to maintain and increase its contribution to the American way of life. In fact, frequently, they are suspicious and, at times, almost hostile to the business men and business institutions whose very existence frequently depends on what actions government agencies take.

Except for polemics, there has been little done to improve the situation. The School of Business Administration of The American University is beginning an ambitious program in this area. Its location gives it unique advantages for successful experimentation.

The University of Pittsburgh, located in the heart area of American industry, has recently established a new Graduate School of Public and International Affairs. Dean Donald Stone of this institution defines the objectives as being to bring students from overseas face to face with students in America who are planning to go overseas and let them study, live, work, and play together. In this way understanding can develop as well as the mere gaining of knowledge of administration. An Executive Development Program in Overseas Operations has been announced, and the Dean describes it in these words:

The course of international developments has opened up new potentials for American business abroad. CED, the Commerce Department's Business Advisory Council, and other business groups have focused their attention on the short and long-term gains in the form of new markets and the growth of free enterprise which can be realized through the greater utilization of American industrial leadership abroad.

Success in such endeavors calls for a broader and more extensive training for representatives of American business charged with the delicate and complex task of conducting foreign operations.

This need for better training is emphasized by the successful steps of the U.S.S.R. in supplanting our influence in many countries. Its agents are skilled in presenting the appeal of the communist approach to economic and social progress, an approach which is producing remarkable impact throughout the world. The wide circulation of the Book of the Month selection of the 'Ugly American' further points up the problem.

Purpose: The specific purpose of this executive development program would be to provide supplementary education for persons selected by business firms and other organizations for overseas assignment or who are placed in charge of foreign operations.

Specifically, it would be designed to help such persons (1) to adjust to and become a compatible resident in a foreign country, (2) to learn tested methods of dealing with persons and organizations of another culture, (3) to gain insight and skill in sharing and fostering the values of responsible and democratic society, and (4) to develop background on international and intercultural problems and practices.

These two institutions, one in the nation's political capital and the other in its industrial capital, are representative of the things going on in dozens of institutions throughout the United States and Canada. The universities are ready to do this type of service to prepare men and women for the future. The big question is whether business will recognize this and follow through in time.

§4. AGRICULTURAL EXTENSION SERVICE IDEA SOUND—INDIA AN EXAMPLE

In 1949, 1950, and 1951, some of us began writing on the general theme of applying overseas our experience in the United States in taking information to farm people in farm communities through local personalities working with local farmers and rural youth. We felt that in the workings of this fine, practical service, commonly known as the Extension Service of the U.S. Department of Agriculture, might be something that could help break the lethargy of the centuries in regard to agricultural producers around the world. In 1949, many people thought this to be an illusionary idea. I stated my views in an article in the *Harvard Business Review,* July, 1951, entitled "Our Economic Policy in Asia." In this, I very frankly said that the best possible way to help the Asian farmer to recognize that there was a place for him in the twentieth century was through the use of the techniques of the Agricultural Extension Service.

Unfortunately the fundamental principles of the Extension Service were seldom transmitted abroad prior to the establishment of the Point Four concept of the Truman Doctrine. In the first rush of the idea, mechanization—tractors and all the gadgets that go with farming in America—was transferred abroad. But this backfired. On my trip through Asia in 1949, with C. Leigh Stevens, in cooperation with the Indian government, we developed the facts that over 80 per cent of the American tractors there were broken down, because of inexperienced handling, with no knowledge of repair and no available parts. Huge tractors were stranded on bunds (or levees). We had attempted to help the Indian solve the problems of a two-and-a-half acre farm by sending a $25,000 tractor that could hardly turn around on such a tiny lot.

Today that is largely changed. Tractors have taken their proper place through the implementation of the Extension Service ideas as readopted for India by M. L. Wilson, former Director of the U.S. Extension Service; Carl Taylor, sociologist in the U.S. Department of Agriculture; Douglas Ensminger of the Ford Foundation, formerly of the Department of Agriculture; and Horace C. Holmes, an American with wide experience in Extension Service and rural credit, along with a carefully selected group of American and Indian agriculturalists. These men studied not how the American extension system could be directly applied in India, but how its principles of research, demonstration, participation, and cooperation could be adapted to the Indian scene. The program they evolved was instituted with success.

Sam Higginbotham, a Presbyterian missionary, was the John the Baptist on this trail, and for forty years at Allahabad Agricultural Institute he directed a praiseworthy demonstration of better education in agriculture. A Horace Plunket of India was Higginbotham, who, dedicated to an idea and an ideal, went to India as a missionary with a Bible in one hand and a hoe in the other, near Allahabad in the Gangetic Plain. With the help of American friends and supporters he built the Allahabad Agricultural Institute, staffed by Americans and Indians. By demonstration and participation they developed one of the model farm patterns of India. When India gained her independence in 1947 this example became a part of the basis for the village improvement which today is bettering the lot of millions of people in the rural areas. Probably the greatest contribution of Allahabad was in its program of "training the trainers." Today, with interdenominational support and under the leadership of its first Indian principal, H. S. Azariah, its influence, through the composition of its faculty and students, is reaching out to other nations.

For a generation William H. and Charlotte Vial Wiser have studied the problems of rural India, and for a period of years lived in an Indian village. Their book *Behind Mud Walls*[5] together with their development of the "village service" idea, was the springboard from which Horace C. Holmes began similar work at Etowah in India. Etowah later became the focal point from which the Indian government, with some assistance from the Ford Foundation, developed the now widely heralded Village Improvement Program of India. The program is carried out by Indian personnel whose background and devotion enable them to lead remote villagers to literacy, sanitation, health, and improved skills in homemaking and agriculture. The role of the Indian farmer is shifting from the primitive meager subsistence level to the efforts of a small capitalist not only to better his own condition but to be a supplier for the better nutrition of others. This cooperative work between a people, a government, a foundation, and dedicated "Johnny Appleseeds" has helped more millions of people to help themselves to a better way of living within the framework of a democratic government than has any similar project in the world's history.

[5] William H. Wiser and Charlotte Vial Wiser, *Behind Mud Walls* (New York: Agricultural Missions, Inc., 1951).

§5. EXTENSION SERVICE TECHNIQUES NEEDED BY BUSINESS

Responsible service capitalism really needs an Extension Service. This may sound facetious, but when we see the success achieved by the agricultural extension idea in India, for example, is it not reasonable that business could achieve measurable success by utilizing the same principle?

Our business system can not merely be transplanted; rather, we must first develop abroad a desire on the part of the people for such business services, operated in their own way in their own communities, developing actually from the experiences which they themselves might gain—a repetition of what happened in North America in the earlier part of this century.

First should come a better understanding of the use of the service cooperative, in order that the farmer, newly emancipated from the drudgery of the centuries and the poverty of the ages, may have an opportunity to work together with his neighbors in the procurement of supplies and services, such as capital, and in the selling of his products. Time has proved that these ideas are sound. They are not my ideas alone, they are the composite thinking of many people. It did happen to fall to my lot to put many of them into writing.

The next step will be the development of industrialization. As brought out earlier in our discussion of land tenure, there must be a surplus of agricultural products before a country can begin to change over to an industrial economy, which seems to be the desire of most of the new countries. This necessitates the creation and use of capital.

The educational program of the American Institute of Banking has done more to change trends in the handling of money in the United States and the public attitude toward banking than has any other one thing. The days when the bank was looked upon with suspicion and distrust, an instrumentality of those who were leeching and literally stealing from the community, have very largely passed. Today, the bank is highly regarded as a part of the community. Much of the credit for this is due the American Institute of Banking, which really is an extension service for bankers, financed by banks. It is a non-profit, cooperative organization that retains local men, professors, and experienced leaders in local communities to meet with young bankers in classes and help them develop ways and means to improve themselves and their organizations.

It can be said without equivocation that the techniques and methods developed jointly by the American Institute of Banking and Rutgers University might well be one of the pivots upon which could be developed, in each country desiring it, an extension service for the financial facet of capitalism. Other organizations have been developed at home to serve other functions of our enterprise system. These might well help to create a similar activity abroad. But the most important thing would be for them to make clear the broad principles of service capitalism, of which their particular activities represent but a single factor.

§6. CORRESPONDENCE SCHOOL IDEA RECOMMENDED FOR WORLD-WIDE EDUCATION

We have seen how, two generations ago, the Land-Grant Colleges became a permanent part of America and developed a better understanding of industry and agricultural sciences in our country. With this increased knowledge came a demand for a wider dissemination of such information among the tens of thousands of young men and women who were unable to attend these colleges, but still wanted the opportunity to secure knowledge over and beyond what they would get in their local experience. There is an old sales adage which says "To find a need and then fill it is the secret of success."

To meet this need, private correspondence schools came into existence. Although not set up with the exacting and traditional academic requirements of many of the established educational institutions, correspondence schools did, and do, fill a great need. Their results have been far-reaching. A great deal of the mass-production efficiency of the American farm and industry can be attributed directly to these correspondence schools. They stepped into the gap and devised a system of education that fitted the needs of the man who had innate intelligence and ambition, but little book knowledge. Their textbooks were so designed that the person who had learned to read and write and had a great desire to learn could obtain this knowledge from his correspondence courses, ultimately translating it into production and a better standard of living. Today a large number of college graduates enroll in these schools for specialized job training, or professional training, or to qualify in the new fields of science, technology, or management which changing times demand.

Why not use this correspondence school technique as the basis for a program to take abroad the fundamentals of American capitalism? Since these correspondence institutions have learned how to translate ideas onto the printed page, why could they not create the beginnings of correspondence courses to meet needs in various isolated spots of the world? This is perhaps the most unlimited market available today for the transmission of ideas and probably has the greatest success potential. The information in these courses and their accompanying texts should not cover merely how we do things in America, but should contain, after careful collaboration with educators of the countries involved, ideas pertinent to those areas.

A trial involving several thousand young people should be made, the material appropriately revised, and then put on the market at suitably low prices. Courses should *not* be given away. This would be a mistake, because the person who is basically motivated to self-study for self-improvement wants to "earn" his knowledge and is not looking for something for nothing, particularly with a "label" or "strings" attached. "Not charity, but a chance" is a way of life that American capitalism operating abroad seems to ignore, but which is the very core of self-respect and personal integrity in the people who can best understand the benefits of democracy and our way of life, and who want to adapt the best that we have to offer to their own way of living. These ideas have already been successfully demonstrated by the world-wide services of some of these schools.

Another asset favoring these correspondence courses is that in much of the world there are so few diversions for people— even a public library is a rarity. There are few places of amusement and, even if there were, most of the people would not have the money to go to them. The average person in the underdeveloped areas of the world has more time, and is more willing to study by any method by which he can improve himself, than is many a person of the present generation in our country.

This is no indictment of our own people; they are normal, natural human beings. But when people do not have things, and are just beginning to turn from illiteracy to literacy, when the intelligence that is stored up in their minds is suddenly freed from the bondage of ignorance and is made available through literacy and discussion with others, then the time is ripe for educational self-help. Responsible business and educational leaders abroad report that it is impossible to get enough instructors, either indigenous or imported, to take care of a fraction of the young people who are today ready, capable, and willing to learn. Correspondence courses could be worked out in such a way as to combine the Socratic question and answer method with the actual course work and problems.

Correspondence schools[6] in the United States have done almost the impossible in the field of education. The techniques learned from the millions of students who have taken these courses should be made available to private organizations in other countries in order to help them develop an educational system fitted to their needs, mores, and environments. As an example, the great need for foreman and highly skilled technicians in the emerging economies of these countries could be largely filled by this development.

Business owners and managers of the enterprises in these countries will be encouraged to cooperate in such programs by knowing that over 6,000 of the larger corporations in the United

---

[6] By "correspondence schools," I mean those whose chief objective is to help the students help themselves to a better and higher education and standard of living. I do not refer to the "diploma mills," but to those accredited and well-recognized schools that offer good courses and qualified educational service— based on sound and ethical business practices.

States have training agreements with the leading home-study schools. The techniques of the correspondence course have been proved and tested among these organizations. This shows what initiative and private enterprise can do to promote industrial progress and human well-being.

XI

SOME SUGGESTIONS FOR ACTION

§1. Junior Chamber of Commerce
an Example of Progressive Action

Americans are justly proud of their continually rising standard of living, their high degree of literacy, and the fact that people can aspire to work in any vocation that appeals to them and for which they think they have talent. However, we err when we try to transmit these benefits wholesale to our friends abroad. We are prone to believe that we must export the things we have rather than the means by which we obtained them. We must untangle our thinking and recognize that people in other parts of the world would like to do things in their own way. We might better communicate to them the fundamental principles by which we have built America and the discoveries we have made in the fields of law, economics, science, and sociology. People abroad want to attain the knowledge and means by which we acquired our technology and political-economic system and to combine it with their own discoveries—in the way that seems best to them. When we begin to think in this vein as a people, then will we begin to make a new, lasting contribution to the welfare of mankind.

One of our groups that has taken this concept to heart is the Junior Chamber of Commerce. In Manila, in 1949, I saw their idea work. Inspiration had come from the United States, but the operation was by Philippine people themselves—young men who, if at the same age just a few years before, would have been considered only as helpers to their elders and whose advice and counsel would not have been thought worthy of consideration. They proved that if officers under 35 could be given important wartime assignments, then they, as young men in business, were entitled to their place in the operation of civic affairs. The Philippine Jaycees were ambitious, energetic, and civic-minded. They enlisted the aid of two or three newspapers which were willing to back their experiment. The elders in the Rotary Club swung behind it, Manila began to clean up materially, look ahead spiritually, and develop the pattern for the new Philippines. This all happened largely because a few young men had taken an idea from North America and put it into operation in their own way in their own land.

As a close follower of events in the Philippines since the beginning of its independence, it is my opinion that the work of the Junior Chamber of Commerce was the dynamic force that set off a chain reaction of other forces out of which the new Philippines is today being constituted. The Jaycees from the Philippines are now helping in Viet Nam as neighbors.

The United States had the Philippines under its control for fifty years. During that time, we made little organized serious attempt to communicate to the Philippines the philosophy of American business. A number of big companies operated there in a more or less unsocial way; a limited amount of education of an antiquated nature was given to the Philippine people. However, there was no counterpart of our Smith-Hughes Act, which promotes vocational education in the United States. Rural education and the development of agricultural cooperatives, free from government direction, were at a standstill. The ordinary Filipino could not look forward to a successful life in the business field. This was not the fault of the government. The government brings law and order; it is a referee between groups. It was business that was negligent in not making it possible for the citizens of this colonial outpost to understand the fundamentals of American private enterprise. We had to wait until the war had been fought to its bloody end before the Junior Chamber of Commerce in Manila took up the cudgels for a democratic approach to a solution of internal economic problems.

My contacts there were most stimulating experiences. In other parts of the world I have also watched the entrance of the Junior Chamber of Commerce idea into the bloodstream of a community. The infusion has been markedly beneficial.

Among business groups that are real crusaders for democracy and that promote the responsibility of capital around the world, the only ones I have observed that equal in enthusiasm the efforts of the Communists are the young, zealous Jaycees.

The Jaycees are now organized in 85 countries in the free world and the Jaycee Creed adopted by all of these member-groups is:

> We believe:
> That faith in God gives meaning and purpose to human life;
> That the brotherhood of men transcends the sovereignity of nations;
> That economic justice can best be won by free men through free enterprise;
> That government should be of laws rather than of men;
> That earth's great treasure lies in human personality;
> And that service to humanity is the best work of life.

§2. THE SERVICE CLUB IDEA—GOOD PUBLIC RELATIONS IN ACTION

In 1947 I wrote "The Place of Public Relations in Business," to be included in *Business Administration,* a course of study in the curriculum of the American Institute of Banking. At that time I recognized that the service club had made and was making a contribution to America that had far-reaching effects.

Rotary, Kiwanis, Lions, Exchange, Optimist, and numerous other service clubs were created largely because of an inherent desire of American businessmen to know their competitors and other businessmen of their communities as individual human beings rather than merely as tools of other business enterprises. Service club organizations spearheaded a movement that recently has crystallized under the term of "public relations." It is doubtful that American business would have recognized the need for community effort and association until a much later date had not the noon luncheon of the service club become a reality. By 1900 business had reached the point where it was considered flippant and undignified to call an adult in business or in the professions by his Christian name unless in close association with him. The service club has set a new, informal fashion in business—that of familiar friendship rather than the strained relationship of formality.

Good public relations is not a technique that can survive under restraint; it thrives under conditions of frankness, fairness and open-mindedness.[1]

The above statements, as true today as they were in 1947, are cited here to draw attention to one facet of North American life that has taken root in distant places. Rotary alone has clubs in over one hundred countries with the Lions as runners-up. These clubs have done yeoman service in helping people to help themselves, which basically is the North American concept of business. The service clubs have not attempted to constitute themselves as little islands of North America around the world—rather they are crossroads of thought and culture and an indigenous part of the land in which their members attend. The Iron Curtain countries will not allow the service clubs to function there because of the clubs' philosophy of free exchange of ideas.

On a recent visit to Ottawa, the capital of Canada, I encountered a national project, "An Adventure in Citizenship," part of an interesting annual program of the Canadian Rotary which has been in operation since 1950. Wherever there is a Rotary Club in Canada (and there are about 200), a senior high school boy or girl is selected by community choice to be the guest of the local club to go to Ottawa with young people selected from the other communities across Canada. At the capital, they are shown the operations of their government and afforded an opportunity to participate as though they were government officials. They return home imbued with a respect for their land and for the things for which it stands.

If this type of operation or a similar program could be developed in each land where there are service clubs of the type described, it would bring home in a major way the value of business, which supports this program; and to business it would give

[1] Reprinted by permission of the American Institute of Banking.

a real live interest in its national government. Good public relations is always a two-way street.

The modern service club performs unselfishly a wide range of services, such as educational scholarship awards, athletic programs for boys and girls, relief projects, and aid to crippled children, the aged, and the blind, to mention only a few. Businessmen working together toward such common goals come to know each other as they never would during the course of business transactions.

There is not room in this book to tell the whole story of the service club and the part it has played and can play in serving the world on behalf of dynamic capitalism. I know, because a large percentage of my interviewees overseas have mentioned enthusiastically the service clubs' contribution to their countries. I have spoken at literally a hundred club meetings overseas and in each case have left feeling that here was something *pro bono publico* of the land where it met. In India I visited a service club project where, under the inspiration of a Brahman member, a club had become neighbors of a village largely made up of the untouchable caste. Those Brahmans had dug ditches with the low caste—had helped make cement for a road and, as one Brahman told me, "We were men together." The inspiration for this project came from an International Meeting of the Rotary Club at Atlantic City, New Jersey.

The only real criticism I have encountered abroad in regard to service clubs has come from those who have visited clubs here in North America. They say they are welcomed and made much of at the club meeting and perhaps even asked to come home and meet the family of a member or to visit a plant or store. However, when they return home they never again hear from the American, except perhaps for a Christmas card. There is no personal letter, no literature from time to time about the business they saw; just a dead silence as though they had been a "casual customer," as one Peruvian Rotarian described his experience to me.

It so happens that the illustrations given are from Rotary because those are ones I have personally encountered (although not a member). Much of the material of this section, however, has come from conversations with D. A. Skeen of Salt Lake City, Utah, former President of Lions International, under whose guidance Lions became truly international in vision. Every service club is making a contribution.

§3. Projects for Service Clubs

The service clubs are doing a magnificent job in international understanding, but they could do a lot more and not hurt themselves. There are two immediate projects that the service clubs might enter more aggressively.

First, those clubs that have associate member clubs in other countries might well consider encouraging their own members, before visiting these clubs, to become sufficiently acquainted with the fundamentals of dynamic capitalism to be able to discuss it intelligently with members abroad. I have encountered some of the most lamentable public-relations results in cases where visiting club members from North America have apparently known little and cared less about the fundamentals of American business. They were against communism and socialism, and told the world off about it. The results were negative as maybe half of their audience was socialist and was fighting communism long before the American ever became alerted to its dangers. The Book of Books says something about first casting the beam out of our own eyes. Unfortunately, the service clubs of America are too prone to list speakers who denounce communism and all its works and then do not take the trouble even to alert their own members as to the values of our own present-day capitalism.

The second project came to me when, in pursuit of this study, I visited with the officials of the European Productivity Agency in several countries and was greatly impressed with the effective work of this organization—whose purpose is well stated in its name. Its aim is to bring to the European manufacturer the best that there is in modern production and public-relations information from all the world. The thought occurred to me: Why do not our service clubs make the proper arrangements to have their members traveling abroad visit the plant of a similar organization just as a neighbor on a two-way information visit.

The visitor and the host would both gain; and the traveler, in addition, might find something new to talk about on his return, rather than just tell how many cathedrals he had visited. I sprang the idea on the vice-president of the European Productivity Agency and never had I made a suggestion with a more immediate affirmative response. This program could be developed with practically no extra effort on the part of anyone, and I hope that some service club member may spark it into action.

The potential for business understanding among our traveling businessmen is staggering, but too often they never get acquainted with other men in common business abroad except at a few big centers. To say that visitors in plants abroad will be welcome is putting it mildly. During the past year I have asked a few of my friends traveling to take the time to visit a businessman in the same business as theirs while on their trip. It has opened up a whole new vista of experience for them and warm friendships have been made. Others can do it too.

§4. BOY SCOUT ORGANIZATIONS CAN
     DISPLAY ENTHUSIASTIC ACTIVITY

In an earlier section we saw how a reform of the Boy Scouts in Thailand in accordance with the American pattern led to a new respect there for the ideals of service capitalism. An example from our own country will illustrate the enormous potential of these organizations throughout the world.

In 1944, Donald Nelson, chairman of the War Production Board, met with a group of business and voluntary-organization leaders in Washington to discuss with them frankly the dire need for more paper to continue the war effort. Paper seems such an everyday commodity that its presence is just taken for granted, although we use a pound of it per person per day. Mr. Nelson said that because of the lack of paper there would have to be a curtailment of its civilian uses if the war effort was not to suffer.

Freedom-loving service capitalists work together when there is a need. Out of that meeting two things came. The National Periodical Publishers Association went into action and through its members' columns the woodlot cutters of America were alerted to the need for more pulp wood. As a result, several million extra cords of wood were cut.

But the immediately spectacular result was a paper drive by the Boy Scouts of America. Elbert Fretwell, Chief Scout Executive, and Elmaar Bakken, National Director of Rural Scouting, were in attendance at the Nelson breakfast, as were several of the national committeemen of the Boy Scouts of America. Dr. Fretwell called an immediate meeting to see what could be done.

General Eisenhower was the great national war hero, and within a matter of days he had agreed to lend his name to a paper campaign to rid the attics and the cellars of American homes of their surplus stored paper. The Scouts were educated as to the need and asked to volunteer to go into action. From farms, villages, towns, and the street corners of the big cities, an avalanche of paper descended upon the central stations, and within one week the drive had netted 240,000 tons of paper. The shortage was alleviated, and Mr. Nelson and his staff could center their thinking on other things.

Each winning Scout team was awarded an Eisenhower medal —and the boys worked like Trojans for the honor.

After the war was won, Dr. Fretwell decided to award a similar medal to the man whose name had inspired the great ingathering of paper. Shortly after the General returned to America, the Secretary of War, at Dr. Fretwell's suggestion, invited seveal Scout leaders to come to his office and there bestow upon General Eisenhower the same token as had been given to the Scouts. It was my privilege to be among the group there that day. As I was presented to General Eisenhower I remarked that this whole affair had happened as a result of Donald Nelson taking people into his confidence and asking for voluntary effort in a national emergency. The man who was later to be our President replied, "Give my best to Mr. Nelson—without voluntary efforts such as this by the Americans on the home front, we could have had no D-day and victory."

This kind of public-spirited activity by American Boy Scouts could spread into many parts of the world. All it needs is the right kind of resourceful leadership and a belief in the effectiveness of voluntary activity.

§5. STOCK OWNERSHIP CAN HELP CONVEY CAPITALISM

The world is in political turmoil and dissension. Some people say that the battle is between the "haves" and the "have-nots." That may or may not be true. But if it be true, perhaps the best way to correct it is to make certain that the numbers of the "have-nots" decrease and the "haves" increase. Under responsible capitalism as we have it in North America that has happened.

We have a rising percentage of farmers, laborers, craftsmen, and small shopkeepers who own or participate in a larger share of their businesses than ever before. They are capitalists. Millions of shares of corporation stocks are owned by wage-earners and others who just a generation ago were completely hostile to what they regarded as the centralization of capital in Wall Street. Although today this number is only about 15 per cent of our population, yet the New York Stock Exchange and large corporations are advocating larger dispersion of stockholding. Today even labor papers carry the stock quotations; and labor unions make large investments in the common stocks, preferred issues, and bonds of various business corporations. Universities, banks, and professional people look upon the corporate stock as a form of savings against a depression and as a hedge against inflation. Particularly during this past generation we have become very capitalistic-minded in the United States. Why? Because, by a living demonstration of what a regulated capitalistic economy can do, our people have come to recognize its value.

With experience the same understanding can be conveyed overseas. A news dispatch from Saigon shows one effort in this direction:

Refugees to Buy Plants

Saigon—Some 200 refugees from Communist North Vietnam are being taught weaving by American and Japanese technicians in preparation for a venture in people's capitalism. They will be weavers in two small textile plants being constructed with United States aid and under a profit-sharing and stock purchase plan they eventually will purchase the plants.[2]

[2] *The Boston Daily Globe* (April 20, 1958).

An encouraging development in the participation in capital stock ownership is reported in *Forbes*, July 15, 1957:

Is our peculiarly American brand of "peoples capitalism" an article for export? The wider spread of stock ownership in such European countries as France, Britain and Western Germany suggests that it *can* be. But for wide areas of the world and for the many hundreds of millions of people there often appears to be little choice between old fashioned capitalistic "exploitation" and the utopian promises of the Communists and the Socialists.

For this reason *Forbes* soundly applauds an experiment being undertaken in Africa by the U.S.—controlled copper mining companies, Rhodesian Selection Trust and Roan Antelope. The companies have announced a plan whereby employees, both European and African, will be allowed to buy stock in their companies under a system of payroll deductions, with the company tossing 50¢ into the pot for every $1 contributed by the workers. Some 4,000 people, all those earning upwards of $11 a week—are eligible for the plan.

The proposed stock purchase arrangement has several interesting features, one of which guarantees the employee-stockholder against a loss. But perhaps the most intriguing thing about the plan is that some 500 higher-paid African workers will be eligible and thus can gain a direct stake in the ownership of the enterprise.[3] Now it is easy enough, and probably an irresistible temptation, to make jokes about African bushmen waving proxies and demanding admission to sedate board meetings, but the idea of stock-owning Africans is far from being ridiculous.

In Africa a great continent is rapidly catching up with the 20th Century. A middle class of skilled workers, shopkeepers and supervisory employees is slowly growing up. It is important that they should learn firsthand the benefits of private ownership. The copper companies, in their experiment, are setting a good example for those in Africa and Asia who would like to see their people take the free enterprise path to freedom.

§6. ANTITRUST PRINCIPLES
SHOULD BE DRAMATIZED

Informed individuals in many parts of the world look upon the antimonopoly acts of Canada and the United States as the Magna Cartas of our peoples for curbing exploitive capitalism. One of the fundamental things we could do to help the world

[3] As of April, 1958, Mr. Robert E. Kerper of the Reading Tube Company reported that some 200 African workers had taken advantage of the offer.

understand our system would be to dramatize the principles underlying these acts. We should get into men's minds everywhere the idea that competition has here proved to be the lifeblood of commerce.

A small brochure could be assembled to spotlight the effect that the antitrust and combines acts have had upon North American business by allowing it to grow and at the same time compete, thus proving to be a materially restrictive force against exploitive capitalism. Some of our court decisions that have been particularly explanatory of the fundamental principles should be included.

This is a project that the Bar Associations of the United States and Canada might well undertake jointly. Their local units, or individual members, should see that such a booklet is available to all interested foreign students and visitors. It could well be used as a study guide to be followed up with question-and-answer sessions for those who are interested.

There is a latent prevalent respect for continuing government controls upon the natural excesses of monopoly that could be one of our most effective public relations weapons. Yet there is another side to the story that deserves attention. Under the Webb-Pomerene Act and other subsequent legislation of the United States, American business in certain instances is permitted to operate abroad under a licensed cartel system without violating the Sherman Anti-trust Act. In the interests of international understanding and, in the long run, in the interests of world peace and the salvation of our type of economy and government, this whole matter of international cartels and the part played by companies based in the United States should be opened for review. A high-level commission from business, government, public relations counselors and the legal profession should be created to make a far-reaching study of the international complications into which we have been precipitated, or may be precipitated, because of our participation in cartels.[4]

We cannot, in all honesty, expect to communicate abroad the fundamental principles of American capitalism and, at the same

[4] See Kingman Brewster, Jr., *Antitrust and American Business Abroad* (New York: McGraw-Hill Book Co., Inc., 1958), p. 454.

time, permit our companies to operate corporate subsidiaries in foreign countries as participants in cartels, even though the headquarters of the cartel is not in the United States. Several jurists in Asia brought this to my attention. They asked if America was sincere, or was really operating on a basis of having freedom at home and business colonization abroad. The antitrust principle is a valid part of the message of modern capitalism, but it must be followed through in all its implications if it is to be really effective.

§7. The Industrial and Business Conference Can Help Interpret Capitalism

Within the past generation, North American business has developed a unique form of self-education—the Conference. Executives and senior personnel of organizations having a common trade, profession, or vocation meet together to present to the group their latest thinking regarding such things as efficiency and business development. For example, the practice of public relations and the applications of automation have been developed as tools of business largely through the "swapping" of ideas at such conferences.

Hundreds of these conferences are held each year. One outstanding example, which I have observed in operation since 1938, is the Boston Conference on Distribution.[5] This unique organization, with no dues and no large overhead or staff, has been, for almost a third of a century, the focal point for information as to economic trends affecting the business of distribution, and what lies ahead for this important factor in our economy. The conference acts as a forum for the presentation of new ideas in merchandising and as a guide to policy-making for corporations and business enterprises. The old hush-hush of the cartel mind is obsolete in the Boston Conference concept. Competitors

[5] Developed by the Boston Retail Trade Board under the leadership of its Executive Vice-President Daniel Bloomfield, and sponsored by the Graduate School of Business Administration of Harvard University, Boston University's College of Business Administration, and the School of Industrial Management of the Massachusetts Institute of Technology.

and new entrepreneurs sit side by side, gaining from each other's experiences. The proceedings are published and through the good offices of individual companies are made available to the students in university schools of business throughout this continent—with some going abroad. During the past several years an increasing number of visitors from overseas have attended the Boston Conferences on Distribution and returned home having experienced North American capitalism at its best.

In some passages of this book I have presented fairly, I hope, although sometimes critically, my observations as to the work of the government in the field of business interpretation. In relation to the Boston Conference the government agencies have operated in a constructive and helpful manner, with the government sector of operations well defined. The Department of Commerce and the Small Business Administration always have personnel there to answer questions and show their latest publications for study and sampling. Government has found its place and is well received. Many of the overseas visitors are there as guests of the United States government under its several programs of bringing people from abroad to see what is happening here. The arrangements are made smoothly, and, having visited a majority of the men from abroad who have attended the Conferences, I have nothing but praise for the arrangements and follow-up.

Men from 28 different countries are on the International Advisory Council of the Boston Conference on Distribution, and give their time freely to this project. The number is growing through the cooperation of our State Department, cooperating around the world through its embassy personnel in helping to alert interested people about the service offered by the Boston Conference.

Here is a combination of a local group of businessmen cooperating with educational institutions throughout the nation, together with leading national trade associations and the United States government, to the end that the effectiveness of what we call American service capitalism may be known on a world-wide basis. The faults of the system as well as its merits are openly discussed and reflected in the printed reports of the Conference.

The President of the United States and members of the cabinets of many of the free nations of the world send their messages to these meetings, which are always attended by men of importance in directing the economic and political life of the free world.

Business groups that are seriously considering what they can do to communicate overseas the fundamentals of American capitalism can probably get as many worthwhile leads from studying the workings of the Boston Conference on Distribution as from any other single source. The beneficial results of this organization in interpreting the dynamics of a free economy are far more widespread and have resulted in more understanding than any propaganda effort in the dissemination of news by government news agencies trying to interpret business.

The proceedings of such conferences should be made available to other areas of the world so that others may have access to the valuable information regarding techniques of better production, transportation, or distribution for the common good. Much headway is already being made in this direction, but more is needed. Here is a ready-made opportunity to let others know what we mean by free-flowing private enterprise, with government taking its proper place as a part of the democratic team.

§8. TRADE FAIRS, IF USED SENSIBLY,
OFFER U.S. BUSINESS OPPORTUNITY
TO DRAMATIZE OUR SYSTEM

The United States government has cooperated extensively in the development of trade fairs throughout the world. This effort can generally be put down on the credit side. However, displays by American manufacturers often have been of goods that were manufactured for the American customer, with too little thought given as to how or why such products might interest people in the country abroad. If American business will really cooperate with the United States government in these fairs, perhaps nothing else could do a better job for less money and with more favorable results.

Many of the new things in the United States are introduced to our people through the medium of state and county fairs. The world enjoys going to exhibits and fairs. But when we cooperate in an overseas fair, we can present to the people there only a few things—often the luxuries. Furthermore, the official representatives from America that we send to these fairs find it impossible to talk with more than a mere fraction of those who come to visit—and that means a job not even half done. American business should take a voluntary interest and send good-will ambassadors, without order books and at its own expense, to get acquainted with other peoples.

A good example of a demonstration of a typical American retail institution emphasizing consumer choice is the supermarket reproduction which the National Association of Food Chains has displayed at trade fairs in several countries, including Yugoslavia.

John A. Logan, president of the National Association of Chain Stores, says in a letter to the author:

> Trade fairs are part of a government program to develop international trade, and build good will and show the American way of life. Government asks assistance of business. At their request NAFC cooperates by providing know-how, technical skills and operating personnel. We get manufacturers to provide equipment and contribute merchandise. It is a joint project—government and business—which USSR does not do. Our experiences in Italy and Yugoslavia convince us that it is tremendously worthwhile—the right kind of public relations, creating at one time good will and good business.

He has had years of experience in this field and reports that his members are enthusiastic about enlarging the program.

There are some American companies that have long studied the needs of countries overseas and have done a magnificent job, such as the Collins Company described in a previous chapter. Such firms should be encouraged to participate in international fairs. I found that the Collins name on machetes and knives used for clearing jungles, cutting sugar cane, and slicing pineapple is as standard all through South and Central America as "sterling" is on silver. American private enterprise most clearly is understood through this type of operation that serves the needs of the people efficiently and honestly. As noted in *Time* of July 1, 1957:

Says Commerce Department Trade Fair Boss Harrison McClung: "Private industry itself is the instrument that can most effectively tell the story of free enterprise."

§9. WANTED: MORE PAMPHLETEERS FOR BUSINESS

The world as a whole is in great need of information, through visual and auditory means, on the economic possibilities of service capitalism in foreign countries. The story of Abraham Lincoln, Woodrow Wilson's Fourteen Points, the pronouncements of President Truman and President Eisenhower are common political knowledge everywhere, but there is little information available about the evolutionary methods by which America has solved so many of its economic problems. The dearth of knowledge about the way our private enterprise operates is appalling.

Much of the educational material in this field which is produced and distributed by industry is so biased in its approach and lacking in an understanding and appreciation of the intelligence of the people to whom it is directed, that it is a mistake ever to file it except in the wastebasket. But there are an increasing number of exceptions to the general rule. One of these is a publication of the United States Steel Foundation entitled "Education for Responsibility," which presents the commencement address given by W. Homer Turner at the 108th Commencement of Pacific University at Forest Grove, Oregon, May 26, 1957. This is an excellent example of a fair presentation of American business responsibility from a university platform as a forum. More material of this kind should find its way into pamphlet form. One pertinent paragraph is quoted:

. . . All government must ever be wary of doing too much for its people, else various well-recited evils ensue. Such is the only known way to productive civilization. As an alternative to over-much governmental action, private and voluntary organizations of all types, safeguarded by self-control—or minimum regulation—if needful, are a primary benefit to nations with liberty as a cardinal goal. The further maturity of such private and voluntary organization, for our century, may be one of the chief contributions to the better articulation of the cause of freedom.

Every schoolboy in America has read of the pamphleteers of the early days of the Republic. Wanted today in the world are pamphleteers for business, in their best sense and not as propagandists.

Throughout this book I have tried at every opportunity to suggest concrete steps that each of us can take to promote modern service capitalism—as individuals, as members of business organizations, or in whatever capacity we may serve. In this section I have outlined a few special projects that stem from my own experience at home and abroad. But this is by no means a definitive list. We must all be on the lookout for new ideas.

XII

SOME OTHER VOICES ARE HEARD

§1. Puerto Rico—A Case Study of Capitalism
in Action

Progress is usually made because a problem needed to be solved. Puerto Rico was acquired by the United States by the treaty concluding the Spanish-American War. During the next fifty years Puerto Rico became an increasing problem, and ultimately its distresses began to weigh heavily upon the conscience of the American people. Within the past decade increasing attention has been given to Puerto Rico; and today, while it still has many problems, the fact is that they are being attacked and in many cases being solved not primarily by charity, but by a planned approach to them through the combined efforts of government, business, and voluntary agencies.

Because Puerto Rico is a microcosm from which we may gain much that may be helpful in avoiding mistakes in dealing with problems in other parts of the world, and in communicating overseas the fundamentals of American service capitalism, a special study made by Robert W. Miller, Executive Vice President of the Public Relations Research Associates, Inc., and Lecturer in the Graduate Division, School of Business Administration, the American University, is attached.

CAPITALISM IN ACTION
Puerto Rico—A Case in Point[1]

by Robert W. Miller

In Puerto Rico there has developed in the past ten years an excellent example of how dynamic capitalism can operate to the benefit of a depressed area. Here, next door, is a ready-made case study wherein the methods, successes, and failures of responsible capitalism and democratic government working together can be observed.

Prior to World War II, Puerto Rico was largely forgotten by the United States. It had progressed little since coming under the American flag in 1898, at the end of the Spanish-American War. Its population was largely impoverished and illiterate.

The war emergency, and especially the German raids in the Caribbean, suddenly plummeted Puerto Rico into an important position as a bastion of the United States. Troops were moved in and bases were built. However, the Puerto Rican people were still treated as little more than serfs—they were in no sense partners in the adventure. Their standard of living was at about the subsistence level, with 650 people per square mile. As one source aptly commented, "If you were to put the entire world's population within the confines of the United States, the area would have about the same population density as that of Puerto Rico."

Congress became concerned with the Island's problems. It approached the matter, in a bipartisan move, undertaking studies of Puerto Rico's past, present, and future. On July 25, 1952, the people of the Island, by a free vote, elected to become a self-governing Commonwealth of the United States. Congress ap-

---

[1] This study points up the success of Operation Bootstrap. It is not to be inferred, however, that all problems have been solved; a tremendous amount of work remains to be done in Puerto Rico. Living conditions are still below the United States standard; literacy and health levels are still behind. This study is merely an attempt to highlight some of the means by which progress can be achieved.

proved the action and, for the first time, our government entered into a solemn compact with one of its territories whereby only the conduct of foreign affairs and a few other powers were expressly retained by the federal government. All else was to be handled independently by the Commonwealth itself.

By this arrangement the Islanders obtained complete autonomy and local governing power—they, however, pay no taxes to the federal government.[2] In short, the Island is virtually a self-regulating state within a free nation, somewhat analogous to the relationship between Liechtenstein and Switzerland.

Capitalism Grows Deep Roots

Concurrent with the development of the body politic, long-range studies were made jointly by Puerto Rico and the United States government contemplating the possible economic development of the Commonwealth. In the beginning there was a tendency for Puerto Rico to operate on a socialistic pattern due to its extreme poverty, underdevelopment, and fervent desire to progress rapidly. For several years after World War II, the Commonwealth at times leaned heavily toward socialism. However, sounder reasoning eventually prevailed and the Islanders began to operate through the use of "enlightened free enterprise."

There was a precedent for this in the experience of some of the states, specifically the Dakotas and Mississippi. In *Eakin vs. S.D. State Cement Commission,* 44 S.D. 268; 183 N.W. 651, dated June 20, 1921, the Supreme Court of South Dakota ruled that the state could legally and constitutionally manufacture cement. A government plant in Rapid City, South Dakota, is still in operation, manufacturing and supplying that commodity. In Mississippi, the Balance Agriculture with Industry Board used the state, as authorized by vote of the people, to offer inducements to industry. These were in the form of manufacturing facilities, the promise of a constant labor supply, and other benefits.

[2] Puerto Ricans became citizens of the United States under the Jones Act of 1917. They, however, cannot vote in national elections.

This balance between socialism and capitalism, which had proved so successful in the Dakotas and Mississippi, was adopted by Puerto Rico and made an integral part of the development of the Island. This was not socialism creeping in from abroad— there was no "ism" forced on the people. Rather, it was an evolutionary process by which responsible capitalism and the vote of a free people cooperated to benefit the entire population.

Puerto Rican Success Due to the People

While it is true that Puerto Rico offers certain benefits in terms of its location and climate, plentiful labor supply, and advantageous tax structure, which have attracted wide interest, the facts show that these alone have not produced progress. Puerto Rico's industrialization, development of better business conditions, improved agriculture, and increased living standards have been referred to as "Operation Bootstrap." The objective has been to make the Puerto Ricans participants rather than mere spectators in the drama of twentieth-century progress. It is, however, the people, under the dynamic leadership of Governor Luis Muñoz Marin, who are now, and have been, the real key to the successful operation of the program. Their willing spirit, outstanding work record, eager optimism, and genuine friendliness comprise the backbone of "Operation Bootstrap."

Small Business Part of Puerto Rican Effort Since Beginning

American business wanted to become a part of the future of this country and has done so; by and large, it has stayed with the Puerto Ricans through both good and bad times. One development of more than passing interest is the fact that small business has been a part of "Operation Bootstrap" from the beginning. There is, of course, a large amount of big business, as there should be, but there has also been from the beginning a constant participation by small business, some of it coming in from the United States, and much of it originating on the Island itself. Today, there are over 500 industrial plants in operation in Puerto Rico, ranging from the very small to the large.

Puerto Ricans Show Great
Capabilities in Modern Industry

A few basic things have become apparent in the Puerto Rico experiment. Among them is that fact that the Puerto Rican is capable of being a partner in modern industry. He has proved again the lesson that science and progress are race blind. The Puerto Rican with his non-Northern European background is no longer merely a helper, a hewer of wood and a drawer of water. He is a partner in the shaping of his own future.

A second discovery was that the Puerto Rican, with training and with consideration and interest on the part of his instructors, can become not only a skilled craftsman but also a trusted member of the management team. "Operation Bootstrap" has helped to destroy a myth too long held by the "upper classes" around the world. It has been said that the "native" who is illiterate and poor will not be a responsible employee; that he will work for a few days, take his pay, get drunk, and wind up in a worse condition than before. People convinced of this can learn the fallacy of it by reading the history of Britain and Northern Europe. The majority of our ancestors in Europe at one time were looked upon by their conquerors as being just a little higher than animals, to be always ordered about, browbeaten, and allowed to live only that they might minister to the comfort of their masters.

The Puerto Rican has proved to be an outstanding worker when given the opportunity. The discovery has been made that he is a human being and, as such, reacts to stimuli in the same manner as anyone else. Absenteeism in Puerto Rico's industrial plants has been on a par with and, in many instances, far lower than that in Long Island, Los Angeles, Boston, or Detroit. One manager of a plant employing several hundred Puerto Ricans doing precision work reported an absenteeism of less than 1 per cent over a three-year span, and a turnover of less than 3 per cent. The manager was the only "continental" there—all others, including superintendents, section chiefs, and office help were natives.

In the last few years the people of Puerto Rico have pulled themselves up from the very bottom to a point from which they can now envision a better economic future. Through the utilization of service-type capitalism the Puerto Ricans have been able to shift the gears from the old to the new by an automatic transmission without the labor of hand-shifting. Puerto Rico received some United States grants-in-aid, but less, percentagewise, than other areas. The vast majority of funds have been internally generated.

During the past five years, San Juan, with a population of just under 500,000, has relocated over 200,000 people from dismal slum areas. The government has built tremendous housing projects. One can stand on a hill and for miles in any direction see only new, modern, well-kept structures. Some are apartments where the rent is charged according to the tenant's income. A person might pay anything from $2 a month up, and this would include his utilities. However, a large number of the dwellings are individual homes sold outright to the occupants. The homes are priced from $3,000 to $9,000 and are sold at cost, on a 25-year payment plan. Another housing program is the $300 rural houses. These houses, built by the occupants and their neighbors, have gained world-wide recognition for Puerto Rico. The houses are constructed of cement blocks, with preformed roofs, and poured concrete foundations. The government provides the materials at cost and delivers them to the site. It lends to the project technical assistance, plans, and a cement mixer. As a final gesture, it arranges for payment of the house and provides the owner with one-quarter of an acre of land free. The payments are made as a thirty-dollar down payment, and two dollars and fifty cents a month until the $300 debt is paid off.

The results of all this have been amazing. Where there was poverty and filth and erosion (both of the soil and of the spirit), one finds many signs of prosperity and progress today. There are beauty parlors, drugstores, self-service supermarkets, clean restaurants, roadside stands, hotels, movies, theaters, and a developing tourist trade, all of which provide employment and opportunity for men and women, creating a climate for a healthful morale without which no people can succeed or be happy. In other areas the literacy rate is climbing rapidly while incidence of disease is dropping almost as fast.

Automation is not a thing to be feared in Puerto Rico any more than elsewhere. Fast transportation, rapid production, and the labor-saving devices that sometimes would seem to diminish the labor opportunities have in the long run provided an ever increasing number of jobs in service institutions. The older generation in Puerto Rico was pleased to see its sons and daughters become electronic technicians, laboratory experts, assembly-line workers. And they themselves grow better crops than ever before while at the same time enjoying the opportunity to earn extra money through part-time employment. Today automatic washing machines, electric stoves, and the like are to be seen all over the island. It is very common to see a television antenna projecting from the roof of a shack.

Just a few generations ago, the average person almost automatically became a member of the class into which he was born—there was almost no social mobility. Today, under the American capitalistic system, this has been changed and Puerto Rico is a good demonstration to the world of how a responsible capitalism operating within a responsible democratic structure can penetrate the rigid boundaries of the past.

Junior Chamber of Commerce in the Forefront

San Juan has an active Junior Chamber of Commerce composed of 80 members, about half of whom are "continentals," the other half Puerto Ricans. At present, this is the only chapter on the Island. However, they are planning to establish another one in Ponce, the second largest city. When I visited the Island recently, Milton Zapata, President of the San Juan group, told me of the activities in which his chapter is engaged, of the stimulus they are providing to the community by arousing interest in good government, welfare projects, social reforms, city-wide clean-up compaigns, and, in short, community improvement. This group illustrates dramatically the Puerto Rico story. Young men who would have had no future ten years ago, or even five years ago, today are eagerly encouraging their compatriots to do bigger and better things. The youth of Puerto Rico is on the march toward progress, and we would be well advised to turn the eyes and ears of the rest of the world toward this Island of the Caribbean Sea.

Puerto Rico Suggested as Case Study for Disbelievers in Private Enterprise

Here is a living example of how responsible capitalism can operate successfully, and its success has probably won us more friends around the globe than any other one project. Over 5,000 observers from foreign countries have visited Puerto Rico to see the results of Operation Bootstrap and to learn what might be beneficially applicable to their own countries.

Puerto Ricans are proud of the part they play in telling the American story. For instance, the manager of a large sugar cooperative told me that his feeling of greatest accomplishment was in the "bridge" he had helped construct between North and South America. He said that Latin-Americans look upon North Americans with a certain degree of suspicion—not understanding North American customs, language, and, in many cases, ideology. However, Puerto Rico shares many of these things with South America, and the people from the lands to the south can see in Puerto Rico, from their own frame of reference, how North America works and what responsible capitalism really is. It is a mirror reflecting North America to South America.

Thousands of overseas visitors come to America to study, their expenses paid by our State Department or by voluntary agencies here. Many of them spend countless days and nights in the large metropolitan and industrial centers of America, but really see nothing of the heart of America out where the farmers, the storekeepers, the housewives, the people on the land and in the small towns work and play. When one sees these erstwhile guests later in their own country after their return, they are often frustrated and disillusioned. What they saw in America was too big, too overwhelming; and much of what they learned is apt to be difficult or impossible to apply to the development problems of their own areas. One cannot but wonder why more of them are not sent to Puerto Rico in the course of their training to see something they can readily comprehend. And, why cannot Puerto Ricans, in turn, be sent to other countries to tell the story of their Operation Bootstrap in the Caribbean?

In a world which is so largely hostile to democracy and to the capitalistic system, it is a story that should be told and retold. The story of Puerto Rico cannot be taken and duplicated in other lands, but it can be used as a case study of what is being accomplished in an area that only yesterday ranked among the worst of the world's depressed areas.

§2. A Proposal for Effective Communication with Latin-Americans

Throughout this book we have emphasized the problem of communication with peoples overseas. I have tried to show that successful communication is always a two-way street—we must open our ears to what others have to say if they in turn are to listen to us. In the following presentation Dr. William S. Barnes, Assistant Dean of the Harvard Law School and Director of the World Tax Series, has some extremely valuable things to say about communicating with our Latin-American friends.

A PROPOSED PROGRAM FOR COMMUNICATING NORTH AMERICAN CAPITALISM

by William S. Barnes

If we are to explain the basic philosophy and operation of North American capitalism, we must translate it into terms which will be understood abroad. The fact is that capitalism is not now putting its best foot forward. We need an active program which will produce an understanding of the elements of capitalism which make it an effective tool for economic development, and a willingness to explore its advantages and shortcomings without prejudice. The economic system under which North America is growing strong and prosperous is often viewed with suspicion and contempt. We must encourage informed curiosity and an open mind as the first step toward effective communication. Developing countries need assistance to achieve good living standards, and are looking for examples of how economic development has been achieved elsewhere.

In this report I propose a definite program based on observations in Latin-America during the last few years. The form of capitalism which we now have in North America has never been widely practiced in Latin-America, and is not properly understood there. Contrary to old-fashioned notions of capitalism, the North American variety encourages close cooperation between labor and management working together to achieve maximum production. Much of the capital is provided by the public, which includes both business managers and working men. There are few countries where shares of stock in corporations are owned by such a wide segment of the working population as in the United States and Canada.

In North America, so-called capitalists tend to delegate control of capitalistic enterprise to management in much the same spirit as voters delegate responsibility for managing the affairs of the nation to their elected representatives. The division of responsibility creates a situation where labor and management can actually negotiate their differences without unreasonable capitalist intervention. Such a system might properly be called "social capitalism" to distinguish it from the more ruthless individualistic type of exploitation which has drawn so much criticism in the past. This form of social capitalism is an expression of democracy in business which supplants more authoritarian or oligarchical control of the means of production.

The influence of a social capitalistic system on the potential development of the Latin-American countries may be decisive. In any event, a proper evaluation of the part which capitalism can play is the first concern of any program of communication with these countries. Our North American system should not be imposed on other peoples; but they should understand how this system works and not condemn it simply because there have been abuses in the past. Like any new product it takes time to work out the "bugs," and it is only beginning to develop into a fair and workable economic tool.

Proposed Program

We should begin the program by acquiring a knowledge of the state of opinion concerning North American capitalism abroad. If we attempt to communicate with people in a single country, we may learn what needs to be done by listening to the attitudes and aspirations of the people there. Such a receptive state of mind may seem the very antitheses of action, but a more positive approach would be doomed to failure. The first step would be informal, perhaps simply mentioning our interest in the problem in the course of correspondence with friends in Latin-America. The next step would be entirely dependent on the initiative of the individuals abroad.

This program would involve one or more small discussion groups in each country and a counterpart group in North America. Each group must be representative of various backgrounds and opinions, not necessarily connected with any particular calling and certainly not elected by any association. The relations between the groups in the foreign country and in the United States would be coordinated by a small professional staff which would stimulate discussion without attempting to indoctrinate the group abroad.

This group should start by answering questions, the first being: How would you describe the capitalism that you see in operation in North America? On what basis have you formed this conception? This presupposes an understanding of the present degree of economic education in Latin-America. Perhaps the answers would lead back to a discussion of fundamentals of economic life of a nation and its people. At any event, the question would be discussed by a cross-section of individuals who represent many different parts of the population.

The coordinating staff would be responsible for assistance in organizing the groups abroad, and for preparing and circulating questions for discussion. Its principal functions as the program developed would be to receive responses and reports from the discussion groups abroad and transmit them to the groups in North America. Under no circumstances should the opening queries be included in a questionnaire; each question should be introduced separately as a basis for group discussion. In one sense this approach is a form of group dynamics in the field of economics. It is designed to provoke interest and inquiry rather than solution, especially in the initial stages. Thus the discussion may evoke a series of requests for information in reply which would provide a framework for research, and the preparation of materials that would help to explain the concept to the group when they are ready to receive it.

The staff would then begin to prepare readings in English and in the foreign language which would supply information specifically in response to the needs of the Latin-American groups. This work would be aided by discussions of the readings in North America. The actual preparation might involve several drafts before readings would be ready for even limited distribution and circulation abroad.

Further questions for discussion might be more specific; for example, what role do you believe that government regulation plays in the process? What is your notion of the relationship between labor and management in our capitalistic society? What is a corporation and how does it differ from your forms of business organization? How do consumers express their preferences? Can prices be established on the basis of free competition? What conditions are necessary in order to permit enterprising individuals to finance their business ventures?

These questions should become gradually more difficult and at the same time more generic and applicable to conditions in the particular country. For example, the groups should be encouraged to seek the answer to the later questions by comparing the situation at home with the situation as they understand it to be in the United States and Canada.

In some instances it might be necessary for the groups abroad to supplement their meetings with a number of local interviews so as to obtain a consensus of opinion which would be reasonably representative of various points of view. These interviews would be conducted by members of the group to supplement the discussion of various questions by the group itself; for example, if the group did not know anything about a particular segment of the economy, say retailing and marketing, the members of the group would interview persons engaged in distribution to obtain their reactions to some of the questions which the group had been discussing.

Organization

The number of persons in each group and the method of organization and operation would vary according to the situation in the particular country. In general, it should be limited to 12 persons and should not include more than 5 or 6 who have had definite connections with North America and knowledge of North American culture and ways of doing business. It should not be considered as an "elite" group. The group need not be large or especially well informed, but it must have local leadership to stimulate response. In some countries the young, industrious professional may provide the most dynamic approach, especially if he has had experience in business and government affairs.

The group should be organized by the leader, who would choose two or three persons to advise him on who should be invited to participate in the group discussion. In choosing members of the group, it is important to remember that an understanding of capitalism is sought not only from an economic point of view, but equally from a psychological or sociological point of view. For example, in his book on *The Anti-Capitalist Mentality,* Von Mises suggests that many people are against capitalism because they are not the ones who have been successful in proving their own ability under the capitalistic system.

In view of the need for developing an adequate set of reading materials and procedure for group meetings and the formulation of objectives for the group, coordination of sources of information will obviously be important. Each group should be given the maximum autonomy in determining its procedure and subject matter, but some pattern or guide lines should be provided. This must be done by the coordinating staff providing suggestions both as to how to organize the group and what kind of materials to use. Such a coordinating group would probably have its headquarters in North America and would be composed of representatives of various points of view in the United States and Canada.

It should include persons who are familiar with Latin-America and as far as possible its members should be fluent in the Spanish language. The permanent staff of this coordinating group would have offices and a regular budget for working with the groups in the various countries.

In addition to this over-all coordination there should be a special North American group organized for each one of the countries in which groups have been active. For example, if a group is organized in Mexico and another group in Argentina, the coordinating staff would be responsible for providing suggestions on procedures and materials, but it should also help organize in North America a group discussing capitalism in Mexico and another group discussing capitalism in Argentina. These groups would correspond with their counterparts abroad, and would develop a relationship based on their mutual interests. Questions raised by the group in Mexico would be referred to the corresponding group in this country and, likewise, the group here might raise a number of questions which could only be answered by the group in Mexico.

In my own experience in developing a series of studies on foreign taxes, I have noticed that the closest collaboration occurred where there is a mutual interest in each others' problems. Our experience in working with correspondents in the various countries which are included in the World Tax Series gives us an example of what can be done in the development of international understanding. When we are studying the tax laws of a particular country, we are in close touch with at least one outstanding tax expert in that country who ultimately comes to the United States to discuss points of interpretation and to check the final draft. At this technical level understanding between the two countries is very easy. It is essential for us to understand their system. The fact that we are so engaged makes it easier for them to explain it to us; in other words, we are naturally curious about all of the details of their system, and they are eager to give us information which will help us to understand it. It might seem that this is an extremely indirect way of developing an understanding of the American system on the part of the correspondent, but as a matter of fact that is just what it does.

In attempting to describe to us his own system, he must naturally learn about the general principles and some of the details of the American system. He is keen to do this so that he can compare points in his system with similar points in our own. The result has been that by asking him to help us explain to the English-speaking world his system of taxation we have in fact succeeded in developing his understanding of our system as an indirect result. This is the principle behind the organization of a group in North America to study the development of capitalism in the particular country involved.

It would be important to include some so-called "experts" on Latin-America in the groups here, but the emphasis should be on other qualities. At this time when individuals in the United States are expressing concern for our relations with Latin-American countries, it should be possible to bring together a group of individuals who would work toward a better understanding of the point of view of Latin-Americans toward capitalism in the twentieth century. *The ability to be aware of the Latin-American's experience with capitalism and thereby to understand his definition of it is the essential characteristic which should be found in all of the individuals in the North American group.* As Spanish-speaking people recognize the quality of being "simpatico," we should seek out those individuals who have this quality of "empathy." We meet many Latin-Americans who are *"muy simpático"*; do they meet many North Americans who are indeed "empathic"?

In finding and bringing together a group of North Americans in a central location, it would be advisable to begin with a series of meetings throughout the United States and Canada of small groups to discuss the background and current problems of the particular country involved; for example, if we plan to organize a group to work with its counterpart in Mexico, there might be as many as 20 or 30 small discussion groups, using a compact set of reading materials concerning Mexico. These would form the basis for a short series of meetings, say once each week for a month, to go over the material and raise important issues; for example, does individual enterprise find free expression in small business in Mexico?

The most effective institutional framework within which such a preliminary program could be carried out would depend on the locality and should not be stereotyped. In some places a university might be a sponsor of the discussions and provide additional materials when necessary. In another it might be the local public library. The attention of these preliminary groups would not be directly on the Latin-American understanding of North American capitalism, but simply on the particular country under consideration; and, therefore, it would help to bring out the empathies of individuals rather than the *expertise* in a particular economic field.

Financing

This report has suggested only the general framework within which a program might operate. I have emphasized attitudes and approaches rather than spelling out details of organization. The groups in the foreign countries and here in North America might incur considerable travel expenses as the program developed, but the major expenses would be the maintenance of an adequate coordinating staff and the provision for research and the preparation of materials. Reproducing and circulating these materials even in an expanded program would be relatively inexpensive. The first steps might require substantial financial support, but they would plant the seed which might well spread without any expansion of staff or consequent increase in expenses.

I can suggest two possible methods of obtaining the funds necessary to meet the expenses. The first method is the conventional support from industry, government, or private foundations and individuals which would be interested in contributing to such a project. This method might require preparation of an elaborate and detailed outline of the proposed project and a budget of annual expenditures. In any project where funds are to be solicited from a number of sources, there is always the problem of the appropriate amount which should be requested from each source. There is also the danger that a project of such wide interest and appeal would be associated too closely with the source of the funds in the minds of the groups participating in the work.

In order to overcome some of these difficulties, I suggest an alternative method which would seek support directly from the people of North America. Any such public subscription has the obvious disadvantages of the high cost of advertising, mailings, and collection of funds, but does provide a means of publicizing the project widely and informing the people of the fact that such a work is being undertaken. For this particular project there is the added advantage of asserting the basic power of broad participation in an enterprise; for example, annual contributions in the United States and Canada under the slogan of "A Penny a Person" would mean a potential goal of almost $2 million a year. This dynamic illustration of the power of the Penny might be worth the tremendous cost involved in launching such a campaign. Even if it would not be realistic to hope to actually receive a penny investment from every man, woman, and child in North America, it would at least provide a yardstick of what could be given by communities or other groups toward the financial support of the project; for example, an institution might be asked to contribute a penny for each employee as an investment in the future of our free enterprise system in the world-wide ideological battle. In one way or another the resources of our "social capitalism" need to be mobilized behind this effort.

Conclusion

There seems to be a general realization that something along this line needs to be done at this time. I have already had several informal personal discussions in Argentina where the change of government has increased the interest in revising relations with the United States, especially their attitude toward our particular form of business enterprise and our desire to invest in certain types of activity there. In Brazil the atmosphere is entirely different; they are already convincing United States business that their economy is stable regardless of the rate of exchange, and they welcome new capital there. In the discussion of this proposed program which I had with several professional and businessmen, I found that there was a considerable interest in

awaking public opinion in Brazil to the potentialities for expansion and development, which the North Ameircan experience
points out so clearly can be accomplished under capitalism. In
Mexico there is no doubt that they can mobilize a number of
leading citizens to make the first stage of the work proceed. In
Venezuela members of a young management course were especially interested, and they convinced me that the program which
I have described in general terms above is practicable as of this
moment. In Colombia there is a strong feeling that a representative group should be brought together to examine the climate
for foreign investment and to learn more about what is needed
in order to understand the North American attitude and to encourage investment in Colombia.

The proposed program will help at least a limited number of
people in North America to explain our system in terms which
respond to the actual attitudes toward capitalism now prevalent
in the various Latin-American countries. One of the obvious
advantages of the particular exchange of ideas which is outlined
above is that we learn to communicate our ideas by attempting
to satisfy the curiosity of the group in Latin-America. In effect
we are concentrating, perhaps unconsciously, on how to articu-
late our ideology. As this program develops, we begin to train
leadership in the ideological calisthenics which must precede any
competitive encounter with other ideologies.

As an ever expanding group of Americans obtain training in
the art of articulating our own beliefs, we gain confidence in our
ability to compete with other ideologies. As we become conscious
of the attitudes abroad, we see how to put our best foot forward
within these attitudes; and thus our small North American group
becomes increasingly effective. The way to explain and express
North American capitalism becomes more clearly defined. Members of the foreign service conceivably could learn much from
the materials developed by the coordinate staff, and all the businessmen, scientists, engineers and tourists who go abroad could
well learn how to put our best foot forward.

Those who develop the ability to explain our system and its
advantages on the basis of this program can teach others how to

do it too. Gradually, we will find that we are winning the war of ideas.

Capitalism can and will compete so long as its adherents are willing to learn how to explain it to our friends and enemies abroad.

§3. Views on Capitalism Expressed by Religious Leaders

To make a completely rounded study of a subject, we in America believe in consulting with our religious leaders. Their opinions are inspiring, timely, and thoughtful, and must occupy an important place in any momentous discussions.

The following pages speak for themselves and I include them with respect and gratitude.

ROMAN CATHOLIC VIEWS OF CAPITALISM

Monsignor L. G. Ligutti—the Permanent Observer of the Holy See to the Food and Agriculture Organization of the United Nations—is one of the keenest observers of world conditions in my Library of Friends. During the past ten years he has averaged over a hundred thousand miles per year going into the far-flung areas of the world. He has the habit of sending home to his friends a series of letters covering his observations— "Sunrise and Sunset Letters."

On the eve of an extended trip to the Far East in the fall of 1955 I asked him if, upon his return, he would report on the general theme of this study at a session of the June Conference at the Harvard Business School. He not only participated in the Conference, as reported in "Management Guide to Overseas Operation"—a report on the 26 June Conference of the Harvard Business School by Dan H. Fenn, Jr., published by the McGraw-Hill Book Co., Inc.—but also included some of his observations in his inimitable newsletters. These paragraphs are quoted for their simplicity and audacity:

Excerpts from *Sunrise and Sunset Letters*, No. 15[3]

by

Msgr. Ligutti

The car ride to Bandung is most picturesque. The rises are not too steep and the turns not too sharp. The Three Sisters Mountains and the upturned canoe mountain, tree covered and deep green, are delightful to see. Bandung is a big new city, lovely climate, broad streets, clean, but growing too fast for its limited public utilities. I drove by the famous auditorium where the Asian-African conference was held. The people of the East are becoming more and more conscious of their numerical strength. The resentment against the West is something to be reckoned with. In many ways they seem to be right; in others wrong. No question about the wrongs of colonial exploitation, of western imposition, of haughtiness, low regard for the human personality of the poor native, etc., etc. Now a complete mistrust of anything the West offers or does. They describe it as a new trick to keep Easterners in subjection, and they don't want any of it. They need technical assistance; they need capital investments, but make limited use of them. They need relief, but almost refuse to accept it. They cannot conceive how the U.S. can help or give away a lot of stuff just out of a sheer spirit of charity and brotherhood. From a military viewpoint, they fear a war that would involve them. Then they fear particularly American capitalism.

U.S. capitalism in the minds of most people in these parts (white, Eurasians, and full-blooded natives) is really and truly a veritable devil. We may sell our products abroad, but our reputation is as low as one can imagine. We are accused of everything under the sun. We are crooks, we are mistrusted, we want to subjugate people, to conquer them, make them pay through the nose. Modern decent capitalism, fair competitive service, lower prices for products, mass markets, higher wages and living standards, plus a fair justifiable profit have not been sold as part and parcel of capitalism. To my mind this sales job has to be done in all the danger areas of the world. What has enlightened capitalism brought to the world? Will statism in any shape do any better? Can it do better? After much looking into, I believe that to save itself capitalism must realize its social purposes, of service to society, and act accordingly. Also, show the world that only through a system of honest competition can better living be secured for the world. I am sorry to say that very few attempts have been made along these lines, and that the results have been nil. Even the most bitter enemies of communism are still thinking in nineteenth-century terms—exploiters, cheaters, crooks, etc., etc. There is

[3] From Djakarta, Indonesia, February 19, 1956, and mailed from Singapore.

plenty of money being wasted in our fight against communism, and our U.S. public relations job is too often a sorry mess.

Now that I have this off my chest, I can go on from Bandung. I met there Bishop Arntz of the Crozier Fathers—a fine group of churches and schools, also the beginnings of a Catholic university . . . a noble attempt, indeed, for such a minority group as the Catholics in Indonesia. I am an inveterate sinner in this regard. I don't believe Christian universities produce a Christian elite, and I don't believe that the so-called "elite" amount to much except in a show window. The finest and most influential Christians we have are just plain ordinary people.

Excerpts from *Sunrise and Sunset Letters,* No. 16[4]

This evening I heard a lecture on fundamental economics by a splendid professor of the local university. From the questions that came out of the audience, I could glean that they were anti-Communists, but also anti-capitalists. For the very reason explained in one of my recent letters, capitalism sells goods, but not itself. A very capable Australian Jesuit who has been making the rounds in reverse to mine, but whose path I have crossed now three times and conferred with him each time, is of the same thought. In his opinion the democracies and capitalism are selling themselves down the river. Communism is selling itself by pointing out the inconsistencies of the democracy; i.e., colonialism, exploitation, race discrimination.

Excerpts from *Sunrise and Sunset Letters,* No. 19[5]

Some time ago [the Burmese] turned out U.S. Technical Assistance, really not because of too many conditions on the part of the U.S., but because they wanted complete and unaccounted for handling of funds. It's sad they don't realize what harm crookedness and inefficiency in government bring about to their own country. There is nothing much the U.S. can do under such circumstances. Here as elsewhere, even among persons of good will and intelligence, the old prejudices exist against capitalism, and by the same token against American imperialism. What a sales job is ours to do. We spend money for so many inconsequential efforts, but nothing to hit at the root of the trouble.

Reverend James L. Vizzard, S.J., Vice President, National Catholic Rural Life Conference, Georgetown University, Washington, D.C., has prepared a statement for inclusion in this book

4 From Singapore, Malaya, February 22, 1956.
5 From Rangoon, Burma, March 7, 1956.

based upon his thoughtful consideration of the problems of men, machines and materialism.

The greatest social and economic contribution the West has for the world is not its strictly technical knowledge and competence, great and necessary though that be. It is not its machines, efficient though they may be. It is not even the accumulated results of its advanced economy, urgently needed though they may be. What the West has discovered, or perhaps stumbled upon, is an economic society in which justice *can* prevail, in which a man's legitimate aspirations *can* be fulfilled, of which the basic elements are in conformity with his nature and his needs. It is a society to which a man can make commitments because it allows for and rewards the energy and intiative he expends. Through his own efforts he can improve his standards of life and his status in society.

No one would be so rash as to claim that this is wholly true and everywhere true in our society, but the basic elements are there. This is the "product" desperately needed in the underdeveloped areas of the world and what we ought to be communicating.

A PROTESTANT VIEWS CAPITALISM

Dr. Cameron P. Hall—Executive Secretary of the Department of Church and Economic Life of the National Council of Churches of Christ in the United States of America—is a long-time friend of mine and a man in whose judgment I have great confidence. Just prior to embarking formally upon this study, I asked him to give me his observations of capitalism. His answering letter was so stimulating that it is being included in its entirety.

Dear Ray:

I enjoyed our luncheon together the other day perhaps more than usual, if that is possible. I found your questions most stimulating and bearing directly upon crucial issues in today's and tomorrow's world. Let me put down a few thoughts that have come to me since we met.

Capitalism today lends itself to a threefold description. One is the way it exists particularly in the United States but also in other parts of the Western World. A second description is the form it has taken primarily on the Continent where its cartelization has been developed by industrialists and encouraged by government; this hardening of the economic arteries, as it were, is contrary to what the American people support as sound economic policy.

A third description is found in the way capitalism is understood by the people of Asia, which means in effect a good portion of the modern world. To put it mildly, this view of capitalism is highly critical and this criticism extends to the Western peoples and their governments. It seems to me to be compounded of two closely related factors.

First, the people of Asia are all out against colonialism, imperialism, and racial injustice. In their eyes the nations who are guilty of these evils are capitalistic. Capitalism is thus historically identified with these "isms" under which the Asian people have suffered and out of which they are presently emerging.

Second, there can be no doubt that in the past, as a matter of record, grave injustices and cruelties have been inflicted on vast populations by practices which have been sanctioned by capitalistic principles and policies. There is a continuity within history which means that the present is always joined to and its problems largely set by what was true in the past, however much the present itself may represent a change. What capitalism is thought of in Asia today is largely colored by what Asia suffered under earlier concepts of capitalism.

In general, I would think that to the peoples in Asia capitalism means a system of values, a set of working principles, and a complex of practices which protect and encourage the strong to take advantage of the weak for the sake of monetary gains and economic power, with little or no regard to what happens to the weak whether they be individuals, nations, or races. The group in a capitalistic society to which this is seen to apply is the business community; businessmen and capitalists are interchangeable in this kind of thinking.

To these foregoing two points three brief comments may be added: (1) While upon businessmen is heaped the main opprobrium, the culture which permits them to operate thus is strongly condemned as materialistic and ruthless. (2) In addition to what he does in his representative capacity, the businessman as an individual in Asia and other such areas has almost uniformly acted with arrogance, snobbery, and a studied indifference to the welfare of the people. (3) Although capitalism is understood as calling for maximum aloofness of government from what the businessman does and plans in pursuit of economic gains and power, people in underdeveloped countries generally feel that in fact Western governments have often gone out of their way to support and even to interfere on behalf of, rather than to restrain the exploitive practices of capitalism.

In line with their ideology, Communists are often quite outspoken about their supplanting capitalism. It would seem to me that this means two things according to the part of the world which is being thought of. In connection with the traditional capitalistic countries Communists expect their economies to collapse and the so-called downtrodden workers to move into the places of power. In connection with the vast areas occupied by noncapitalistic countries, the Communists, it seems to me, affirm that the future of these countries in their march to economic strength and political power lies not along the capitalist—but instead the Communist—highway. In other words, communism is the dynamic and successful force that will make the world of tomorrow.

I have had personally only a marginal, firsthand contact with the non-Western world. On the other hand, through contacts with missionaries and leaders of the missionary movement, with churchmen who have taken on special assignments for an extended period in Asia, and through my relationship over the past years with the World Council of Churches, especially in its program dealing with economic, social, and political issues, I have been in touch with what is reported and thought about the character of the crisis of the free world within a total world context. Out of this background I am prepared to make the following observations.

First, that large populations in Asia may succumb to the apparent promise and hope which they see in communism is, indeed, a threat of major proportions. Viewed from the background and perspective of Asia, the likelihood that this could happen lies in some countries between the possible and the probable and in other countries between the probable and the certain.

Second, because capitalism has traditionally stood against both government restraint upon the individual and government planning for the social welfare, by way of reaction there is in the present historical situation what might be called a built-in favorable disposition toward reliance on government in the economies of Asia's lands.

Third, somewhat supporting the above trend is the desire to reap the benefits of technology and industrialization rapidly. The attendant need for capitalization and the allocation of resources to get on in a hurry could well lead to a maximum of government activity. In the short run this might well help economic progress, but in the long run it could well lead to unfavorable consequences both to economic progress itself and to the essential freedoms in accord with the dignity and worth of the individual.

Fourth, because of the association attributed to capitalism of economic injustice on the one hand and government inactivity toward the public interest on the other hand, it may seem logical to peoples with newly won independence to insure economic justice by mobilizing the place of government controls.

I would say that these four considerations at their worst could lead to widespread Communist domination and, at their best, might lead to an unfavorable unbalance between the private and public sectors in the economy with grave consequences to the individual and the nation as well as to the free world as a whole.

That we of the Western World should be concerned about this goes without saying. Also that the situation is one of urgency requiring effort both to understand and to deal with it should become apparent to a growing number of responsible leaders, including those in business.

What can be done? I make two general but in my view crucial observations.

First, within the revolutionary dynamics moving the people of Asia there is a positive appreciative attitude toward the United States. Observers at and students of the Bundung Conference hold that the occasion showed the power of the United States on the *level of ideas.* I am told that on opening the Conference President Sukarno of Indonesia declared that what underlies the ferment in Asia and Africa in throwing off the Western yoke comes not out of Marxism but out of the American Revolution; he went on to recite parts of Longfellow's poem about "The Ride of Paul Revere." That contact with the spiritual dynamics within our American history is not seen to be related to our economic as well as to our political and social history is perhaps our main neglect. But whatever the reason the spiritual force moving large numbers of leaders in Asia, as well as their followers, issues from our heritage, and, as such, offers us a decisive means for basic rapport.

Second, it seems to me that we are in a strong position because we have made ours a mixed economy. We are committed to keeping the private sector dominant, yet at the same time we have recognized the need and made room for the place of government. In theory and practice we are not doctrinaire either on behalf of an absolute individualism or an absolute collectivism. We have taken the values that lie in each with emphasis on those that lie in individualism. We might be described as illustrating both responsible individualism and responsible government. In this connection I am thinking of an address by Mr. Charles P. Taft at the Evanston Assembly of the World Council in the summer of 1954 in which he elaborated the evidence of responsibility in our economy.

In connection with the above I might mention the current studies on Ethics and Economics in Society which this Department of the National Council of Churches is conducting under a grant of the Rockefeller Foundation. Already these studies have resulted in seven volumes published by Harper & Brothers with six others to appear within the next fifteen months. We have taken a rather comprehensive look at our economy within the context of dominant American values from the perspective of Judeo-Christian principles.

In pursuing the question of what can be done at this time, I have not had the opportunity to think this through further beyond suggesting a partial analysis of where the answer might be found. You suggested that your interest is in what might be done through businessmen themselves. Presumably their most natural point of contact would be with their counterparts in Asia. This leads to the question what the businessman of Asia could do to deal with the situation. While recognizing that the forces that move in history have a mass foundation, there is no warrant in today's situation in my judgment which precludes effective contribution from the business community within Asia itself. This contribution would be made by themselves understanding and adhering to sound economic policies in respect to the relation of private and government enterprise, and also demonstrating ways in which their own interests and the public interest are intertwined.

This leads inevitably to the question about how the business community in the United States can be of help, if any, toward this objective. One thinks of the printed word and the personal contact as the most promising media. The development of both of these means of communication of ideas is fraught with extreme difficulties, many of which are subtle and delicate. I cannot help but think, however, that our American ingenuity can come up with some solution which would contribute to this problem which is so central to the future of the free world.

With warm personal regards, I am

Sincerely yours,
CAMERON P. HALL

A JEW VIEWS CAPITALISM

My friend and associate Professor Benjamin M. Selekman of the Harvard Business School suggested that excerpts from the article, "The Businessman's Moral Failure," by Louis Finkelstein, Chancellor and Professor of Theology at the Jewish Theological Seminary of America, published in the September, 1958, issue of *Fortune,* contained material that would be an important contribution to the part of the book covering attitudes of religious leaders.

Before I had an opportunity to follow through on his suggestion, I found that the editors of *The Executive, a Guide to Reading for Top Management* had selected Professor Finkelstein's article for abstraction in the October issue of this publication. With this double endorsement, I present a Jewish view of the businessman as published in *The Executive.*

The Businessman's Moral Failure

by

Louis Finkelstein[6]

If American businessmen are right in the way most of them now live, then all the wise men of the ages, all the prophets and the saints were fools. If the saints were not fools, the businessmen must be.

---

[6] *Fortune,* LVII, No. 3 (September 1958), pp. 117–18, 194.

Too many businessmen never stop to ponder what they are doing; they reject the need for self-discipline; they are satisfied to be clever, when they need to be wise. They worry about their place on the economic ladder, but are not concerned sufficiently about whether the civilization in which they work is likely to collapse. They can defeat a local competitor, but may well be defeated by the competitor of us all, which is moral decay.

The American executive is very often a man of some vision, motivated by a spirit that generates great energy. But he is losing his insight into the moral sources of American economic strength. Ask him why he is successful today, and he may explain to you the advantages of capitalism, the profit motive, and the "American system." But he will largely ignore the philosophic foundations of the American system. He tends to ignore the great ethical laws as they apply immediately to his work. He is preoccupied chiefly with gain, coasting on the spiritual momentum of the past.

Why is the American businessman singled out for indictment, when he is probably no more materialistic than any of the rest of us? Because his role in American society is so great. Ours is an industrial society, and the customs and morals and attitudes of businessmen pervade our whole life.

The American tragedy is that we fail to see the signs of our decay. The signs are apparent in our general toleration of wrongdoing, which is itself an evil and corrupting force.

Competition is the basis of our free enterprise and of our industrial success. But to compete in ways that are designed to destroy someone else is very different from competing in terms of doing better than your rival. A management worthy of success remembers that the true justification for profit is an incentive to serve the community. Success is paid to business by the community for the services it renders.

Unquestionably, ethics have a practical value, inseparable from their ultimate one: the creation of better men and women. Rivalry for goodness should, in the long run, make for pragmatic gain. But it is not enough for the individual to mean well. Men as individuals and as corporations must make an effort to understand what they are doing and why they are doing it.

A businessman can develop an awareness that *every* decision of his life involves moral considerations. He should *place ethics on the agenda*:

• His calendar should include regular meetings of management to discuss the moral dimensions in his specific business.

• He should seek expert advice on ethics.

• He should put moral health on the same level as mental and physical health, in fact above them. He should work for the establishment of research in ethics, as he has worked magnificently for the development of research in science and technology.

Today's crisis demands the businessman's leadership in the area of human behavior. Morally sensitive and informed businessmen can compel American philosophy and religion to focus on the basic problems troubling mankind.

Does all of this sound as though the businessman had to take on new burdens, and rush even more prematurely to his grave? On the contrary, one of man's primary duties is preservation of his life on earth, so that he can realize his potentialities for good. The businessman who will take time to contemplate and to ponder the ethical dimension of life will discover new realms in which he can develop his talents, freeing himself from the bondage to private gain that menaces the maturing business executive.

XIII

LOOKING AHEAD

§1. WHAT WILL HAPPEN WHEN COMMUNIST IMPERIALISM COLLAPSES?

So far in this book, most of our attention has been focused on the practical problems of the immediate future. There is another phase of this whole subject that deserves thought and careful study, but seemingly very little is being given to it. When the Iron Curtain collapses, and the satellite countries are suddenly freed from Soviet dictatorship, will we be ready? Militarily, yes. Civilly, no. What of these people who have been reared for centuries under feudalism, who now have been for a generation under the dictatorship of state capitalism, with their industries of five employees or more, even in Yugoslavia, being operated by the state? Suppose the people in those countries were suddenly free and asked us for advice and help as to how they might bring their business into the realm of private enterprise, integrated with some state operation, as it is done in the United States or even more in Scandinavia? How many trained men have we ready to do something about it?

When General Douglas MacArthur was training his men in Monterey, California, for proposed Japanese landing operations, he also had a group of men being trained to help operate the civilian part of Japanese life. Men from American business, labor, and the professions were studying every facet of the

Japanese economy, and at a moment's notice were ready. That was war-planning. It was also the beginning of the rehabilitation of Japan. Can American service capitalism organize to do a similar job? This would require an over-all organized project of American business, clearly not in violation of antitrust laws, but broader in its cooperative organization and operation than anything yet developed. Yet something on this order is what is needed to meet the organization and operation of communism in its avowed determination to destroy capitalism.

Following the MacArthur plan, one man, John Cooper, and a few associates were able to work with the Japanese until 35,000 Japanese communities within a period of months had begun the formation of community-owned and locally operated, nonprofit capitalistic cooperatives for the benefit of their patrons. Their success was accelerated by the fact that in introducing their work they identified themselves with the backgrounds of the people with whom they dealt rather than with the Occupation.[1]

And when the Korean war broke a few years later, what happened? General MacArthur was able to move his troops to Korea, leaving the military bases in rural Japan undefended in many cases, save by a few Americans. But they were defended by the Japanese people! There is a village in the central part of Japan near a large U.S. military establishment that typifies this concept. Apparently, there were few U.S. personnel around on a visit I made there during the Korean War. While at a dinner hosted by the Japanese mayor, I asked, "Who guards this camp?" He was sitting at a low Japanese table. He got so excited he jumped up and knocked the table into my lap, saying, "We do!" Those farmers in rural Japan had learned the fundamental principles of American government and business through the stern necessity of war.

---

[1] It is interesting to note that the cooperatives still survive, whereas Occupation-imposed changes in the Constitution and in decartelizing business have subsequently been modified.

For the past several years Mr. Cooper has been an adviser to the governments of the Philippines and Korea on the development of cooperatives in the villages. The development of these has again proved that taking information from where it is to where it can be used through the medium of a dedicated individual is the best method.

We should have groups in training today in business, ready to help whenever and wherever the Iron Curtain cracks, prepared to go in when invited as friends and not as invading conquerors.

Dr. Philippe Zuger, the well-known Swiss student of international affairs, has recently visited a cross-section of European and Latin-American leaders to discuss the economic and social problems of the world. In a letter to the author commenting on the present world situation he concludes:

> The peoples in the captive satellite countries have conclusively demonstrated that—although fervently desiring to join the Free World again—they will not agree under any circumstances to accept the old economic and social conditions and institutions of the pre-communist times. They do not want to give back the factories; they do not want to give back the land.

As it looks toward the future, American service capitalism faces ever more stimulating challenges. It must be ready to face them clearly and confidently.

§2. WHAT I BELIEVE AMERICA SHOULD "EXPORT"

Four forms of business activity in America are invariably of interest to everyone overseas with whom I have discussed the subject. Some indicated a deep interest in one form and some in another, but all have told me that either one or all of these forms of American capitalism would be of interest to their compatriots.

All four of these vital areas are treated more or less in detail in several earlier sections but for emphasis they are grouped together here as the four pegs upon which any future program must hang.

The cooperative, the nonprofit corporate association, as it is used in North America, is something that fascinates overseas leaders, but unfortunately only a few coming here under any auspices get acquainted with it. Unless the visitors are farmers or actual operators of consumer cooperatives, they seldom hear of our cooperatives; or if they do, they are told: "Cooperatives are not good for America—they are socialistic." Nothing is more capitalistic than a corporation for service without entity-profit but with profit to the members who use and own it—such as the Associated Press, Sunkist, Railway Express Agency, Land O'Lakes, Equitable Life Assurance Society, our credit union finance companies, and agricultural purchasing associations.

The Scandinavian countries are "loved" in all parts of the world largely because of their "middle way."[2] We have a similar development here, but we do not talk about it enough. B. J. Patel, of India, a businessman devoting his life to the betterment of his people, was in the United States, and we talked for hours about this whole situation. He visited cooperatives in many sections of the country, and then at the request of his government went to Red China to study their state-dictated "cooperatives." His minority report[3] pointed out that the cooperatives in China are not truly cooperatives, but are really economic divisions of the government; that while real democratic, capitalistic cooperatives can build men of independent thought, will, and initiative, government organization destroys all this.

Small business is a facet of American life that is devastating to the promoters of Soviet communism. The mere semantics of the words has a drawing power that startles one when talking with a leader from overseas. The fact that we have small businesses, and that they are able to compete with the "big" ones, is a story so unexpected that I recommend that the reader try it on the next visitor he has from overseas.

The word "capitalism" is under world-wide attack. The words "small business" are the end of the rainbow for multiplied millions. The fact that we, as a nation, have recognized small businesses as a vital part of our economic life and have shown governmental interest in them is revolutionary to the thinking of those who have condemned America as being materialistic and dominated by "big business."

Nothing will appeal to people in distant lands more than to be brought face to face with the fact that small business is a vital part of America. We have an "atomic bomb" here in the world

---

[2] Marquis W. Childs, *Sweden: The Middle Way* (New Haven: Yale University Press, 1936).

[3] *The New York Times* (June 3, 1957).

of ideas that for some unaccountable reason has never really been tried. Our big business is largely considered out of bounds for serious overseas study because its size makes it impracticable and unattainable there. On the contrary, small business has an appeal by its very terminology.

We sometimes forget that Communist theory eliminates small business almost immediately upon taking power. In Yugoslavia, where I studied the situation, all establishments with five or more employees had been taken over by the state.

The Washington *Sunday Star* of November 9, 1958, reports:

> The Prague newspaper *Svobodne Slove* reports the Czech capital's few remaining independent hotels and restaurants will be nationalized soon. The national council recently recommended liquidation of the last free enterprises.

Nothing is more American than private small business; and even President Eisenhower showed his interest by accepting an honorary membership in the National Small Business Men's Association, Inc.[4]

Labor unions, as stated elsewhere, have done a better job of interpreting America overseas than has business. This trend was noted in the speech entitled "Dynamic Capitalism" that I made before the Third Annual Conference on Institutional Relations, University of Utah, November, 1952. Our trade unionist is not suspect, nor does he operate under a cloud when he goes about in foreign lands. For one thing he is usually a visiting American who knows the difference between European socialism and Soviet communism. Unfortunately too many of our well-intentioned industrial leaders and politicians use the terms interchangeably. This has caused more local friction in Europe than any other single factor in my experience. The stand that our labor unions have taken against the seductive wiles of the state-

[4] Following excerpt is taken from a letter from President Eisenhower, dated October 26, 1956, to Mr. A. F. Mathews, President, National Small Business Men's Association: "Mrs. Eisenhower and I are deeply appreciative of your kindness in awarding to us a certificate of honorary life membership in the National Small Business Men's Association. Particularly, we are delighted that we qualify because of the operation of our farm in Gettysburg."

controlled labor organizations behind the Iron Curtain is well known.

Highly organized American labor is part and parcel of our present-day capitalistic system. Our laborers are in many cases stockholders. Not in a generation have our labor leaders advocated the taking over of industry by the state. Together with business and agriculture, labor has made possible the great revolution of the past fifty years whereby we have achieved universal participation in capitalism by all segments of our society.

Reference has been made earlier to the activities in the field of communicating the fundamentals of American capitalism overseas by the labor groups. As trade associations for labor transferring American knowledge overseas, they are in a unique position. They have seen the opportunity and have performed probably as great a service as any group in America. The fact is that they, as free trade unionists, believe enough in our system to fight for it. If the trade associations of the companies for which labor works would take a fraction of the interest in this international program that labor does, we could turn the tide of history. A step in this direction is the successful training program here for men from the steel industry in India through a combination of Ford Foundation, members of the American Iron and Steel Institute, and the labor unions. This should develop into a pilot project of great value. It has its problems, of course, such as the frustration of the men returning to India at a wage rate infinitesimal compared to ours—but that must be a calculated risk. The main result of the project is not only to help men to become better steel workers but to give them a better understanding of the partnership here between labor, finance, and management. That is dynamic capitalism at its best.

With its own resources, labor has done much already in communicating overseas the fundamentals of American capitalism (of which labor is a vital part). The mere fact that our labor leaders encouraged European trade unionists to work with business in common development has had as much to do with the success of the European Productivity Agency as any one other thing.

Voluntary agencies are as representative of American capitalism as any other contemporary institution. Reference has been made earlier to several of them and the part they play in good international public relations. Those mentioned are only examples and typical of what can be done by many others. There are hundreds of trade associations here that might well apportion a part of their income to send true businessmen abroad, without government subsidy, to do a job of interpreting America. The National Association of Food Chains is doing this with amazing results. Europe is now becoming conscious of modern markets largely through the efforts of this association. The modern self-service food market is probably the best actual example of what we mean by freedom of choice that has yet been sent abroad.

CUNA (Credit Union National Association), of Madison, Wisconsin, the trade association of the credit unions, whose aggregate membership totals some 9 million, has for years made men and resources available to interested people in other countries.[5] In 1953 an Asian group needed some information about credit unions and requested it from them. Within a matter of days the New Delhi group received several books via air mail from CUNA. Maybe it cost CUNA ten dollars postage—from the point of view of understanding America and the service motivation of this credit union form of capitalism, it was of inestimable value. I was with the group at the time the package arrived. There were perhaps fifty men in a conference on how to control moneylenders. No one who has not experienced a similar session can understand the enthusiasm with which the information in the material was discussed—but even more than that, the lesson it taught of America was inestimable. One thing that took an hour of discussion was how the headquarters of this organization, representing billions of dollars of business, could be in Madison, Wisconsin, a place that they had never known of before. CUNA did a good job of public relations for both its cause and America.

The farmer is a part of the real backbone of capitalism—no

[5] Surprisingly enough, the basic concept of credit unions was originally Asian. Edward A. Filene was surprised to find them in India in local indigenous forms. He came home inspired with their value and devoted much of the rest of his life and fortune to promoting them here.

group of individuals is more capitalistic than the farmer. We sometimes fail to recognize this, but the independence of the farmer is the end of the rainbow for millions of farm-owners overseas. Through the cooperation of the United States government, The National Grange, The Farmers Union and the 4-H Foundation, the Future and National Farmers of America, and the American Farm Bureau there has been, for several years, a small trickle of young farmers from abroad coming here for a few months of study and residence with American families. A like number has been going overseas from here to live in farming communities. While the outsider might consider this an exchange of farming information, it has proved to be much bigger than that. In some respects it has been the most effective tool I have observed in communicating overseas the fundamentals of American capitalism. When I talked with some of the erstwhile visitors in their homes abroad I encountered people and communities that understood America and what it means in the way of improved economic life.

The Heifer Project is another effort of a voluntary agency—this one in the field of religious effort—spearheaded by the Church of the Brethren but from the start interchurch, both Protestant and Roman Catholic. This organization has shipped overseas thousands of bred heifers, baby chicks, and other farm animals for distribution to refugees and others trying to re-establish themselves after dislocation. The great value of this organization, as a lesson in communicating an understanding of America, lies in the way it distributes its animals. They are given to a farm family, the family having been selected by its neighbors, not by the Heifer Project. The recipient agrees to deliver the first female progeny of the heifer (and other animals in similar ways) to another family in need, and that family to another—an endless chain of friendship. Pages could be written of my observations as I have studied this program in Europe and Asia. All I can say here is that it works, and there are now great-grandchildren of the first heifers being delivered to new refugee families. This is another illustration of what dynamic capitalism in action can do.

The nonprofit foundation, even though its money may have come from "big business," is not suspect abroad. In all fairness much of this credit must go to the Rockefeller Foundation that has set the pace throughout the world. Briefly, the situation is as follows: Such foundations as Ford and Rockefeller and a few others are liked and taken at their face value. They are evaluated as an expression of capital at its best—money made and then expended to help others. The following quotation illustrates this point:

> . . . One effect of the [Fulbright scholarship] program in its first decade, according to Dr. John F. Mead, executive secretary of the West German Fulbright Commission, has been gradually to give bearers of Fulbright scholarships a distinction not unlike that usually associated with the ultra-choice Rockefeller, Guggenheim, Ford, and even Rhodes scholarships.[6]

Foundations, when divorced from the business itself and operating in the general interest, are a medium that are successfully communicating abroad the fundamental principles of American capitalism. Even though it is known that, because of their tax-exempt status the government indirectly makes a sizable contribution to them, they receive a minimum of criticism. Take an equal amount of money and employ a Foundation to do a job for the government and most of the public-relations value comes through. Spend the same money through the welfare departments of a "big" company, and it boomerangs.

These various examples from the efforts of voluntary agencies —from profit entity business, the chain store; from nonprofit corporate associations, the credit unions; from trade unions; from agriculture; and from a cross-section of religious groups and foundations generally—are just a few examples of what can be done. If just a few more organizations would light their own candles, study the situation, and find where their members' particular talents and resources fit, world tensions would be considerably eased.

As stated at the beginning of this section, these four forms of American activity—cooperatives, small business, trade unions, and voluntary agencies—hold the most vital keys to solving the riddle

[6] *Newsweek* (May 27, 1957).

of how and what to communicate to others of things that have brought America to its present greatness.

§3. Questions for American Businessmen

American business concerns today have thousands of employees from the United States and Canada working overseas, whose families are there with them. A cross-section of the employees and their families has been interviewed as to their reactions to the job and what they think might be done to help communicate overseas the fundamentals of American capitalism. A large volume could be written on this subject, and it is my understanding that the Maxwell School of Citizenship and Public Affairs of Syracuse University, under Dean Harlan Cleveland, has completed such a project.

The results of my interviews are presented in a series of questions, each one of which is a composite of many conversations. They represent a sizing-up of the situation by the men and their families who are in the field. They might well be analyzed by business executives, looking toward the future.

For convenience of the reader the questions are placed in two groups. The first is for companies with overseas operations; the second should be of concern to *all* American businessmen.

1. Does my company operate in another land to make a profit alone or to also help others there to develop local businesses?

   Can my company survive in its foreign operations if other business is expropriated by the state?

   What is my company doing to help create an understanding climate of the value of capitalism?

   Has my company ever considered introducing "multiple management" in its overseas operations?

   Does my company train and orient its men going overseas to realize that they are guests of a sovereign people and act accordingly?

   Does my company brief its overseas-bound people on the history, cultures, religions, ambitions, and needs of the people of the land to which they are going?

   Does my company ever "kick upstairs" misfits here by sending them overseas?

Does my company have a patronizing or neighborly attitude toward the nationals of the other land with which it does business?

Do executives of my company when going overseas demand the best local housing to an extent that it disrupts the living of executives and officials of other companies or of local people?

Does my company deal with the government officials of other countries on a basis similar to that with American or Canadian officials?

Do my company's executives and employees going overseas know enough about American business and government to carry on a real discussion?

Do our employees realize that as foreigners in other lands they are really the ambassadors of capitalism, and do they behave as such?

Does my Company "open the doors" for overseas appointments at the executive level to "natives" or American citizens of non-European ancestry?

In dealing with foreigners, do we do unto them as we would have them do unto us?

2. Is dynamic capitalism of enough importance to me and my family to take time to inform myself of the difference between it and Marxism?

If the objective of Marxism is to expropriate all business to the state, then do I have any right to expect the government to conduct all the education relative to the value of private business to the world?

Do I know enough about the difference between Marxism and capitalism to intelligently carry on a discussion about their relative merits with a Communist?

Have I ever realized that science is "color blind"?

Are we going back to the "good old days," or is the twentieth-century adaptation of "socialism in the chair" a permanent part of our economic life?

Does "creeping socialism" surge of its own momentum, or is it sucked into a vacuum where business has failed to perform a necessary service?

When I meet a foreign visitor socially or at the plant, do I take an interest in him as a person or is he just another visitor?

Do I or my associates who have met him carry on any correspondence with him after he has returned to his homeland?

Do my wife and I ever invite students or businessmen from overseas who are not the top brass to our home or encourage our company employees to do so?

Have I ever studied what part of my business is dependent upon overseas imports-exports of goods and services?

Do the men and their families in our business have an opportunity to readily inform themselves of the public-relations problems of foreign affairs?

Is economic geography of enough importance to spend some time on it, or do my opinions of overseas problems depend upon political opinion only?

If I or members of my family have traveled in other nations have we made an attempt to know anyone and continue the friendship through correspondence?

If I have been overseas, have I ever visited businesses of the same or like nature to my own and established permanent lines of communication with it?

Do I personally, or do I encourage my associates to, take a real interest in the international work of service clubs, churches, schools, and business organizations?

Do I have "the unconscious arrogance of conscious wealth" when thinking about the economic conditions of other nations?

§4. CAN CAPITALISM COMPETE?

Can Capitalism compete? Webster defines "compete" as: "To stand comparison as to fitness or value; to seek or strive for the same thing." Capitalism and communism are in a life-and-death competition for the loyalties of mankind. This little book has attempted to evaluate the battle as seen from the vantage point of an eye-witness to many of the thundering events of the mid-twentieth century, the century of human destiny. I have tried to present not a mere travelogue, tempting as that might have been, but rather an attempt to conduct the reader on a mental excursion into the extensive fields of conflict where the precarious future of mankind is being determined.

Two ideologies are in open warfare. One is statism, where the all-powerful central authority looks upon men merely as hollow tiles to be used in building a structure of human society as it sees fit. The other is freedom and self-determination, where man makes certain concessions for the common good, but reserves his own decisions on fundamentals, even retaining the right to be wrong.

Most of the discussion of this subject has stormed around the state. This is natural because the attack upon the liberties of mankind is being engineered by a group of men who have captured governments and made them do their bidding. Our North American governments have thus unconsciously been drawn into a field of battle not of their choosing, and one in which they are ill-equipped to attack or defend. We have, as individual North Americans, given the state the power to represent us in protection against enemies within and without. But that enemy, within and without, against whom we now compete is a "wolf in sheep's clothing." The disciples of Karl Marx took the lamb of innocence of New Testament communal practice and used its skin as a covering for the diabolical wolf of Bolshevik imperialism.[7]

By a planned prostitution of the science of semantics, our enemies in the war for the loyalties of man have delegated unto themselves the protection of "democracy" and are espousing the cause of "socialism." They have caused the world to use the words "communism" and "socialism" when describing them and yet there is no actual communism or socialism there. True communism, as described by New Testament writers, was a harmless device enabling a group of people to live together for the common weal. It has been tried during the course of the centuries, however, and has usually ended in dismal failure; but never before has it been the fraudulent basis for such a militant crusade for power as we now witness. The Soviets have appropriated the word "communism" and, playing on the heartstrings and prejudices of humanity, have made black veritably appear as white.

"Communism" may be compared metaphorically to a slender stream flowing from the past into the present, having been polluted by Marx, Lenin, and Stalin with the poison of fraud,

[7] See, *The Ideology of Freedom vs. the Ideology of Communism,* a Consultation of the Committee on Un-American Activities, House of Representatives, with Dr. Charles Wesley Lowry, June 5, 1958 (Washington, D.C.: Government Printing Office, 1958), p. 13.

falsehood, and deception, and fed by the criminal inventions of the Kremlin until the spark of original truth in it is no longer discernible, so that "communism" today is the convenient and inexhaustible reservoir of imposture and entrapment wherewith to delude, ensnare, and enslave mankind.

An armed militant power openly claiming world domination is a far cry from the men who taught "Utopia." They were dreamers, but not conquerors. They were evangelists, but not dictators. They were teachers, but not deceivers.

The moguls of the nineteenth-century commercial enterprises against which Marx hurled his invective pen have been largely liquidated in North America by the peaceful process of enlightened public opinion, together with the power of the ballot box and parliamentary procedure. Yet the world attack on capitalism goes on as though the nineteenth-century version were still present. Our generation has found the way to preserve the material benefits of combined investments, which is what we call modern corporate capitalism, that simultaneously serves the general public as well as returning a fair profit for the stockholder. We have come to use capitalism as a responsible servant within a responsible society.

Largely because the attack upon capitalism came as a thief in the night, we turned to the government to meet the issues, military, social, economic, and spiritual. In this we made a grievous error. The government under our system is primarily our defender collectively against the "power of the sword," and I have unlimited confidence in its ability to protect us. But the attack upon the "power of the spirit" is directed against us as individuals. Because we have retained the right of individual choice in these matters we are the only ones who can win this war for the minds of men. Our governments are geared to fight physical battles. But we have the privileges of liberty, which entails the obligation to engage in this war of ideologies.

If capitalistic business will not engage in this battle for understanding of men, it may well lose its very all. If it really attempts to carry abroad its message of profit combined with service, it will find a ready response, one which the government alone can never obtain. If business will embark upon an educational program within its own organizations, if individual businessmen will go the extra mile, then modern capitalism will have a chance to be welcomed throughout the world. Men around the planet are all motivated by the same basic impulses. The material needs for food, raiment, housing, and health may or may not be provided under a dictatorship; but in the field of the spirit, present-day capitalism has a rare opportunity to serve mankind and provide him with the opportunity to be appreciated, to participate, to belong, to have security of person and property, to have freedom of belief and worship, and have the love and respect of his fellow-man. Never in the history of man have these ineradicable desires been fulfilled until the advent of our new humanistic concept. While not perfect, it is a closer approximation than ever before. What was said by the soapbox orator a generation ago, is now an accomplished fact. To export the "show-how" of this new world is the task of the private businessman; otherwise, he is derelict in his responsibilities to his family, his country, and mankind.

Seldom does an author have the opportunity to follow an experiment that proves his point as has this one. Several references have been made in this book to my traveling companion in Asia, C. Leigh Stevens. He became involved in 1949, in this adventure of helping the world to help itself as a result of a lunch with Donald K. David, then Dean of the Harvard Business School, and the author. I had just returned from a world-circling trip as Consultant to the Director General of the Food and Agricultural Organization of the United Nations. I had seen the restless striving for active participation in the blessings of the twentieth century. I had visited several countries so new that they hardly realized they were independent of foreign domination. I saw that there was a need and place for good solid advice from an American businessman as to how to make things work. During the lunch Don and I told Leigh that he might perform a great service to mankind if he would go to Asia on his own and take a look. He cheerfully accepted the challenge and subsequently he and I made three trips there together. Never had I seen an experiment work so successfully. A short time ago news dispatches from New Delhi said that Mr. Stevens has helped the

Indian obtain hard brick from the soil of the Gangetic Plain, and both electricity and increased water from the wells by a bullock-powered, dual-purpose mechanism of which all the parts can be made in India.[8] The Prime Minister and an entourage of leaders attended the opening demonstration of these developments. Mr. Nehru is quoted as having said:

> . . . the progress achieved in industrially advanced countries like the United States, Japan and Russia is not the result of magic but through the hard work of their people through the centuries.
>
> In India we have to compress within a few years what others took a century to achieve. Therefore, we must tighten our belts and work harder with firmer determination to stand on our own legs.[9]

Yes, modern capitalism can compete if it is intelligently and universally demonstrated by dedicated individuals who believe in it sufficiently to give of their time and talents to a waiting and receptive world.

The rules of communication of the ideas of the spirit are simple. They are: Do it clearly, completely, correctly, conscientiously, and courteously. These rules Stevens did follow. You and I can do likewise and help save capitalism and freedom if we but have the will to do so.

Thus will we be faithful to ourselves, our fellows, our families, our country, and humanity, and thus will we do honor to the name of America and her allies in the epic struggle to free men from a dread new tyranny over the mind and make the technological revolution safe for freedom.

---

[8] "One imaginative American often accomplishes more than our whole government. Such a man is Leigh Stevens, an engineer on a Ford Foundation project. He became so engrossed in Indian problems that, when he returned home, he spent much money and time perfecting four inventions: a bullock-operated generator that can light a village at night and supply power by day; a bullock-powered well to furnish double the normal amount of irrigation water; a cheap, durable brick; and, finally, a new-type cart wheel. The inventions answer Indian needs within Indian resources. I was told that Steven's ingenuity will have more impact in India than ten Explorers." See *Look* (May 27, 1958), p. 46.

[9] The *Evening Star* (Washington, D.C., July 26, 1958).

INDEX

Italy
  antitrust study, 74
  Italian Social Democratic Party, 24

Japan
  baseball in, 9
  cooperatives organized in, 234
  emergence in scientific field, 162
  Girard case, 155–56
  how to use capitalism in, 45
  inflation, example, 67
  textbook selection, domination of, by Marxists, 170–71
  U.S. specialists, training in business economy of, during World War II, 233–34
Jenson, Dr. A. Ladru, 61
Jewish view of capitalism, 230–32
Johnson, Edward F., *quoted*, 150
Johnstone, Henry W., *The Restraint of Competition in the Austrian Economy*, 73
Junior Chamber of Commerce
  active in Puerto Rico, 211–12
  beneficial program in Philippine Islands, 188–90
  consists of needed young men, 146–47
  Jaycee Creed, 190
Jussawalla, Mrs. M. F., study of American capitalism, 70–71

Kerensky, A. F., 26
Kerper, Robert E., *cited*, 197
Khrushchev, Nikita S.
  described Soviet industry practices, 30
  letter to Eisenhower, *quoted*, 33
  party-government official, 26
Kibbutz, 24
Kirkpatrick, Evron M., *Target: The World*, 106
Knapp, Joseph G., *Are Cooperatives Good Business?*, 49
Knapp, Seamon A., developer of Extension Service, 141
Knappen, Dr. Marshall, *An Introduction to American Foreign Policy*, 53–54, 59–60, 104
President's criticism as to treatment of American Indians, 76

Korea
  shipping of U.S. rice to, 86

Labor
  fundamental part of American capitalism, 237–38
  part of socialist movement in Europe, 148
  unions
    as backers of private enterprise, 147–49
    in U.S. and Canada, 51
    unique position of, to export private enterprise fundamentals, 237–38
  U.S. Department of Labor, *The American Workers' Fact Book*, 147–48
  What Labor Means by "More," 147
Lacoste, Robert, *quoted*, 161
Lage, Oskar, *quoted*, 28
Land O'Lakes, 236
Land tenure; *see* Agriculture
Laski, Prof. Harold J., *cited*, 172
Latin-America
  program for communicating North American capitalism in, 213–23
  relationship of Technical Cooperation Administration to, 84
  study of public relations in, 127
Laubach, Frank, *cited*, 170
Lawrence, William, *Memories of a Happy Life*, 175
Lenin, Nikolai
  activities, 27
  on world domination, *quoted*, 32
  philosophy, 25–26
Lerner, Max, *quoted*, 152–53
Lewis, John L., *quoted*, 148
Liberty, individual, largely unknown, 77
Lieberman, Henry R., *quoted*, 172–73
Ligutti, Msgr. L. G.
  excerpts from *Sunrise and Sunset Letters*, 224–25
  quoted, 85–86
Lincoln, Abraham, *cited*, 174